Ford Sterling

Ford Sterling

The Life and Films

WENDY WARWICK WHITE

McFarland & Company, Inc., Publishers
Jefferson, North Carolina, and London

LIBRARY OF CONGRESS CATALOGUING-IN-PUBLICATION DATA

White, Wendy Warwick, 1954–
Ford Sterling : the life and films / Wendy Warwick White.
p.   cm.
Includes bibliographical references and index.

ISBN 13: 978-0-7864-2587-7
(softcover : 50# alkaline paper) ∞

1. Sterling, Ford, 1882–1939. 2. Motion picture actors and actresses—United States—Biography. I. Title.
PN2287.S6783W45   2007   791.43092—dc22   2006101495
[B]

British Library cataloguing data are available

©2007 Wendy Warwick White. All rights reserved

No part of this book may be reproduced or transmitted in any form or by any means, electronic or mechanical, including photocopying or recording, or by any information storage and retrieval system, without permission in writing from the publisher.

On the cover: Publicity portrait of Ford Sterling; (background) the actor's famous "Dutch" persona

Manufactured in the United States of America

McFarland & Company, Inc., Publishers
Box 611, Jefferson, North Carolina 28640
www.mcfarlandpub.com

To my late father,
who introduced me to silent comedy;

my son Harry,
the next generation of silent comedy enthusiasts;

my late mother,
for her patience;

and James,
for his caring support and enthusiasm

and in memory of my mother, Muriel.

Acknowledgments

I would like to thank the following people for their help, shared material, and support. So many people have helped me over the years. Some offered photographs, others film, and of course there were those who gave me access to the research they had done. I hope I have remembered all who were so generous; if someone has been forgotten, I apologize profusely. The names have been listed in alphabetical order so as not to give the impression one was more important to this endeavor than any other. I would, though, like to give a special mention and thanks for their help and encouragement to Sally Dumaux and Annette D'Agostino Lloyd. They made sure I got the project completed and in a timely manner.

So, thank you: Robert Birchard, Lisa Bradberry (Florida), Bruce Calvert (stills), James Cozart (LOC, film restoration, and preservation), Sally Dumaux, Rob Farr, Judy Finelli (circus), Natasha Gerson (circus), Paul Gill (baseball), Sam Gill, James Golini, Buckey Grimm (paper print), Jack Hardy (film), Tommie Hicks, Ed Hulse, Annette D'Agostino Lloyd (proof), Jon Mirsalis (film), Glenn Mitchell, Joe Moore, Richard Roberts, Patricia Tobias, Brent Walker, David Wyatt (film).

I would also like to thank the following institutions: Academy of Motion Picture Arts and Sciences Library, Beverly Hills, California; Arizona State University Library, Tempe; Arlington Public Library, Arlington, Virginia; Chicago Historical Society; Chicago Public Library; Library of Congress, Washington, D.C. (Film, Television, and Broadcasting); Los Angeles Public Library; Phoenix Public Library, Arizona; Society for American Baseball Research, Inc., Cooperstown, New York; University of California at Los Angeles Film Archive; University of Notre Dame Archives, Hesburgh Library, South Bend, Indiana.

Contents

Acknowledgments	vii
Preface	1
1. His Youthful Fancy	5
2. His Smashing Career	19
3. Our Dare Devil Chief	26
4. A Dramatic Mistake	38
5. Roaring Lions and Wedding Bells	48
6. Out and In	54
7. His Wild Oats	67
8. Peeping Pete	80
9. Day of Faith	88
10. He Who Gets Slapped	99
11. Stout Hearts and Willing Hands	118
12. The Unhappy Finish	136
Ford Sterling Filmography	145
Notes	181
Bibliography	189
Index	191

Preface

Early comedy has fascinated me since childhood. It was introduced to me by my late father, Douglas, who had a passion for silent comedy, English music hall, the Marx Brothers, and W. C. Fields, to name a few. Over the years, the collection of short and feature films grew and so did my family. It wasn't long before my young Master Harry followed in his mother's footsteps and caught the silent comedy bug. Inspired by my son's interest and his questions about silent comedy, I decided, as a way of answering his queries, to put together a booklet about the genre. Along with the history, the booklet was to include techniques, restoration, and the making of silent film. Because it was aimed at young people, I thought it might be interesting to add mini-biographies of various silent comedians and stars—one of whom was Ford Sterling.

As the research for information on Sterling's career in contemporary newspapers and magazines bore fruit, so did the realization that much of what had been written in recent times was somewhat different from what was written in his day—not to mention less than flattering. It appeared that over the years Ford Sterling's reputation had suffered, chiefly through the perpetuation of misperceptions, rumors, and outright inaccuracies. Finding those discrepancies between contemporary newspaper articles and more recent biographical material further piqued my interest.

Where had the negative press come from? Why was there a belief that Sterling had been rude and difficult to work with, and that he was a washed-up has-been upon leaving Mack Sennett's Keystone Studio? And this was only a few years after he had started working there. What was the truth behind the Sterling Studio debacle? Who was Ford Sterling, anyway, other than a slapstick comedian, and was the modern reputation deserved?

Being inquisitive and one to enjoy a challenge (especially if it involves research and cinematic archaeology), I decided to expand the mini-biography into an article in an attempt to answer these questions.

It turned out that this man was interesting. He was far from a one-trick pony. During his life, Sterling was recognized as a world-class photographer, exhibiting and winning prizes internationally. In addition to his baseball interest and his signing with a major-league team, he gardened, played golf and tennis skillfully, painted and sculpted, and enjoyed traveling the world. He was a well-rounded and learned man who got the most out of life and gave much back.

My article painstakingly progressed, with new information coming to light and sending me off in new directions. Now more intense research was required — hours of sitting in front of microfilm, reading trade magazines and newspapers dating from 1911 to 1939, and watching all the available films I could lay my hands on. Letters had to be written to institutions and persons who might have some information. Then came the task of trying to find someone who had actually worked with or known Sterling. This was hard, as he died in 1939 and had no surviving family — but someone was found.

One summer, on one of several trips to the Los Angeles area to do research and view films, my idea for writing an article was somewhat altered. While there, I had lunch with a group of fellow silent film and silent comedy aficionados at a restaurant on the site of the old L-KO Studios at Gower Street and Sunset Boulevard. Most were writers and researchers with far more knowledge and expertise than I. This was one of those regular events where the group would meet to swap stories, research, and gossip. When I mentioned I had been working on a Ford Sterling article, one member of the group suggested I expand it and write a full-blown book instead, and all the others were enthusiastic about the idea. There was certainly more material than could be used for a decent-length article and, as has been said, Ford Sterling was proving to be quite a fascinating study. The group felt that because nothing substantial, or even particularly accurate, had been written about Sterling in the past, it was about time someone righted that wrong. Sterling had been, after all, one of the more important pioneering film comedians in the early days of silent comedy, attaining international stardom by 1913. The group was as good as their word when they offered to give me material to use in the book; and as I scoured through every available source of information, Sterling's life continued to unfold before me.

Ford Sterling was born into a wealthy middle-class Chicago family and educated at a renowned college, but circumstances led him to leave his comfortable life. The fates were with him all the while. By way of the circus, vaudeville, burlesque, Shakespeare, Broadway, and baseball, Sterling made his way to the top in the early days of silent film comedy. But he didn't stop there. During the mid–1920s, Sterling acquired a reputation as one of the most sought-after character actors of the day, and when the sound era came he made the transition effortlessly. So successful was Sterling that he was able to retire a millionaire. That is, until fate stepped in yet again. As the twists and turns in Sterling's life occurred, so are they chronicled within these pages.

Work on the book has not always been straightforward; some encouragement has been needed along the way to stick with it. Three fine and learned ladies and one gentleman have been instrumental in its completion. The first of the ladies was the late Sally Dumaux, author of *King Baggot: A Biography and Filmography of the First King of the Movies*, whose encouragement, generosity, and expert knowledge of the various Los Angeles Library systems have been invaluable. The second is Annette D'Agostino Lloyd, world authority on Harold Lloyd and author of *An Index to Short and Feature Films in the Moving Picture World: The Early Years, 1907–1915*, as well as two books on Lloyd and his films. She has been my long-suffering proofreader and remains a friend. The third is my mother, Muriel, and the gentleman is James Golini, drummer extraordinaire and avid film collector; these two encouraged me and pushed for me to get the manuscript to the publishers, even though neither had any idea who Ford Sterling was. They do now.

So now is the time to set the record straight and restore this silent film comedy legend, Ford Sterling, to his rightful place among the greats. I hope that this chronicle of his life and times, which were filled with adventures, great highs, deep lows, and immense joy shared along the way, will assist in this endeavor.

1

His Youthful Fancy

To the modern audience, Ford Sterling's name is not necessarily the first that comes to mind when the question "Who's your favorite comedian?" is asked. It used to be very different. Moviegoers in the first few decades of the twentieth century adored him, shrieking and laughing at his antics, and a smile will still creep across the face of those who recall his films. But what made him so popular? He was so popular, in fact, that between 1911 and 1914, until Charles Chaplin took the crown, many considered Ford Sterling to be *the* comedian. It was as the nose-biting, bespectacled, grimacing, lecherous, mustachioed villain in a crumpled top hat, half-mast pants, and vest, or as the equally expressive Chief Teheezal, leader of the Keystone Kops, with his goatee beard, "Dutch"[1] makeup, and ruffled dignity that he was so loved. This angry, harassed, grumbling, Daffy Duck forerunner created by Sterling led the way. It wasn't only as a comedian that he was famous in his day; there was much more to Ford Sterling, and he left his mark on more than just the silent movies. Sterling may be largely forgotten now but the image and comedy legacy are surprisingly familiar. His influence is still seen in the work of actors, directors, and cartoonists today, whether they are aware of it or not.

The rude behavior was reserved for the screen only. According to his contemporaries, Sterling was anything but angry or antisocial. At Mack Sennett's Keystone Studio, the stage that Ford Sterling was working on was an immensely popular place to be. It was packed with fellow comedians, studio workers, and visitors watching his every move. Sterling vociferously ad-libbed his way through scenes with an adopted German accent and this, along with his antics, had his impromptu audience in hysterics. Unfortunately, as these short films were made before the advent of sound, Mr. Sterling's vocalizations in them are lost to us forever, with perhaps one exception, his dialogue in *Keystone Hotel*. In this 1935 film he reprised his role as Chief Teheezal for a Sennett-style sound short written by Joe Traub and directed by Ralph Staub, in which many of the old team reunited to run around and cause mayhem. With Sterling were cross-eyed Ben Turpin, walrus-mustached Chester Conklin, energetic Hank Mann, pretty Marie Prevost and Vivian Oakland, and of course the Keystone Kops. After its success a series of these shorts was planned, but salary demands from some of its stars unfortunately put a stop to that.

If imitation is a form of flattery, then Sterling must have been very flattered. His

Sterling's "Dutch" persona became recognizable the world over. The inscription, "To Edward ———?/Moving Picture Playactor/Frame anothers hand. Ford Sterling," was for actor/director Edward Dillon. The two had both worked at Biograph in the pre–Keystone days.

immense popularity led to other performers imitating him and directors requesting that their comedians use the "Sterling style." Thus his influence started to spread. Charles Chaplin himself, when he joined Keystone, was asked by Mack Sennett to "act like Ford" but, with a few exceptions, he declined, choosing to continue to evolve his own Tramp character brought over from the British music hall. Before long, Chaplin was being impersonated, too. The first Chaplin impersonator, ironically, was Henry "Pathé" Lehrman in none other than the first offering from the short-lived studio that bore Ford's name, The Sterling Film Company. *Love and Vengeance*, made in 1914, was being filmed at the same time and location Chaplin was impersonating Sterling in the Mabel Normand short, *Mabel at the Wheel*. As it was early in Chaplin's film career, well before he had found his niche, Lehrman's parody was probably intended more as tit-for-tat than as homage to Chaplin's later recognized genius and popularity.

But how did this well-educated son of middle-class parents come to be the nemesis of many a Keystone maiden and the instigator of dastardly plots? And what about his other achievements, completely forgotten today? Ford Sterling was born George Ford Stich, Jr., on November 3, 1882,[2] in La Crosse, Wisconsin, the son of George F. Stich, Sr., a first-generation American born of German immigrant parents in Louisiana, and Mary Kirby Stich, also a first-generation American, whose father was from England and mother from Scotland; Mary was born in Ohio.[3] Although there were both Stich and Kirby relatives living in the La Crosse area, the family did not stay there long after young George's birth. The infant George and his parents were soon on the move to Texas, where his father was involved in the cattle business. By 1898 they had made the move back north, this time to Chicago, Illinois, where George was to grow up.[4]

The Chicago to which young George and his family moved was a pioneering new city, part of which had risen out of the famed fire of 1871. Tall office buildings were being built by a new generation of brilliant architects and engineers, including Dwight Perkins, William LeBaron Jenny,[5] Ernest Graham, and Daniel H. Burham. These peo-

Will Rogers (R), impersonating Ford Sterling's Chief Teheezal, confronts Chaplin lookalike Charlie Hall in *Big Moments from Little Pictures* (1924).

ple and their innovative designs would be the inspiration for buildings all over the country. The parks, considered an important part of Chicago social life, were being landscaped by Jens Jensen, and the whole made a vibrant and modern multicultural city. Outside the larger commercial area the buildings were more modest in height and usually reached no more than three stories. These buildings ranged from workingmen's cottages to the elaborate mansions of the wealthy, and, to serve the residences, small commercial businesses were springing up in these areas to form neighborhoods.[6]

This is not to say the entire city was idyllic; the fact was far from it. Chicago, like all cities, had its vices, some of which were more or less tolerated and kept in segregated areas. Prostitution and gambling were confined to their own zones, usually bordering on ethnic areas referred to then as the "Black and Chinese residences."

The segregated ethnic enclaves had little or nothing to do with the vices in their neighborhoods; it just seemed to be that the poorer areas, as happens today, had the vices of the better-off deposited on their doorsteps. Some of the less reputable saloons and flophouses were also allotted their own areas and this was to remain so until the early years of the twentieth century. The cost of living was much lower than it is by today's standards, although in Chicago it was comparatively higher than in most other areas of the United States. Wages did not really keep up with the higher cost of living. The working-class wage, for a job that was not guaranteed and often dangerous, was paid daily or weekly and was low. Construction workers were paid around 17¢ an hour, foundry laborers 16¢, machine woodworkers 25¢, and plasterers the princely sum of 50¢. Businesses would sometimes be closed for months at a time because of bad weather or a lack of customers. In most cases the whole family needed to work to make ends meet, and this included the children. Women's and children's wages were substantially lower than men's for the same work.

It was estimated that, for a family of five, as much as $600 per year was needed to provide for basic food and shelter. As for food, you would expect to pay per pound for cheese 17¢, flour 2¢, chuck steak 13¢ and sugar 6¢; eggs were 18¢ per dozen and a quart of milk 6¢.[7] It was the cost of housing that took the largest portion of the wages. For just a tiny dingy two-room apartment the working-class had to find money to pay rent which was anywhere from $4 to $7 per month; and this was one rung down the ladder from the slum accommodations with their shared toilets, no bathroom, and heating extra. These averaged $8–10 per month. The middle class, into which the Stich family fell, could rent the older houses in fashionable neighborhoods for $25–60 a month. If they wanted to live along the very fashionable boulevards, $100–300 had to be found each month. It was there, on Grand Boulevard, that George and his family lived. These homes were equipped with the luxuries of modern living: bathtubs and flushing toilets. Some even had electricity, telephones, and steam heat.

Chicago had parks, beautiful parks dedicated to the promotion of public health through outdoor activities and recreation. And what recreation they provided — golf, tennis, baseball, cricket, and football. During the summer months boating was available on the lakes and, in the South Park District (Douglas, Humboldt, and Garfield parks), musical concerts were given on bandstands in the evenings. In the winter, ponds were available for ice skating. By 1900 there were sixty rinks throughout Chicago. Those that were not within walking distance of the Stich house were accessible by public transportation. There was a 500-mile network of streetcars at that time. Cycling was another popular method of transport. Chicago had become the center of bicycle manufacturing by the turn of the twentieth century, and the Schwinn Bicycle Company, established in 1895, kept up the standard almost through to the next century. Other industries that made Chicago the city it was to become were agricultural implements, railcars, meatpacking, and steel mills. Chicago was also a major financial center, with banks, stock exchanges, and insurance companies. But what made Chicago a central hub for railway connections all over the country was the cattle industry that George F. Stich, Sr., worked in and its wholesale and retail trade businesses, specifically the Montgomery Ward and Sears, Roebuck mail-order companies.

Such an important city naturally had a large library and arts and cultural events with varying degrees of sophistication. Performances ranged from lowly, often vulgar, shows put on in the taverns that had stages, to vaudeville to Shakespeare and opera. There were the Opera House and the Dearborn, Great Northern, Bijou, and McVickers theaters which provided entertainment for nineteenth-century Chicagoans. It is probable that young George and his family visited the theaters at some point in his childhood.

It was from the prestigious Chicago neighborhood of 4142 Grand Boulevard that, on September 2, 1898, Ford Sterling, or George Stich, Jr., as he was still known, went away to be enrolled at Notre Dame College in South Bend, Indiana. Although Ford Sterling had the estimable college of Notre Dame as his alma mater, it was not the same college it is today. Then it was a private Catholic preparatory boarding school, which catered to Catholic and non–Catholic students alike. The students were offered a variety of college-degree courses if they wished to continue their education, but Sterling didn't take advantage of this. Sterling was not a Catholic and it is unlikely his parents were.

By all accounts, the Notre Dame George was sent to was very different from the forbidding Dickensian institution often envisioned as turn-of-the-century public schools. There was electric lighting installed in all the residence halls, and the youngest pupils, called Minims, had a "play hall" complete with a roller rink. The classrooms were well-equipped, light, and airy, and the boys' rooms were homey and welcoming. Picnics and outings were planned and if the boys were required to stay over for Christmas and Easter their places were warmly decorated. The students were even allowed to have pets. It was generally a place of happiness and security; surprisingly enough, there is no reference in the *Scholastic*, the school's newspaper, that corporal punishment ever took place. It was expected of the students that they would behave with decorum and manners. Although some of the student body was non–Catholic, the practice of the Catholic faith was an integral part of daily life for all and the students were expected to follow its code of ethics without question.

Fortunately, George, Sr., had been successful in the cattle business, allowing the family to be financially comfortable. Private education, then as now, was not cheap and Notre Dame was no different. The fees alone for George were over $100 per semester in addition to his clothes, books, uniform, outings, fares, and other expenses.[8] This was a sizable amount of money for the last years of the nineteenth century, especially when taking into consideration the family's household expenses.

The purpose of sending young George to Notre Dame had nothing to do with any problems with the Chicago schools; it was for a far more personal and sadder reason. It was to allow him to continue his high school education relatively uninterrupted while his parents traveled for the sake of his father's frail health. George was unaware when he left for Notre Dame that his father, whom his mother claimed in a letter had always been devoted to the boy,[9] was suffering from a serious kidney ailment.[10] George was somewhat overwhelmed by the idea of leaving his parents and felt homesick.[11] As it was the first time he had been away from home unaccompanied it took him a while to settle in, and it wasn't until eighteen months later that he was reporting back to his mother that he was happy and well.

It appears, though, that young George continued to have mixed feelings about life away from home throughout his stay at the college. One thing that seems to have been on the plus side for his new school was that it gave him his first taste of acting. During his first few months at Notre Dame, Mary Stich, in another letter, spoke of George's fondness for the teacher who coached him in a little play he acted in.[12] There would be other chances to perform: on April 3, 1899, Easter Monday, he appeared as Cecato in *If I Were a King* put on by the Philopatrian Society[13]; a few months later, on November 29, George had another part in a play, this time William Shakespeare's classic, *The Merchant of Venice*. The seventeen-year-old took on a role worlds away from a future Sennett comedian, that of Portia, Shylock's young daughter. A spark had been ignited.

George Stich, Sr., continued to be in very poor health, so much so that George, Jr., was allowed home in 1898, for one day, during October of his first semester.[14] His mother made the request that George visit his ailing father after his father returned from receiving medical treatment in New York. The following May, George, Jr., was summoned home again.[15] This time, his mother asked the school if her son could stay a week as his father's health was now failing rapidly. This would prove to be the last time young George saw his father alive. By the latter part of the month, George, Sr., needed throat surgery; and although Mary reported to the fathers at the college that he was making a good recovery it would appear this was not the case.[16] June 10, 1899, is the likely date of death of George F. Stich, Sr. Unfortunately, no death certificate has been found to corroborate this; most Chicago records of this time were lost in a fire. What makes this likely (other than the very poor state of Mr. Stich's health, as well as Sterling saying the death of his father made it eventually necessary for him to go to work) is that there are no more mentions of George, Sr., in his wife's letters after this date, and Mrs. Stich started to sign her name Mrs. Mary Kirby Stich instead of Mrs. George Stich. By the propriety of the day, a married woman was known by her husband's name, only reverting to her own after his death. Mary Stich's lifestyle changed, too, as did her address.

(There is one thing that gives rise to doubt on the matter of the date of death. Although likely referring to a different person, there is a mention of a George F. Stitch in 1900 taking an active role in the Chicago Republican Party, first on October 21, 1900, where he was a speaker at the Kuehl's Hall on Grand and Armitage Avenues at the twenty-sixth ward's party meeting.[17] Later, in November, this Mr. Stitch was identified as the chairman for a joint meeting of the Workmen's Republican Club and the Hamilton Club held at the Auditorium.[18] As there are no more mentions of this gentleman at other meetings and with the two he attended being so close together, he may have been a visitor from out of town brought in for the meetings and no connection to the Stich family. It is worth mentioning, though, in case anymore information comes to light.)

After his father's death, there is an implication that George and his mother had different agendas. George spent most of his 1899 summer vacation at Notre Dame, rather than in Chicago with his mother. Mary Stich had written to George asking him to come home in August to be fitted for suits for the coming year, but he wrote back saying he "didn't care to come."[19] Mother duly sent money for his train ticket home and dutifully George obeyed, although he was looked after, certainly for a while, by someone else, as his mother had left for La Crosse in September before George returned to school. Mrs. Mary Stich admitted to doing a lot of traveling and happened to be out of town at the bedside of dear, sick friends at the time of George's departure. She did plan to visit George at Notre Dame for a day once she had returned to Chicago, though. The fact is, he nearly didn't return to Indiana at all. In the same letter, she relates how George had been influenced by some local boys and had suddenly decided school and life away from Chicago wasn't for him anymore. With all that Chicago had to offer there was plenty to keep a teenager, or a group of teenagers, busy and amused. George's mother informed the fathers at the college that it took her "quite some work" to restore his interest in his education but that he never openly disobeyed her wishes and would be returning.

Even so, George's schooling was cut short by illness in January 1901, this time his own. Academically he was doing well: he was intelligent and a good scholar, coming first in his class in arithmetic, bookkeeping, reading, and spelling, and second in grammar; he also studied French and technical drawing. In the fall of 1900 George again had problems leaving home and going back to Notre Dame.[20] He did return, but a mysterious illness struck him down around mid January 1901. He remained ill throughout February, and finally went home on March 2, 1901. The nature of this illness was not recorded, but whatever the ailment, it permanently delayed George's return to college. At the age of eighteen, he ended his formal education.

The family finances may also have been an issue, considering the outgoing expenses they had to meet for George, Sr.'s medical treatment and George, Jr.'s schooling. With his father sick, it was unlikely any money was coming into the household at all. After the death of his father, Sterling did say it was necessary for him to hustle for work,[21] although he and his mother obviously managed to get by until George left school. Even so, some of the payments to Notre Dame were late.[22] His mother moved from the Grand Boulevard house[23] in the spring of 1900 and, after a visit to Mount Eagle, Tennessee, she spent June at 305 36th Place, Chicago. By July she had moved George and herself to 3139 Michigan Avenue,[24] not far from their old home. This would be George's last home in Chicago. When the subject of finding employment came up, young George, being well-educated, would have had several apprenticeships and employment opportunities open to him had he wanted them, but he apparently didn't want them. It was a young school friend of George's we have to thank for Ford Sterling the comedian.

James O'Neill,[25] namesake and tragic son of writer James O'Neill and brother to Eugene, had joined the school in 1885 at the age of six[26] and continued his education there for nine years. When George joined the school, he and James became good friends. When it was James who suggested that young George should go on the stage to earn a living, on the stage he went. And O'Neill was right — his suggestion set Sterling on the road to a career that by 1913 would make him a household name. Having lost in a short time his home, his father and the security of his family, it is not surprising George had difficulties with his health. It would not be the only time in his life that Sterling would reportedly fall ill during a time of change and crisis. He had also been ill before leaving for what would be his last semester Notre Dame[27]: apparently, according to his mother, he had a stomach disorder from eating "green fruit."

There has been the romantic notion postulated that Ford Sterling entered show business at fourteen, or as a child, after running away from his home in La Crosse to join a visiting circus. This is not quite correct in spite of the fact that he did work in two circuses later on in his career. Sterling himself lists his first professional engagement as being in the theater, not the circus ring. In a December 1914 interview with *Motion Picture* magazine,[28] "the circus," he said, "came later," which suggests that the rumor about his running away to join the circus was already in circulation by the time he was a comedy star. Although Sterling was a baby when the family left his birthplace, there were other family members still living in La Crosse. His mother was also traveling quite a lot in the year Ford left home and they were in a shaky financial state, so it was quite possible he was sent to stay with family in La Crosse. As for age, Notre Dame's school records show that under his given name of George F. Stich, Sterling didn't leave school until he was eighteen. George Ford Stich may have been legally a minor by American standards when he left home, perhaps without parental consent, but he was not exactly a runaway child or particularly young to be going to work. Many Chicago and other American children were working well before eighteen.

George had lofty ideas of stardom and realized that if he wanted to rise in the profession he would have to change the honest but plebeian name he had inherited. It would hardly be an appropriate name to appear someday on billboards next to Hamlet, Lear, Romeo, or Marc Anthony. So he chose the name Ford Sterling. He never legally changed it like some performers did, although the spelling of his legal name changed from Stich to Stitch. Even so, like many actors, Sterling found that getting into the theater was not easy, name change or no. In a 1914 interview he admitted that "it was after much persuasion and sundry promises that were almost threats to make good" that he got his first job with George Whittier's Shakespearian repertory company. He was given some small parts in *Tangled Relatives* to begin with but, although he gained experience in a wide variety of plays and got the chance to act and do a song and dance, he found himself mainly responsible for props and helping to load the cars. Sterling felt this didn't do him any harm, though, and in actuality it taught him a lot.

Ford's next venture was worlds away from musical comedy but a good training ground for a future Keystone comedian. It was at this point that he joined the circus.[29] First, according to Sterling, he found employment with John Robinson's Circus, starting out at the very bottom as handyman, roustabout and errand boy. He persevered and was rewarded with a "real" job as a member of an aerial troupe. This turned out to be the Flying Lees, regarded as one of the most outstanding troupes of aerial artists of the day. Billed as Keno the Boy Clown, he was tossed from hand to hand as the acrobats swung from their flying trapezes. This was hard and dangerous work, especially the part where the acrobats would pretend to let Sterling fall. He wondered if the audience would laugh louder if they actually did drop him.[30] In order to perform his part in the act Sterling had to have been a very adept and dedicated acrobat. An added danger was that no safety equipment could be used in that type of act. This was important because of the surprise element; nobody expects the ring boy to end up on the trapeze. From records of the Flying Lees' performances, the type of act Sterling was participating in was hair-raising. The ring boy was caught by the ankle or jacket; in some cases the jacket came off and then he grabbed onto the trapeze or an acrobat. His timing had to be impeccable and he had to know exactly when to stop moving, otherwise he could upset the balance of the catcher and both would fall. Aerial acrobats are usually quite contained, quiet people, not given much to facial expression except for their smiles; the aim is to look natural while performing apparently impossible tricks. But someone who plays the ring boy has to have the ability to really clown, change expression many times, look frightened, shocked, hopeless, hopeful, apparently effortlessly while concentrating on the acrobatics.[31] Still, Sterling stuck it out until the circus went into its winter quarters. Then the boy clown took what jobs he could get in small stock companies during the first year, which gave him his early experiences on the stage and enabled him to make his living until the circuses reopened. Spring would again find him haunting the circus quarters. There is a glimpse of Ford Sterling the clown in Victor Sjöström's 1924 classic *He Who Gets Slapped*, starring Lon Chaney, Sr. Sterling played Tricaud, the head clown, in this circus drama: in one scene he was seen helping the great master of disguise, Chaney, put on his clown makeup. Allegedly, Sterling spent the four summers of 1902–1905 as an acrobat and clown with Forepaughs Amalgamated Circus which toured the Western states.[32] How much of 1902–1905 was actually spent *in* the circus is debatable and may have increased with subsequent tellings. Although it is possible Sterling did spend some of this time with Forepaughs as he claims, he could not have worked the entire 1904 season, for example, as he is documented as being elsewhere up until the end of March.

It was not just by working with repertory companies and circuses that Sterling learned his craft; he also took formal acting lessons, and the time period he would have been taking these classes would have clashed with the opening of the circus season. It wasn't with just any old acting coach that he was taking classes either; he enrolled in the prestigious American Academy of Dramatic Arts in New York, graduating in March 1904.[33] The Academy, the first acting school in America, had been founded twenty years earlier by Franklin Haven Sergant as the Lyceum Theatre School of Acting. Within two years, the Academy had moved to Carnegie Hall and was to boast such alumni as Cecil B. DeMille (1900), Edward G. Robinson and William Powell (1913), and Pat O'Brien and Spencer Tracy (1923).

Sterling could have returned to the West Coast and rejoined Forepaughs after the circus season started, as his next recorded sighting is not until March 1906, in a review for one of Sterling's early appearances but unlikely the first. After leaving the Academy, Sterling was in a one-act piece at the Berkley Lyceum in New York called

Keystone Comedies publicity photograph ca. 1913. These photographs of Sterling belonged to a set of color montages that included Mack Swain and Roscoe Arbuckle.

A Woman's Pity. (This was the same Berkley Lyceum where Mark Twain had given a speech on November 23, 1910.) The play was apparently "prettily staged." The plot involved a wealthy young woman (Frances Fontaine), her maid (Margaret Langham), a young man in love with the wealthy young woman (Ford Sterling), and "several minor personages." The young man had known the maid when she was a shopgirl

Zuzu, the Band Leader. Released December 24, 1913, by Keystone Film Company. Ford Sterling (Zuzu) in center. Second from right, half-hidden by a cornet, is Fred Mace. Sources also indicate that Charles Haggerty and Hank Mann are pictured but do not identify them.

and had evidently paid her attentions. When he foolishly lingered in the wealthy woman's house after he had been dismissed and they had said their good nights, he was captured by the night watchman as a burglar. The wealthy young woman said she had never laid eyes on him before. Then the maid (though a woman scorned) stepped forward to protect him and said he came to see her. This saved him from the lockup. The maid was discharged at once, of course; the young man says that the maid has restored his faith in womanhood; and that's all, play ended. The *New York Times* said that "Sterling isn't effective here."[34]

Sterling knew what he wanted to do: he had made up his mind to be in musical comedy. Stardom in this branch of the entertainment world was not instant, as he admitted in the 1914 article: "My start in this profession was by no means prepossessing," he said, but he did get his wish. In 1907 Sterling appeared in *Down the Pike*, a musical comedy starring Johnny and Emma Ray. He was mentioned in the *Atlanta Constitution* when the company appeared at the Bijou, "In support of the two stars—Mr. and Mrs. Ray—will be seen some of the cleverest people in their particular lines including Dan Coleman, Ford Sterling, Sam Goldman, backed up by a chorus of thirty charming and bewitching girls, who know how to sing and dance."[35] By November they were in New York at the Majestic Theatre[36] on Grand Circle with another musical, *King Casey,* referred to as "a hodge-podge of mirth and melody."[37] The Majestic was then one of the largest theaters in New York; it opened in 1902 with the musical extravaganza *Wizard of Oz,* which was followed by the equally lavish

As well as having drawn cartoons himself, Ford Sterling became the topic of a cartoon strip published in the United Kingdom in **Kinema Comic**. This example is from its May 25, 1929, issue, p. 16.

Babes in Toyland. The Ray Company had returned to the Bijou in Atlanta with *King Casey* by the new year, and Ford Sterling was getting a reputation. The *Atlanta Constitution* said the play "embraces some of the leading comedians of the day including Dan Coleman, Ford Sterling and Jack Clabane."[38]

There is an irony here: when Sterling appeared in musical comedy movies later in his life, he hardly got to sing or dance, that is, if he got to sing at all. So far there has not been any surviving footage found of a singing Sterling, save for three notes in the beginning of the 1931 RKO short *Trouble from Abroad*. We do get to see him hoof from time to time, oddly enough, mostly in silent shorts. *Hearts and Flowers* has a nice example with Sterling doing a little comic dance number while conducting a band, as well as some pretty fleet footwork as he takes Phyllis Haver around the dance floor.

Sterling's career was not confined to acting; although he was still acting for three-quarters of the year he branched out, seeing what he could do with his other talents. During the summer he tried his hand at another one of his passions, baseball.[39] He claimed to have joined such teams as the Gulfport Crabs in Mississippi; the Mobile Sea Gulls; McKeesport in Pennsylvania; Saginaw Wa-Was, and Toledo Mud Hens for a season each, and the Duluth team for two seasons. It is certain that Sterling tried to break into professional baseball as an infielder, as those records still remain.[40] He received a tryout for McKeesport of the Ohio-Pennsylvania League in 1908, but was fired by the owner of the franchise and local magistrate, Squire William D. Mansfield, before the season started and no reason given. Sterling tried again in 1910 to gain a place on a team and was signed by Duluth of the Northern League, but history repeated itself; he was released just before the season opened.

This did not stop him from playing in a more minor capacity. In fact, he devoted a good deal of his spare time to the all–American pastime, playing for his old friend and employer, Johnny Ray, who sponsored a team of ball-playing actors. Sterling played on other teams as well, for fun and for various charity events. Later, he was to thank Squire Mansfield. Although in 1908 Sterling had been angry at his failure to become either the infielder or outfielder he had tried out for, by 1914 he had changed his mind. He considered Mansfield had done him a favor, as he had become a star in the movies.[41]

In 1914 a California department store, B. H. Dyas,[42] organized a baseball league between the different film companies operating in Southern California. They supplied the umpires and a ball field as well as a silver loving cup for a trophy. Universal Studios also had a team, The Big U, and Sterling was its shortstop, dressed as his film persona in full costume and makeup. In June the team had a benefit dance on the stage at the studio to raise funds for uniforms and equipment, which Universal did not supply. In 1916 the Sennett studio played a comedy one-inning game as part of the Chance Day celebrations honoring Los Angeles' winning of the pennant.[43] Their two teams, the Never Sweats and the Meat Hounds, boasted the likes of Billy Gilbert, Bobby Dunn, Al St. John, Edgar Kennedy, Harry Gribbon, and Ford Sterling as the Meat Hounds' pitcher. Also, in 1937, Sterling played a softball game at Wrigley Field for Benny Rubin's Screen Stars against Jack Daro's Wrestlers. Sterling played center field; other members of his team consisted of Parkyakarkus, left field, The Three Stooges, second base, and Bert Wheeler, third base. The Ritz Brothers were also on the roster.[44]

The aforementioned game wasn't played at *the* Wrigley Field, home of the Chicago Cubs, but rather the park which was home to the Pacific Coast League's Los Angeles Angels from 1925 to 1957, and the Hollywood Stars from 1926 to 1935. The park was designed to be the image of Wrigley Field in Chicago, even down to the ivy growing on the fifteen-foot high outfield wall. However, one feature made Los Angeles' Wrigley Field different from the one in Chicago: a twelve-story office tower at the entrance of the ballpark (from the playing field a clock was visible on the tower). As in Chicago, the Los Angeles Wrigley Field was named for William Wrigley, the chewing gum magnate who owned both the Cubs and the Angels. The ballpark was built to replace the 15,000-seat Washington Park, which was used from 1903 until 1925.[45]

Yet another career helped boost Sterling's salary as an actor in the off-season. He returned to Chicago and, like fellow silent comedians Larry Semon and Harry Langdon, became a cartoonist and illustrator. Among other exploits, he was the originator and artist of a series of cartoons that appeared in the *Chicago American* in 1910 called "The Sterling Kids."[46] His acting training actually helped him in his artwork: to get the proper facial expressions for his cartoon characters he would sit in front of a mirror and screw his face up, drawing what he saw. This in turn taught him what expressions raised a laugh and how he could use his face in the animated cartoon manner onstage and later on the screen as a member of the Keystone Studio.[47]

In conjunction with his other ventures, Sterling's stage career seems to have been moderately active and varied. He toured the entire United States and appeared fairly regularly in New York. While touring, Sterling played in stock and vaudeville; he also found work on the legitimate stage and, for a while, a Mississippi riverboat. He was appearing with headliners such as the actor synonymous with *Kismet*, Otis Skinner,[48] who also performed one-act plays as well as the classics, including Shakespeare. Then there was actor/playwright William Gillette,[49] another classical actor of his day and Essanay Studio's 1916 Sherlock Holmes. Among others, Sterling appeared with the comedy teams of Emma and Johnny Ray, and the Four Mortons, led by Sam and Kitty Morton, one of the first great family acts in vaudeville. Like the Three Keatons, their performances were wild and roughshod. But it was on the silver screen that Ford Sterling would find his true niche.

2

His Smashing Career

Sterling's film career began with the Biograph Company[1] in the second half of 1912. There are two documented versions of how he entered the movies, differing only in the names involved. At the time, Sterling was appearing in New York on Broadway in the musical comedy *Sidewalk Chatter,* in which he had a featured act. This was one of his return visits to the theater capital after touring the country as a featured player in vaudeville, stock companies, the Mississippi riverboat, and musical comedies. As his specialty, Sterling had mastered the art of dialect which when combined with his facial gymnastics proved popular with audiences.

These were the days when all actors were expected to have literally hundreds of roles on hand; adding the accents helped Sterling to stand out. Sterling's own memory of this time was a little vague, except that he did recall he was in an act in *Sidewalk Chatter* with Tom McEvoy, billed as McEvoy and Sterling, entitled "Breaking Into Society." Sterling sometimes said that after this act, "Pathé" Lehrman spoke to Sterling, telling him he was convinced he would make good in pictures. Lehrman, a man of French or Viennese or some other descent, depending on which story he was telling at that time, was employed at Biograph with future comedy impresario Mack Sennett. Sennett had apparently been looking for another comedian to join the company within the Biograph Studios he had been put in charge of and Sterling fit the bill.

Sennett claimed, though, that it was he who saw Sterling in his act and not Lehrman and, after visiting him in his dressing room, decided to sign him up. In other interviews, Sterling concurs with this, stating that Sennett spoke to him in the spring of 1912. The movies were a hazardous financial risk in those days, but Sennett managed to persuade Sterling to leave the stage for pictures. Mack and Ford may have known each other from the theater and, being familiar with his work, Mack had no qualms about putting Ford forward in a prominent role in his first film. Sterling already had a good reputation as a comedian across the country, judging by the reviews he was getting, so who better to have making films for you?

Sennett had been successful enough with his directing and writing to be given the comedy unit at Biograph in March 1911, and Sterling was now one of his team. Tracing Sterling's Biograph film roles is not as straightforward as with some of his later Sennett offerings. Those have been, and continue to be, well documented. Biograph did not credit their actors until 1915; consequently, the only cast lists accompanying Biograph titles for films prior to this date were later either made up from cast names appearing in the production data, from interviews with those connected with the studio, or by contemporary reviewers putting names to faces they recognized from other credited films or stills.

Sennett's team also included Biograph players Vivian Prescott and Eddie Dillon. Eddie had joined D. W. Griffith in his first movie stock company and was later seen in *Intolerance, Judith of Bethulia,* and *Fisher Folk.* Dillon would go on to successfully write scenarios for movies and direct, and he would remain a friend of Sterling's.

Also on the Sennett team was the lady who would become Keystone's superstar comedienne, Mabel Normand. Originally an artist's model, Mabel started her moving picture career with Vitagraph in 1911, later moving to Biograph where she met Mack Sennett. Soon Mabel and Mack began a romance, which lasted for many years; why they didn't marry has never been clear. There circulates a strong rumor, however, that Mack Sennett was already married, albeit unhappily, to an opera singer; with both being Catholic, divorce was out of the question. This made Sennett, for all intents and purposes, both available *and* unavailable to Normand. After Mack and Mabel broke up she was plagued by ill health, drug addiction, and scandal. Prime items of gossip were that Mabel was the last person to see director William Desmond Taylor[2] alive before his murder on February 1, 1922, and that Normand's chauffeur shot a guest at a New Year's Eve (1923) party given by fellow comedienne Edna Purviance. Mabel was married for less than four years to actor Lew Cody before her death from tuberculosis on February 22, 1930. Sterling, who had remained friends with Mabel, was one of the pallbearers at her funeral.[3]

Fred Mace originally intended to become a dentist but traded in his drill for the lure of light opera and musical comedy. After a career on the stage he was persuaded by Sennett to join Biograph in 1910. In 1917, Mace was found lifeless in his hotel room; official reports stated he had died from a heart attack, despite rumors of his taking his own life because of unrequited love.

Many surviving Biograph and Sennett shorts from this period, including Sterling's, have been made available for viewing thanks only to the quirks of early copyright laws. In the early days you could not copyright a moving picture; however, still pictures *were* protected. Movie studios tried several methods to protect their product — hanging or painting the company logo on the set in a prominent place assured viewers would know who owned and produced the film. Copyrighting the film's images as if they were photographs was another shrewd technique. This required transferring some or all of the camera negative to contact paper, thus making a paper print,[4] which was then lodged as a paper reel at the Library of Congress. In 1940, Howard Lamarre Walls rediscovered a series of paper rolls in a basement vault at the Library of Congress. After the reels were catalogued, pioneer cameraman Carl Louis Gregory was approached to see if he could make projectionable prints from these paper positives. Gregory converted a printer he had designed for working with shrunk nitrate film and was able to process the reels by painfully photographing each perfectly lined-up image one at a time. It worked, although it was a little shaky at times,

Ford Sterling as George Fitzgerald in *The Galloping Fish*. Released March 10, 1924. First National Pictures.

but the end result was that the films could be projected onto the screen as originally intended. Fortunately, Biograph had lodged all their material for copyright protection with the Library of Congress. If these paper prints had been destroyed or had remained tucked away in the old musty basement, there would be practically no film record of any of these early, pre–Keystone Sennett films. The Library of Congress Motion Picture Preservation Lab has taken over a long-term project involving rephotographing the rolls of paper in the archive using new technology with great success. Film preservation lives on.

A number of Ford Sterling filmographies cite his film debut as the nonsurviving Mack Sennett–directed Biograph short *A Dutch Goldmine* (released June 1911).[5]

However, this (as well as five other credited film appearances in 1911) cannot be verified or authenticated. Neither has he shown up in any extant films made at Biograph in the first half of 1912. Sterling's first confirmed appearances are in *Tragedy of a Dress Suit* and *The Interrupted Elopement,* both released on August 15, 1912; *He Must Have a Wife,* released on September 11; and *Stern Papa,* released on September 16, 1912. These are only release dates—not the period when the film was actually in production—so this also blurs the issue of when Sterling actually worked at Biograph. Given that his first definitive appearance on film was at the end of Mack's tenure at Biograph (just before Sennett went off to make movies under the Keystone brand), it would be logical to presume Sterling only made the four films for Biograph before joining Sennett at Keystone. In fact, the release dates of Ford's first two shorts came three days after the press release announcing Keystone's inception, on August 12, 1912.

If Sterling had made an occasional film with Sennett before the August releases, as some filmographies suggest, he probably would have combined his film appearances with his New York stage career, as he would have had to fulfill his contract for *Sidewalk Chatter.* It was not unusual for a performer to make occasional short films while working in the theatre, despite the fact that filmmaking was not considered a legitimate field for a stage actor to ply his craft. In the United States, film was an art form frowned upon by those in the "biz." Interestingly, however, the anonymity provided by the studio's lack of on-screen credit for performers actually allowed actors to appear in the movies with at least a little bit of secrecy. Actors in other countries didn't seem to have this attitude; they thought the movies were a good way to advertise their acts and were pleased to be seen on the screen.

There is the possibility Sterling had a role in one earlier film at Biograph, which he spoke of later in the mid–1920s; however, certain blatantly inaccurate Paramount press releases[6] put doubts on the whole issue. The story: Sterling recalled that, having been a vaudeville comedian for two or three years, he thought he was a "pretty big guy" when Mack Sennett hired him to play in his comedies. On the first day that he reported for work he was asked by the director if he could play a woman. Sterling claimed that he could. He then went up to the dressing room, put on makeup, and proceeded to rehearse in front of a mirror for three hours, so he could fulfill the claim he had made to the director. Eventually the assistant director called him and they started out.

According to Sterling and the press release, the scene was filmed on a Hollywood street corner. Sterling apparently was to play a woman caught in a traffic jam — and he worked hard. He carried bags, was hit by a streetcar, and took about a dozen hard falls. Later that day, after returning to the studio, he was heartily complimented and went to his dressing room believing he had done a marvelous comedy sequence. A few moments later, the assistant director came up and demanded the women's clothing. Sterling wondered why but gave the clothes to him anyway. About an hour later, as he was leaving the studio, he saw the leading woman in the picture wearing the identical outfit Ford had just taken off. Not until then did Sterling realize that he had been doubling for her.

Was this Ford Sterling's film debut, as some have concluded? Hardly. Given the source of the story — a studio publicity release designed to pique interest and generate buzz — it is highly likely that it is entirely fictional and that it never even happened. Besides, considering that Sterling was at that point a successful stage performer, it is questionable whether he would even take such a small role in a short film when that was considered in the industry the lowest rung on the ladder.

Another erroneous assumption made by some film historians is that in the late 1910s and early 1920s Sterling was forced to tone down his characterizations and change his makeup after his popularity waned. The rationale was that he had to reinvent himself due to the changing fashions and expectations of more

Producer and director — and the force behind the Keystone Studio — Mack Sennett.

sophisticated audiences. The Biographs featuring Sterling nicely show that he had a wide range of acting styles, well before we see the more subtle Sterling in his later silent post–Sennett features. This also illustrates that it was not so much a new toning down of Sterling's comedic technique but rather a conscious decision to return to a pre–Keystone stage persona that he undertook. He simply performed in a way the role demanded. It is unlikely that such eminent actors as Otis Skinner or William Gillette would have appreciated a frenetic Dutch comedian mugging his way through one of their productions.

In the early films, Sterling is seen with various makeup designs, often favoring nothing more than basic movie makeup and the pencil-thin mustache which he sometimes sported in real life. What is apparent is that Sterling brought part of his stage act, including his characteristic makeup, with him, to the screen. This, though, was only part of a galaxy of characters he portrayed. A 1913 *Moving Picture World* article refers to how many of "the funny situations that used to have his audiences in roars [in vaudeville] were utilized in his films with great success." It also refers to Sterling as "a past master in the art of facial expression and makeup that set a new mark in this sort of work."[7]

As confirmation, examples of the subtle later Sterling performances are found in two extant 1912 Biograph shorts, *Tragedy in a Dress Suit* and *The Interrupted Elopement*. Sterling's performances in these can be paralleled to those used in both the Keystone short, *Hearts and Flowers* (1919), and the Mal St. Clair–directed Famous Players feature, *The Show Off* (1926).

In Biograph's *Tragedy in a Dress Suit*, Sterling, in the guise of his Dutch character, is the manager of a boardinghouse. Apparently he is the only person in the building to own a dress suit and he is very proud of the garment. When he finds the dress suit has been "borrowed" by a young penniless lodger, Sterling is furious. The young man is bent on impressing a local heiress who has invited him to attend her house party, and he simply has to have that suit. Sterling's character, upon discovering his suit missing, remains relatively calm — a very different reaction from the ballistic anger he would portray in later Keystone films. The trademark hand gestures and thinking out loud (in the guise of chatting to himself) are there, but without that degree of threat and agitated animation of Sterling's future characterizations of Chief Teheezal or Cohen. Off Sterling goes in search of his elusive suit, running down a path through the park in a perfectly normal manner. He thinks he sees the culprit and after deftly swiping the top hat back and placing it on his own head (it is highly likely that this was the first time Sterling wore his trademark headgear on-screen), he tries to remove the jacket from the back of an unsuspecting stranger. The stranger retaliates, violently shaking Ford. Does he launch himself at the man and try to bite his nose off? No. Realizing this is not the thief, he apologetically cowers back before returning the hat and heading off across the park to find the real culprit. The Keystone character would have continued to attack unless the victim had been an authority figure. In that case, the victim would have been brushed down and ingratiatingly saluted.

Later, when Ford tries to gain admittance to the party *persona non grata*, he is ejected down the front steps of the mansion where it is being held. This is not a problem; he merely dusts himself off, thinks of a plan, and scuttles around to the side of the house so he can affect his entry via a window. Once inside, he makes a beeline for the young thief and confronts him: there is much angry fist shaking, yet no physical contact is required for Ford to get his suit back. The young man is left to face his shame hiding behind a screen in his underwear. In the closing shot, Sterling uncharacteristically appears more shocked at the young man's situation, rather than being smug at having won back his precious suit. Sterling has also, for all intents and purposes, won the fought-over object. In the Keystones, whether it was an inanimate object or a woman, he normally lost and was the recipient of the comeuppance.

In *Hearts and Flowers*, although Sterling is playing one of his sophisticated characters rather than his Dutch character from *Tragedy in a Dress Suit*, his behavior is similar to that in the earlier film. Sterling plays the conductor of a high-class band performing in an elegant hotel restaurant and sports bow tie and tails and his pencil-thin mustache. He has all sorts of problems with Louise Fazenda and her family, as well as a rich heiress and her boyfriend, but he reacts in the same restrained manner to all the trouble he gets himself into. Case in point is his technique in disposing of Louise Fazenda's boyfriend. Instead of out-and-out attacking him, Sterling, leaning on the hotel desk with his back to the forlorn man, simply bends his knee behind him, plants his foot squarely in the approaching boyfriend's stomach, and propels him back across the room with a quick shove.

2—His Smashing Career

In the Biograph short *The Interrupted Elopement*, Ford's character—sporting a fashionable straw hat—would form the basis of the role Aubrey Piper in a later, more famous feature. *The Show Off* (1926) was directed by Mal St. Clair for Famous Players and starred Sterling. (In more recent years, this film has tended to be thought of as a Louise Brooks vehicle, even though she was only a supporting player appearing in one of her early films.) The plot of *The Interrupted Elopement* has Ford as one of Bob's friends, Bob being the intended fiancé in the elopement of the title.

Sterling's character is outraged when the girl's father turns down Bob's request for her hand; so incensed is Ford that he hatches a plan for the two to elope. Sterling delivers a letter (which he of course concocted) to the girl containing the elopement plot; he then suggests kidnapping the minister so they can be married in secret. After the plot is discovered by her father, Ford blusteringly encourages the fiancée in his actions, boasting bombastically about the clever scheme he has thought up concerning the minister. Unfortunately, when he goes to the minister's house to kidnap him, father has arrived first. Ford inadvertently bags father (literally), kidnaps him, and brings him back to the others in a sack. "I did it," he mouths proudly as he pulls the sack off father's head. He sure did.

Again there is no sign of Sterling behaving in his Keystone manner; there are none of the gesticulations associated with the Sennett period apparent at all. Although still full of energy, it appears to be Sterling's most subdued performance in a Sennett-directed short. In the later feature, *The Show Off*, with Louise Brooks and Lois Wilson, Sterling plays Aubrey Piper.

Piper is a bombastic, loud, irresponsible, and self-important egomaniac whose boasts and exaggerations get himself and his future wife teetering on the brink of disaster and nearly dragging her family with them. The only remotely slapstick moment in this feature is a car ride after Aubrey wins a car. He insists to the car salesman that he not only knows how to drive but has also won auto races. Of course he has never driven a car in his life. His ensuing trip home is fraught with complications and lack of road rules right up until the moment he pins a policeman to the fence of a large building with his fender, at which point he is arrested. Sterling did all his own driving for the car chase sequence, including the dangerous stunt of driving through the crowd while chasing the policeman across a courtyard and up some steps.

In these initial roles played by Sterling his characters are varied. We are seeing Sterling the stage actor, performing without previous film experience or training (something not available at the time). It wasn't until later, after he gained experience with Mack Sennett and was able to experiment at the Keystone Company, that he perfected his film style and achieved worldwide recognition and stardom.

3

Our Dare Devil Chief

In 1912 Sterling, together with Mack Sennett, Mabel Normand, Fred Mace, and Henry "Pathé" Lehrman, had left Biograph to form the nucleus of Sennett's new Keystone Film Company. To be accurate, Sennett did not own the Keystone Company but was its managing director, or director general as he liked to be known. He pretty much had *carte blanche* over its films, though, and the day-to-day running of the studio. Although founded and funded by Adam Kessel and Charles Bauman[1] through their New York Motion Picture Company, Keystone was a separate entity. Kessel became the president and Bauman the treasurer of the new studio. Sennett was paid $100 per week to begin with and got one-third interest in the company, plus being able to contribute the talent. Kessel and Bauman maintained control of the finances, any expansions to the studio, and the quantity of the studio's output. The NYMPC released the Keystone product through Mutual, with whom they were contracted; this also obligated Sennett to provide a certain quota of split- and one- and two-reelers per month.

Soon after making the first few split-reelers, the Keystone Company left New York and headed for the growing movie colony on the West Coast. It is very easy to see which of the films were made on the East Coast by looking at the surrounding scenery and buildings. Victorian houses, trees, and paved roads: New York. Palm trees, dirt roads, and clapboard houses: California. Sennett, Normand, and Mace were familiar with the area, as the Biograph Company spent the winter months filming in California's less inclement weather conditions. Sterling, too, was familiar with it through his years of touring with the circus and theatrical companies. Thus it was in Edendale, California—with Sennett, Keystone, and the anarchic, chaotic band of comedians who formed around them to make movies—that Ford Sterling fit in so well. The new Keystone Company's move out to California, according to *Moving Picture World*, began with the advance guard of Sennett and Normand on August 28, 1912; Sterling, Lehrman, and Alice Davenport arrived shortly thereafter.

Alice Davenport was a gallant lady and a marvelous foil for Ford. Born Alice Shepphard, she had been a child actress, making her stage debut in 1869 at the age of five. Her first film, a comedy titled *The Best Man Wins*, was made for Nestor in 1911. The Keystone clan affectionately called her "Mother Davenport," and she would often play opposite Sterling either as his nemesis or his more homely love interest, as in *Toplitsky and Co.*, or both, as in *A False Beauty*. She lampooned her formidable presence with the typical Edwardian ample-bosomed, wasp-waisted, corseted figure, hair piled high on top of her head, but she could just as easily look elegant. She also appeared to have been game for anything Sennett could put her through. Alice acquired the name Davenport through her marriage to silent actor, director, and later talkie character actor, Harry Bryant Davenport. Their daughter Dorothy became a successful actress, director, screenwriter, and producer in her own right. (Alice died in 1936.)

An old face also became part of the team on its arrival. Former Biograph comedy unit actor Fred Mace was already on the West Coast. He had left Biograph after the company's earlier season in California to work for IMP; problems with that studio soon left him without a job but he remained on the West Coast. He was eager to join the new venture with the old team.

Sennett didn't waste any time getting started after saying good-bye to Biograph. The first shorts made by the new company, *Cohen Collects a Debt* and *The Water Nymph* (a remake of *The Diving Girl*, which Sennett had made for Biograph in 1911), were released on September 23, 1912. These are split-reel shorts, each movie consisting of half a standard reel and lasting approximately five to six minutes. These two films were unquestionably made on the East Coast before the company moved to the West Coast, as were the first few Keystones. It is easy to see that the scenery in *The Water Nymph* is East Coast rather than West, boasting older houses and not a palm tree in sight. The Keystone release was made with the same major players with one exception: Ford Sterling. Sterling plays Sennett's father, a recurring role for him. This time they are both after the hand of the same girl, Mabel Normand, the Diving Venus, complete with her one-piece bathing suit—very daring for 1912. *Cohen Collects a Debt*, unfortunately, is presumed lost.

So eager were they to make movies that when the team first arrived on the West Coast they had to improvise for a studio. The old Bison studio in Edendale, which was to be turned over to Sennett for use as the Keystone studio, was not ready. Temporary accommodation was found for them at Thomas H. Ince's[2] Inceville Studio in nearby Los Angeles. The studio was not the only venue used by Sennett: he liked to go on location, and Echo Park[3] proved a favorite outside venue which, over the years, was used many times for their shenanigans.

As the Keystone films gained in popularity and their comedians became famous, location work became more than just turning up in a park with a camera and a couple of actors. In February 1913, Sennett had made arrangements with the Los Angeles Railway Company to use a streetcar and the mile of track running from Central Avenue to the barns in the neighborhood of Central and Vernon on the south side of Los Angeles. This was needed for the chase in Sennett's latest picture, starring Sterling as a nickel-grasping streetcar conductor. The impromptu audience was begun by normally dutiful housewives neglecting their household obligations to spend the day on the sidewalk enjoying the performances. During the lunch break and later, after school, several hundred youngsters joined the crowd, which now required two real policemen—and some of the Keystone variety—to keep the interested bystanders out of the picture. This would be a scene repeated wherever the unit tried to work.[4]

Sterling immediately became one of the principal players of the early Keystone comedies, often portraying standard Jewish characters or the comic villain playing off Sennett's rube. His popularity grew rapidly with the audiences, and when Fred Mace left to form his own ill-fated company in April 1913, Sterling took over as top banana. He wore different types of makeup and costume in the Sennett comedies, varying them to suit the character. He did not constantly use the Dutch makeup usually associated with him, with its tufty goatee, heavy eye makeup and glasses; that character was used only occasionally. Later, however, it became his trademark. Back in the Biograph days, Sterling's makeup sometimes consisted of nothing but the standard film makeup of the day[5] and his own pencil-thin mustache which he occasionally sported. At other times, presumably when clean shaven, he glued on a huge, handlebar mustache which he would twirl à la grand villain. For a man of his build, a stocky 5'11", Sterling took some pretty spectacular and acrobatic falls, a technique learned in the circus of his youth. His larger-than-life strutting and gesticulation, even more grandiose than stage melodrama required, were also learned in the circus ring, as well as from his cartoons and transferred well to the screen for his comic and flamboyant characters.

In these early movies, Ford Sterling created characters that were well-honed caricatures rather than characters. Even when not wearing his regular villain or Chief Teheezal costumes, his most remembered roles, he is unmistakable. There is Sterling's gait, which was not so much a walk as a slink with knees turned out and slightly bent. He deliberately placed one foot after the other as if the slightest noise would bring dire retribution upon his head. When he ran, he maintained this creeping, bowlegged gait but rose to his toes, or he would spring along like a demented ostrich, unless making a fast getaway, and then he purely up and sprinted. Usually these sudden bursts of speed were preceded by a surprised spring in the air or a turn to the side and a split jump before he sped away. Another Sterling trademark was how he sprang through doors or other entrances. With feet together, he would grab the door frame with both hands and pull himself through the opening in one bound. Sterling used this as a punctuation mark for his clumsy stealth. One such instance occurs as he enters the Toplitsky household in *Toplitsky and Co.* (1913) (on the occasions he illicitly visits Mrs. Toplitsky) through the conventional house entrance. He loiters in front of the door just long enough to casually examine his surroundings for onlookers, then he springs through the aperture like a kangaroo. Sterling used it again to board the locomotive that was intended to run over Mabel Normand (who was tied to the tracks further up the line) in *Barney Oldfield — A Race for a Life* (1913). After facing the camera in defiance and twirling his mustache, he hops straight up the cab steps in triumph in one bound instead of using the steps.

What could be called the Chief Teheezal salute, although it appeared before the Keystone Kops, was liberally used by Sterling for a variety of characters. He didn't necessarily have to be saluting a physical presence; he used it when chatting away to himself to show his feelings toward someone he was thinking about, as a sort of sarcastic "yes, sir" or "yes, ma'am." He ingratiatingly saluted a lot as Chief Teheezal and as a soldier in *Cohen Saves the Flag* (1913) and *Stolen Glory* (1912) and the salute remained the same. Does this little bit of business hark back to his school days and the military suit his mother sent to him?

Then, of course, there was Ford in attack mode, with his penchant for biting people's noses at any given moment and at every opportunity. This occurred especially during arguments, sometimes simply because someone had irritated him or just happened to be in the wrong place at the wrong time. It is quite something to see the avenging Sterling wrap his legs around rotund Roscoe (Fatty) Arbuckle's girth, grab the sides of his head, and try to bite his nose off in *Speed Kings* (1913). Arbuckle's crime? He was a bit brisk in removing Mabel Normand (Sterling's daughter) from the racetrack for her own safety. The ultimate in this activity: envision the identically dressed Sterling and Henry "Pathé" Lehrman spinning around each other, each trying to turn the other's nose into a snack food in *Love and Vengeance*—slapstick at its wildest.

It was not only Arbuckle and Lehrman who came under attack. Charlie Chaplin was another worthy opponent in *Tango Tangles* (1914), where he as the drunken partygoer and Sterling as the bandleader battle it out for the hand of the hatcheck girl. They threaten to take off their clothes for their battle, but think better of it when they see the shocked faces of the onlookers. They whirl and spin together, swing and miss, swing and hit, and ultimately fall, working their way from the dance floor right into the foyer, where they both topple in unison backward onto the floor.

One of the best of Sterling's regular early Keystone characters was his villain. Sterling was the archetypical melodramatic villain that audiences loved to hate. This image, reminiscent of the Victorian and Edwardian stage, has been copied in movies and cartoons and continues to the present day. Witness British comic Terry-Thomas doing his sterling best in such films as *Those Magnificent Men in Their Flying Machines* and *Monte Carlo or Bust,* and the cartoon character Dick Dastardly in the *Wacky Races* television series. Ford's appearance on-screen was accompanied by enthusiastic hisses and boos from adults and children alike. He was wonderfully outrageous, just plain out-and-out conniving and nasty, as he brought turn-of-the-century villainy to the silver screen. Never was he better than in *Barney Oldfield—A Race for a Life* (1913).

In this film, Sterling was the Victorian melodrama villain personified, completely over the top with whisker twirlings, eyebrow wigglings, cigar fiddlings, and dastardly asides to the camera. He abducts Mabel Normand (not a willing subject this time), ties her to the railway track, and proceeds to steal a locomotive with which to run her over. The day is saved only by Mabel's rube boyfriend's (Sennett) presence of mind when he enlists the aid of real motor racing ace Barney Oldfield. Oldfield promptly outdrives the speeding locomotive, allowing him and Sennett to rescue Normand from certain doom just in the nick of time. When the law, on a railway hand cart from one direction, and Barney and Mack from the other catch up to Ford, he produces a gun and shoots the five pursuing policemen, saving the sixth bullet for himself. He puts the barrel to his head, pulls the trigger, and—nothing. There doesn't seem to be a sixth bullet. Egads! He has to be content with *strangling himself*, another useful device for getting out of a sticky situation.

Through the courtesy of a Mr. E. W. McGee, general passenger agent for the Santa Fe, Sennett was granted the use of a late-model locomotive, baggage car, and passenger coach. A special permit was granted by the authorities of Inglewood for Barney Oldfield to race down the old Redondo Road, well above the speed limit.

Ford is not much nicer in *Dirty Work in a Laundry* aka *A Desperate Scoundrel* (1915). His shifty, sneaky character is established right in the opening scene, as he steals the bottle from a baby. The child is contentedly lying in its perambulator, taking in the fresh air at the local park and having a nice drink of milk, when Sterling happens along, places his hat over the baby's head, takes the bottle, drinks the milk, and refills the now-empty bottle with water from a nearby drinking fountain before returning it to the baby.

His character goes downhill from there.

Sterling had an outrageously mobile face which was especially good at portraying sneaky or disgusted countenances. There is a wonderful example of the Sterling disgust-shock-horror in *A False Beauty* aka *A Faded Vampire* (1914).

In it, his face goes through the full gamut of contortions as he watches his fiancée, played by Alice Davenport, get ready for bed. Sterling has hidden in the bushes just outside Davenport's dressing room window and is expectantly waiting to see her undress. Initially, he is enthralled by the profiled figure in the window, but then, as she pulls down the shade, Sterling has to be frustratedly content with watching the backlit silhouette of the lovely Miss Davenport as she undresses. But all is not as it seems. First, her *wig* comes off, displaying a virtually bald pate with just a few wisps of remaining hair; she proceeds to give her scalp a good scratching once it's free from its covering. Then her *dentures* come out and Miss Davenport makes a good deal of business placing them into a glass of water and stirring them round and round with her finger. Poor Ford is beside himself: he writhes and grimaces at the less-than-flattering image of the lady to whom he has just become engaged. As soon as she disappears into her bedroom he is climbing through the dressing room window in panic to get his ring back.

Alongside his Dutch character and without, seemingly, the need for much change of makeup, Ford also specialized in the then-popular archetypical Jewish caricature as personified in the Cohen character. Like most burlesque Jewish caricature of this period, Sterling's could perhaps be accused of bordering on the anti–Semitic. No one was beyond being lampooned: fat, thin, old, young, Italian, Spanish, Jewish, English, rich, poor, bald, shrewish, or fey, and in those days most people had the self-confidence to be able to laugh at themselves or their own shortcomings. Sterling had several outings as Cohen. *Cohen Saves the Flag* (1913) has some pretty spectacular battle sequences for a comedy short.

Cohen is the unwitting hero of the film and a sergeant in the Union Army opposite Mabel Normand's Rebecca. Sterling's rival and nemesis is Henry Lehrman. When Sterling and Lehrman fight they use the same tactics and, as they are both wearing similar clothes before they sign up for the army, it is at times difficult to tell them apart, especially when they are wrapped around each other.

The spectacular battle scenes were actually staged by Ince for one of his Civil War films, and Sennett utilized a few clandestine shots to include in his short. Toplitsky, in *Toplitsky and Co.*, along with Sterling's other Jewish roles, Snitz and Hofmeyer, are primarily the same character and with a quick change of name could easily have been included as part of the Cohen series.

But what of Sterling's other characters? Usually he is remembered as either the villain or the Keystone Kop's Chief Teheezal, although he was one of several to lead that honorable band of men. In 1920, an article referred to Ford as being best remembered for his role in the 1919 five-reeler, *Yankee Doodle in Berlin*, in which he played the humorously villainous Kaiser. Perhaps this was just the last major role the author had seen Sterling in before the article was written. Granted, in his nonvillainous roles Sterling invariably came off as a conniving ne'er-do-well, but more often than not there were mitigating circumstances to his behavior. As some of these characters wore makeup similar to that of the Sterling villains, audiences may have simply expected the sort of behavior from him that could be hissed and booed at.

In *The Gusher* (1913), Sterling plays an almost sympathetic character that remains agreeable throughout the film. He is the one who is wronged; he is swindled and when the swindle (a fake oil well) turns out to be a real gusher, he becomes a rich oil baron and can marry his girlfriend (Mabel Normand). Unfortunately, the villain has set fire to the oil and Ford loses the lot.

Sterling is a domestic victim in *He Wouldn't Stay Down* (1915). His friend (and assistant director) Charley Chase tries to get Ford to drown himself, telling him to jump off a pier into the sea with a rope round his neck while his wife (Minta Durfee) is watching to give her the impression he is committing suicide. However, Chase rigs the rope so that it is not there to help him pull Ford out as they planned. It is actually weighted, so that Ford will really drown! Chase not only wants to marry Minta, with whom he has been having a secret liaison, but also wants to cash in on a newly acquired life insurance policy Ford's wife has taken out. The plot, of course, fails: Ford is hooked out of the sea by a fisherman in a boat and taken to the local police station by a handy policeman who gives him a hard time, thinking Ford did try to drown himself. Sterling again is the sympathetic victim, although when all is discovered, he is not above contemplating keeping the insurance payment on his own life for himself, that is, until the insurance man arrives with the police.

But is the Ford Sterling villain really out-and-out villainous, or is there more to him than that? With the exception of *Dirty Work in a Laundry* and *Barney Oldfield — A Race for a Life*, Sterling doesn't usually start out with malice aforethought. In his marginally more congenial roles he is pushed into villainous activities through mitigating circumstances. Although always ingratiating, scheming, and somewhat of a shady character even before he becomes bent on revenge, he doesn't start out being particularly vindictive; he needs provocation.

Usually there is a lady in the piece with whom he is enamored and who proves to be the cause of all his troubles. She will encourage him and then one of the following hiccups occurs: A typical circumstance can be found in *A Muddy Romance*, when he thinks he is going to marry Mabel Normand. But when he is thwarted by another suitor, he takes revenge on them by draining the park lake.

Here the couple, complete with parson, have rowed into the middle, falsely believing they are safe from Ford's interference and will be able to get married in peace. The second scenario has the flirty young lady's spouse or gentleman friend and his chums wreak vengeance on Sterling for his attentions toward the said young lady, against which, naturally, Ford retaliates.

Even in *Dirty Work in a Laundry*, when Sterling is at his nastiest, Minta Durfee merrily flirts with him. It is the subsequent treatment he receives, from her fiancé and their boss, when he reciprocates that sets him off plotting trouble.

Sometimes he just plain gets himself into trouble with women, as when he pursues Toplitsky's wife in *Toplitsky and Co*. Mrs. Toplitsky (Alice Davenport) certainly doesn't dissuade Ford from making advances and, like Minta, flirts unashamedly with him; but again circumstances gang up on poor Sterling. Mr. Toplitsky magnanimously forgives his wife in front of his friends for her indiscretions with Ford. All seems to be well but, unfortunately, Ford does not know about the forgiveness and looks for a place to hide. If he hadn't gone to the public baths to hide from Mr. Toplitsky and his friends, if he hadn't been chased by a bear, and if he hadn't been forced to make his escape by jumping through Mrs. Toplitsky's bedroom window, Mr. Toplitsky and the friends wouldn't have found Ford hiding under Mrs. Toplitsky's bed in a bathing suit while Mrs. Toplitsky occupied said bed, supposedly asleep.

He similarly gets into trouble believing someone else's wife is not only interested in him but also single, in *Only a Messenger Boy* (1915). When he is under the false impression that the local mayor's wife is in love with him, it leads to all sorts of complications, including his rather wet demise trapped in a safe on the bottom of a river.

Sometimes his problems arise from pure competition, when he simply wants the same woman as several other people and is not the type to step aside. Such is the case in *Tango Tangles*. In this film, Sterling believes he has as much right to the hatcheck girl's affections as either Roscoe Arbuckle, a fellow band member, or Charlie Chaplin, a drunken patron. Just because Arbuckle saw her first doesn't give him *carte blanche* over her affections. Sterling simply employs some devious maneuvers to rid the stage of his competition. He sends Arbuckle from the bandstand on a fool's errand to get a drink for him, and as soon as Arbuckle is out of sight Sterling is on the dance floor with the hatcheck girl. Ford is prepared to fight for her, too, as Chaplin finds out, although neither seems particularly efficient in the pugilism department, both whirling around together, ending up dazed on the floor, each with an arm through the sleeve of the same coat.

Rivalry in love occasionally gave Sterling a chance to be the hero, as in *Love and Rubbish* (1913), set in a park supposedly kept free of paper and litter by two park keepers, Sterling and Charles Avery. Sterling and Avery trade their white park-keeper uniforms for top hats and frock coats (which they keep hidden in a garbage can) to make themselves more attractive to the assorted ladies frequenting the park. Among the visitors are a woman with a small child (Paul "Little Billy" Jacobs) who appears to be habitually put in a large wooden barrel instead of in a playpen, an older lady (the durable Alice Davenport), and, briefly in two scenes, a rotund acrobatic young man in a derby hat (Roscoe Arbuckle). Naturally the park supervisor comes along and to avoid capture Avery hides in Paul Jacobs' now vacated barrel. The barrel is knocked over and rolls down a hill with the entire cast chasing it because they believe little Paul is still inside. He is safe and sound, of course, happily playing with three small friends and oblivious to the concerns of the adults. At the bottom of a steep incline the barrel plops into a pond. Sterling bravely offers to dive in and save the small child from a horrible fate. Assisted by police officers who have also come to the aid of the floating barrel, Sterling pulls the barrel ashore and after acknowledging the gathered crowd's appreciation for his heroism removes the lid only to be greeted by a water-spouting Avery!

Chief Teheezal is not exempt from woman troubles, either, but these are not necessarily of a romantic nature. Where women are concerned, his angst is usually caused by either their rescue or a rescue necessitated because of wheels put into motion by their actions. *Hide and Seek* (1913) is a short which would appear to be spoofing silent star King Baggot's *The Time Lock Safe* (1910).

The Kops are called upon to release a small child suspected of being accidentally locked in a bank's time vault. This situation was due to Mabel Normand's failure to look after the small girl in a responsible manner. Attempting to open the safe, Sterling's inept bumblings first result in his trying to drill out the lock with the wrong end of a hand drill. The bit of the drill twirls into his stomach, thus inducing discomfort until the proverbial light bulb goes on and he, realizing his error, turns the business end toward the vault door. After the drilling activity fails, his next attempt is to blow the lock out with explosives. This only succeeds in blowing the door outward off its hinges and onto Sterling, knocking him to the ground where the door lands on top of him. Now prone, he can be conveniently trampled on by Mabel and the rest of the Kops, who are oblivious to his whereabouts as they examine the empty vault in confusion. Like Little Billy and the barrel, the girl is playing outside with her friends all the time.

Teheezal, of course, does not require the help of women to get himself into trouble. A heroically inept maladroit among men, he also appears to suffer from somnolence. When the Kops are needed, how many times is he found asleep at his desk?

Hide and Seek, Keystone Film Company, April 1913. Front row, L–R: Mabel Normand, Nick Cogley, and Ford Sterling try to release the small girl presumed locked in the bank's safe.

But then, the rest of the Kops are usually dozing. Or, if not, they are sitting in a crumpled line on the police station bench awaiting action or they are somewhere about the police station twiddling their thumbs. Maybe it's just a very low-crime area. The majority of Chief Teheezal's Keystone Kop chases are practically interchangeable. When called into action by Teheezal, the Kops certainly jump to it, knocking themselves, Teheezal, and anyone else they happen upon over in the process. Once out in their wagons, the fearless, or rather unwitting, Teheezal takes on the aura of a leader of men in the battle against crime. He stands on the passenger side of the advance car, truncheon held aloft like a general's, sword in hand, leading his troops. Doesn't last long. However hard the chief tries to maintain his dignity, with his men flying off their vehicles in all directions and some being dragged behind like a string of sausages while others wrap their automobiles around lampposts, trains, trolleys, each other, and anything else they can find and manage countless variations without cars, any illusion of dignity tends to wane. Maybe Teheezal's tiredness is due to being up all night filling out accident reports.

Although the Keystone Kops remained popular and familiar characters long after the last Sennett short featured them, they were, strangely, never given their own series. No Sennett film was built around them, nor were their appearances as numerous as is sometimes presumed: there isn't even so much as a Keystone or Sennett title with their name in it. The Kops were more a familiar entity called upon toward the end of a short starring one of Sennett's leading comics (probably drawn from the Kop's own ranks); their purpose was to keep the momentum of the movie's climactic chase and the laughs going. Sterling's Chief Teheezal in *Our Dare Devil Chief* is the only member of the force to be singled out as a main character for any of Keystone's one- or two-reelers, and that wasn't until Sterling's return to Keystone and Sennett after a brief hiatus from the studio.

Minta Durfee was Sterling's leading lady in many of the post–Sterling Studio films by Sennett. With her exquisite timing and classic beauty she was one of the best comediennes of her time. In real life Minta was Mrs. Roscoe Arbuckle. This Hartsook portrait was taken in 1917.

As in other Keystone shorts, *Our Dare Devil Chief* has Sterling teamed up with comedienne Minta Durfee, a vivacious actress full of courage both on and off the screen. She was at the time married to the popular comedian Roscoe Arbuckle, whom she also appeared with at Keystone. Arbuckle went on to have his own studio, Comique, where he persuaded the twenty-one-year-old Buster Keaton to join him and try his hand at making movies. Keaton went on to be considered one of the most important and influential comedians of all time. In 1921, Arbuckle was accused of causing the death of Virginia Rappe, a minor actress and Henry Lehrman's girlfriend, and allegedly a lady of dubious morals. She died at a party Arbuckle was hosting in San Francisco. After three very public trials he was unequivocally acquitted but his career was ruined. Controversy still surrounds the actual events that took place at the party. Minta stood by and supported him — something many of his old friends failed to do for fear of having their careers tainted by association or because their studio

heads advised them to stay away. Even Keaton stayed away. Minta went on to have a career that lasted until the 1970s, after which she lived at the Actors Home until her death on September 9, 1975.

Because Sterling's Teheezal character and his villains were so stylized and his makeup heavy and recognizable, Sterling was not that hard to impersonate, a fact Andy Clyde and Will Rogers successfully demonstrated. It was also relatively easy for Max Asher to double for Sterling's Snookee character when he was employed by Sterling Comedies and—after Ford departed from the company named after him—to take over the character in order to allow production of the Snookee series to continue. Other comics dressed like Sterling, wore his makeup, used his mannerisms, and did quite passable impersonations but

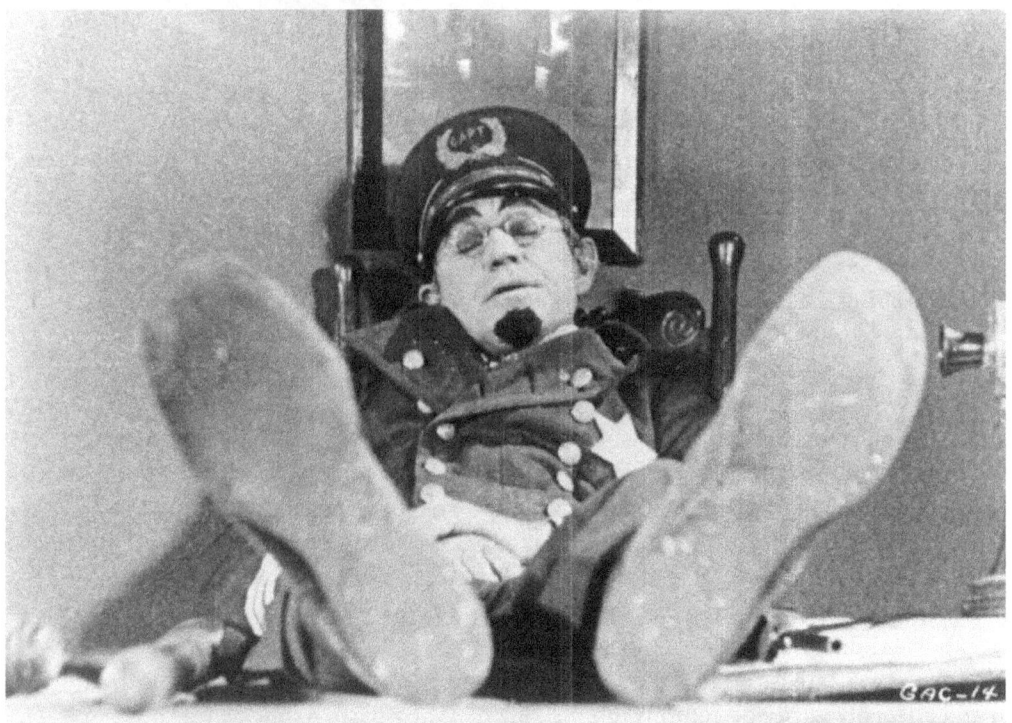

Top: Roscoe "Fatty" Arbuckle appeared with Sterling in many of his Keystone roles. On Sterling's return to Keystone after the fall of the Sterling Studios, he and Arbuckle were teamed together in *That Little Band of Gold*. *Bottom:* Will Rogers, as Sterling's Chief Teheezal, asleep at his desk, in his 1924 short, *Big Moments from Little Pictures*.

it was not so easy to copy Ford's energetic spontaneous expressions. Will Rogers perhaps came the closest in *Big Moments from Little Pictures* (1924).

Sterling's recognizable face may well have been the saving grace of the entire company, literally. There is a dubious but worth-telling tale of escape to Mexico by the Sennett team to avoid the law.[6] The year was 1913, and Mack received a phone call from the district attorney informing him that one of the bathing beauties, a seventeen-year-old minor, was in his office complaining about a certain condition she was in. The young lady had been "friendly" with several members of the Keystone studio, not to mention a local grocer. This would mean serious trouble for the perpetrator, possibly a stay in San Quentin. Mack wasted no time. He called for his car and rushed around the studio gathering up Sterling, Lehrman, Mace, Normand, and Polly Moran. They were instructed to get into the car with a camera and supplies and told they were all going to Mexico until things cooled down; the rest of the company would have to follow the best they were able.

They ended up in Tijuana, where an insurrection was taking place between a group of American bandits who were stirring up the locals against the Mexican government. Their leader was one Zeph Crocker, an American wanted back home for several murders and other indiscretions. When the Keystone group arrived at the local hostelry they were met with suspicion, shots were fired, and the manager mysteriously had no idea where the travelers could find accommodation. Suddenly, Mr. Crocker came in and started accusing Mack of being an agent sent by the American government to round up his gang. Crocker noticed Ford: "Hey pal, you're the funny Dutchman. I've seen you in the movies." Instantly rooms were found for all. Polly and Mabel shared one small room with a mouse; Mack, Henry, and Fred shared another; and Ford was honored with an invitation to share Crocker's own personal domain.

Ford's tenure there was fraught with horror. On his arrival to the objectionably smelly room he was confronted with the sight of a young lady lying on the floor in a drunken stupor. "Want her?" inquired Crocker. Sterling declined and the woman was unceremoniously kicked out of the room. Sterling got little sleep; Crocker insisted on keeping a kerosene lamp burning all night, the fumes of which made Ford nauseous and stung his eyes. Sterling also found his roommate somewhat intimidating, especially when Crocker told him that his own sweet mother was in jail for murdering his father. One night Crocker was assumed not to be returning, so just before dawn Ford blew out the lamp and proceeded to get the best sleep since they had arrived. Crocker did return, however, and didn't buy it Sterling told him the wind had blown out the flame. He had jabbed Ford with the hilt of a machete to awaken him. To his horror, Sterling saw that Crocker's hands were spattered with blood. Crocker had just decapitated a gentleman whose remains he had stuffed in the water barrel outside! "Mein Gott in Himmel" was Ford's only comment to Crocker's query as to whether he wanted to view the body before someone came to take it to the morgue.

The company gladly returned home a week later, after it was determined that it was the grocer who was responsible for the bathing beauty's dilemma.

4

A Dramatic Mistake

Early in 1914 Ford Sterling took what would turn out to be an ill-advised hiatus from Keystone. By the end of 1913 and the beginning of 1914, Sterling's workload was enormous: he was writing, directing and starring in his own films for Keystone.[1] Sometimes he was making multiple pictures, running between sets to shoot scenes requiring shots so close that a stand-in simply wouldn't do.[2] A section of the release schedule for this period demonstrates quite nicely the sort of pressure Sterling was under. At the turn of 1914 he was directing and acting in *Double Crossed*, which had been booked for a January 26 release; in production for *Baffles, Gentleman Burglar*, due to be released February 16; directing *A Thief Catcher*, promised for three days after *Baffles*, and acting in *A Robust Romeo*, which was to be released on February 12.[3]

With this sort of output expected from its comedians, it is not surprising Keystone was running behind schedule with its product. This was made clear to Sennett in one of a series of telegrams and night letters sent from Charles Kessel of the New York Motion Picture Company. The NYMPC not only owned the controlling majority of the Keystone Studio shares, but also acted as the holding house for the Keystone films. The NYMPC then arranged for the release of their films through an alliance with the Mutual Film Corporation. Kessel wrote specifically about *Baffles* on January 13, requesting a completion date which apparently was not forthcoming. By the twenty-sixth he was getting impatient. Another wire ordered *Baffles* to be sent to the NYMPC as soon as possible, and as it was; it would be released in regular two-reel form. Perhaps Sennett was trying to push two-reelers when Mutual had been insisting on singles, because the telegram went on to say, "*Mutual would absolutely refuse to take anymore two-reelers.*" And that proved to be the last Keystone two-reeler for a while. The NYMPC was also getting impatient waiting for delivery of Sterling's *Double Crossed*. In a January 13 telegram, Kessel asked why they hadn't received the negative yet, as it was booked for release on January 26, and ended with a rather angry-sounding "Figure it out for yourself." With Sennett being hassled from New York about the lateness of two of the four shorts Ford was working on, the urgency was probably passed down the line to his overworked star who under the circumstances may not have been all that impressed.

It seems Sterling considered he deserved more for his pains than his current weekly salary, reputed by various sources to be an unlikely $250.⁴ At the time, the public hailed Sterling as one of America's most popular comedians. With the type of workload and pressure that was being put on him, it was no wonder Sterling might have been asking for a pay raise. Sennett and the NYMPC, though, were known for paying their comedians and crew somewhat poorly compared to other studios. It was not only the comedians who were leaving to make their fortunes, or at least better pay, but also writers, directors, and crew members.

The reason for Sterling leaving Keystone has been documented in various articles and books by both contemporary writers and modern authors. The stories, which come from two main sources,⁵ conflict with each other, primary sources, and the record. Could the reminiscences of Mack Sennett and (mostly) Fred Balshofer, with their varied recollections, have been the premises for rumors that Sterling was difficult to work with, unprofessional, spoiled, and greedy? Did he really ask for a raise, or did Fred Balshofer try to poach him from Keystone first and then Sterling asked Sennett to better the offer? Or was there another scenario? One thing is clear: Sterling left Sennett to make comedies which were to be released by Universal. Other than that, it is hazy territory, distant memories, egos, and ax grinding—and one piece of evidence that throws a rather large monkey wrench into the works.

In some sources Sterling was asking for what he considered an appropriate remuneration, three times his present salary of $250. Seven hundred fifty dollars is a very high weekly sum, considering it was way above the accepted expectations and earning power of major stars in what were considered legitimate features. Even two years later, in October 1915, Karl K. Kitchen wrote in *Photoplay* magazine that, with the exception of Mary Pickford, Charlie Chaplin, and possibly Marguerite Clark, there was no film star in America who received more than $750 a week as salary. He stated that Mabel Normand at Keystone received $500 and that famed rotund comic John Bunny was never paid more than that at Vitagraph. The same magazine carried an article less than six months after Kitchen's showing an astronomic jump in the stars' pay. Salaries of $1,000 were common, and Keystone was paying some of its comedians more than $2,000 per week. But that was not the same Keystone as the one Kessel and Bauman controlled in 1913. If Sterling's outlandish $750 per week request was true, it is no wonder Sennett claims he balked. Sennett could not authorize this sort of expenditure; he would have been forced to put it in the hands of Kessel and Bauman, who controlled the Keystone purse strings. This he claims he did, and when they got the request Kessel and Bauman reputedly stalled for a while, then offered Sterling an extra $100 per week.⁶

Story number two, which is a Mack Sennett version, tells of Sterling going to see him to state he was quitting. Sterling's salary was still $250 a week, but he had already made *Dirty Work in a Laundry*, which was not released until July 1915 after Sterling's return to Keystone.⁷ Could Sennett have been confusing the first two times Sterling left the studio? If he was, then this would have been in 1915, at a time when twice Sterling's reported salary of $250 would have given him parity with Mabel and John Bunny and triple would have made him the highest-paid comedian on the lot. That would have been more understandable, but this was still 1913.

Now, a variation: Sennett stated he knew Sterling wanted more money and was unhappy at Keystone, so it was he who offered Ford a raise to $400 per week, thinking that would shock Ford into staying with Keystone. It didn't, so Sennett offered to keep raising Ford's salary until "he would need stevedores to carry it home in bales." When Sterling asked Sennett what this raise would entail he was told he would be given an ironclad contract, no options, and seven hundred and fifty a week.[8] Here's the seven hundred and fifty again, and wasn't that a problem? Sennett couldn't sanction that sort of raise without Kessel and Bauman's okay.

Story number three is yet another Sennett version. In the summer of 1913 Sennett still had Sterling under contract for another six months at the salary of $200 a week, but there were rumors that Sterling was not satisfied and was actively looking for work elsewhere. Sennett, concerned, tried everything to pamper Ford. This included purchasing him a brand-new custom-made chief of police uniform. Sennett summoned Sterling to his office to try to put all thoughts behind him of his leaving Keystone. Sennett offered Sterling, who he said was in a class by himself, the $750 per week and a brand new contract. Ford was over the moon with excitement, whooping and dancing wildly around Sennett's office. Sennett, pleased with the results, told Ford that "it did him good to see him so happy and it was a hell of a big salary." Sterling controlled his exuberance for a moment, looked at Sennett and said, "Mack, I always had a suspicion I was pretty good. Now I know it. If I am worth seven hundred fifty dollars to you, I ought to be worth at least that much to myself. I'm quitting and going into business on my own. Rule number one: There will be no uniforms in my new company."[9] There were plenty of uniforms in the new company, pretty much the same ones Ford had been wearing at Keystone. But there is a smattering of truth in this version.

Another reason bandied about for Sterling leaving Sennett was the arrival of Charles Chaplin. Both Sennett and Chaplin claim in their biographies that Chaplin was hired to replace Sterling, but was that in fact so? Sennett went as far as to claim that he sent a telegram asking Chaplin to join the company after Sterling had left,[10] presumably hoping no one would notice the films they had made together at Keystone. Chaplin did join Keystone in December 1913, when Sennett was more than likely getting wind of Ford's discontent with his lot at the studio, and, on the face of it, it looks probable. But — the original telegram requesting Chaplin to join Keystone was sent on May 12, 1913, exactly one month to the day that Fred Mace left. Chaplin could not leave Fred Karno's Company until his contract ran out. He also had to travel across the country and this did not allow him to join Keystone until that December. There were no rumblings that Sterling was thinking of going that early in the year; therefore, was it Fred Mace whom Chaplin was intended to replace and *not* Ford Sterling?

It is almost certain that Sennett had seen Chaplin in New York at the American Theater in 1912 performing his drunk routine with Fred Karno's Company; it had left such an impression on him that the memory of the performance stayed with him.[11] Sennett is insistent that in 1913, when he got wind that Sterling was looking to go elsewhere, Sennett requested Kessel and Bauman in New York to wire Alf Reeves.

He was Karno's North American business manager and they wanted to make arrangements with Chaplin (or Chaffin as it said in the telegram) to sign up with Keystone at a salary of $150 a week. Chaplin signed to join Keystone after his contract with Karno ran out in December 1913. He did so, though, with some trepidation. On his arrival at Edendale Chaplin was given Lehrman as director, and to say they did not get on would be putting it mildly. Chaplin found the art of filmmaking confusing and, without any concept of editing, he could not understand the logic of shooting scenes out of sequence or in unrelated settings. Sennett was also unsure how to use his new acquisition: he and his style were different from anything else they had. Chaplin also had difficulties under the direction of George Nichols and apparently had major problems working with the much-loved Mabel Normand at the helm, too. His unwillingness to accept direction from her in *Mabel at the Wheel* and their ensuing quarrels allegedly gave Chaplin a rather unpopular reputation at the studio, especially as everyone admired Mabel greatly. It got so bad that Chaplin decided to quit, but veteran comic Chester Conklin advised him to stick with it. Had he quit, it might not have been a completely one-sided decision. Sennett was ready to fire the little comedian but his mind was changed by a telegram from New York asking for more of the popular Chaplin films. Chaplin was allowed to direct himself from that point on and a legend was born.

When Sennett spoke about his discovery of Charlie Chaplin, he painted a picture of instant creative genius and harmony and a sad, sometimes bitter, demise for Sterling, whom he insisted he had hired Chaplin to replace. Sennett said that Ford derided Charlie's style as being too slow and obscure (but aware of impending calamity, Ford prepared to defend himself). Sennett claimed Lehrman and Chaplin had a wonderful rapport, swapping ideas and learning from each other. He also stated that *Between Showers*, starring Sterling, was a battle for the comedy crown between the two men, in which Chaplin brought Sterling to earth as in the battle between David and Goliath. Sennett was so impressed by Chaplin's performance that, instead of calling for Ford when he needed someone to save a picture, he requested the presence of Charlie instead. Sennett said that Ford was made "fully aware he had to quit Keystone." This is the same man who was reputedly offering Sterling $750, according to another of his remembrances!

Sennett has another version of the relationship between Sterling and Chaplin. In this version, he refutes the later reports of unease between Sterling and Chaplin as being legend, which it certainly seems to be. Chaplin and Sterling worked together on several pictures, including *Between Showers* and *The Jazz Band*, neither of which starred Chaplin but featured Sterling. Chaplin was not a threat at that time, nor did there seem to be any deadly rivalry between them. They seem to have behaved in a friendly manner toward each other. Chaplin relates that Sterling used to console him when there was little work coming Chaplin's way and would drive him downtown to the Alexandria bar for a drink with friends.[12] Another point: had Chaplin and his Tramp character been threatening to topple Sterling's place at Keystone Sennett would certainly have been astute enough to realize this, which poses a question. Why would Sennett have had Chaplin impersonate Sterling in *Mabel at the Wheel*, made shortly after Sterling left the studio? It is more likely he would have pushed Chaplin and the little Tramp character forward as his new star and dropped anything to do with Sterling. Why would Ford find Charlie a specific threat when this was occurring at the Keystone Studio, which he was considering leaving anyway? Sterling had no such difficulties with any of the other comedians on the lot, some of whom, like Roscoe Arbuckle, had the potential of becoming far bigger stars than Ford. It was not as if he was the only leading player in Keystone comedies either. Obviously there were problems between Sterling, Sennett, and Keystone, but these would not prove to be insurmountable or filled with animosity, as Sterling eventually came back. Where does this put the various tales of Sennett imploring Sterling to stay with Keystone? If the former were true then the latter surely would not have taken place as well.

Sennett did say that Sterling and Lehrman were in cahoots and looking to start a company of their own. Lehrman's beef was not so much pay (although he didn't object to a pay raise) but more the lack of billing and acknowledgment for the work he did for the company; "everything," he said, was "Mack Sennett." With that and the comment Ford made to Sennett—"I ought to be worth at least that much to myself. I'm quitting and going into business on my own,"—we are getting nearer to the truth than most of the stories' surrounding events. In May 1914 the incorporation papers submitted in February for The Sterling Motion Picture Corporation completed their trip through the appropriate offices and became official. What makes Balshofer's claims very suspect is that the incorporators listed were Fred J. Balshofer, George F. S. Stitch, and Henry M. Lehrman. Sterling had to revert to his given name for legal purposes as he never officially changed it. The capital stock at the time was $10,000 with a subscribed amount of $300. These official documents put a whole new slant on Balshofer's claims of sole ownership, total control, and of certain actions he claimed he was able to take on the presumption it was his company. This is what his memoirs concerning events at the Sterling Studio are based on. Balshofer conveniently forgot he initially had partners once they were both deceased.

There was another player in the scenario: the head of Universal, Carl Laemmle, and his connection with Sterling's exit from Keystone. Surprisingly, there is more than one version to this, too! When talk of Sterling's initial discontent with Keystone started to surface it was made known to Sterling that Laemmle would be interested in financing a separate company with Sterling as the star. This would pay Ford not only a salary, but also a share of the films' profits. That sounds as if Laemmle was suggesting Sterling would own at least part of the studio. This would pose the question of whether it was Laemmle who was initiating the trio's forming of a studio rather than Balshofer; perhaps Laemmle was using Balshofer as the legman. It was also a guarantee that Universal would release all the one- and two-reelers made by the new studio. If Laemmle had courted Sterling, as has been speculated, it happened in October 1913; but this could just have easily been an offer made on Laemmle's behalf by Fred Balshofer, if he was the one setting up the deal.

The alternate Sennett version of these events takes place in the summer of 1914, not 1913, but is otherwise initially accurate if one ignores Lehrman's employment status, as he was still with Sennett. Sennett said that "Sterling teamed up with Lehrman,

4—A Dramatic Mistake

who had already quit Keystone and, with Fred Balshofer, a pioneering picture executive who had worked with Kessel and Bauman, formed a company of their own." Sennett said that trouble began between Sterling and Lehrman before the studio even had a name. Lehrman insisted Ford was not to call the studio the Sterling Motion Picture Company because he was of German descent and, the First World War having just started, this might alienate the anti–German customers. Okay. Stich or even Lehrman might have sounded German, but *Sterling*? Then, Lehrman demanded that Ford stop playing German roles; Ford's answer was that over the previous two years, he had established himself as a Dutch comedian and he was not giving up the character now. It would be pretty silly for Sterling to change, or to be expected to change, his beloved character, with its popularity and box office draw. So what we have in this tale is the director telling the popular star, a man called Sterling who plays a Dutch comedic character, that he might insult those with anti–German feelings and lose out at the box office. It all sounds a bit cryptic and is missing the Laemmle Universal connection, not to mention Sterling's continued popularity at the box office regardless of what character he was playing. Sterling got his way. His name and Dutch character were transferred over to the new studio, one could say almost completely unchanged.

Balshofer told a different story, naturally. He said that as far as the naming went, "Sterling" was incorporated into the company name solely on the basis of Sterling's popularity. Sounds logical. There was also a movie magazine competition for the purpose of naming the studio. The names that were entered are lost, but whatever they were, "Sterling" won the day and the studio became the Sterling Universal Comedy Company, which is probably what it was going to be called from the beginning.

The Balshofer account, and the probable source of Sterling's negative reputation, is in his book, *One Reel a Week*,[13] published in the mid 1960s, long after the event and with hindsight and animosity. Balshofer claimed Laemmle wanted a comedy series for the Universal program. Balshofer told him he believed he could get Mabel Normand, Ford Sterling, or Charlie Chaplin away from Keystone to star in a series as none were presumed under contract. Laemmle didn't think Chaplin important enough to star, which at that time he was not. Laemmle agreed to draw up a contract in which Universal would release any comedies Balshofer might make, provided they starred either Normand or Sterling. By the time Universal's lawyers had drawn up the contract, word had been leaked to Sennett that Balshofer was after Mabel and she was hastily signed up by the NYMPC. However, no one knew Balshofer was also after Sterling, and he got Sterling's signature posthaste, before he was out of reach as well. Presumably Sterling was either between contracts with Keystone — Sennett had mistakenly referred to his contract having six months to run in the summer of 1913 — or Balshofer was wrong in his assumption and got him anyway. Balshofer also seems to have forgotten to mention the business deal between him, Sterling, and Lehrman.

Jack White tells the story that he himself lost his job at Keystone due to passing cryptic messages between Sterling and Lehrman. In *Behind the White Brothers*, by David N. Bruskin, White claims that a teenaged messenger boy (White) delivered a very important coded message to Sterling. It was an offer from Lehrman and Universal to start his own company. A livid Sennett asked who got the message through to Sterling and when he learned who the culprit was he fired White on the spot. It seems strange that Lehrman would be sending coded messages to Sterling when both of them were working at the same studio and often on the same film. Wouldn't it have been easier just to have gone up to Sterling and spoken to him?

Incidentally, Balshofer said that Universal's contract with Sterling paid Ford a salary of the much bandied about figure of $250 a week. Balshofer claimed that, while he was at it, he also signed up Pathé Lehrman for $200 a week and, "about twenty other Keystone players—Louise Fazenda, Peggy Pearce, Bob Thornby, George Jeske, Chester Franklyn, Beverly Griffith, and several of the Keystone Kops. Billy Jacobs, Carmen LaRue, and Olive Johnson headed up a child comedy series that I assigned Bob Thornby to direct. My wholesale grab of Keystone players, as well as their best comedy director, Pathé Lehrman, brought Kessel and Bauman hightailing it out in a hurry for a pow-wow with Sennett, and they made a pretty unhappy trio." Perhaps just a tiny bit of an exaggeration: even though Sterling and Lehrman were partners, they were probably paid a salary for their work.

Indicative of Sterling's universal popularity and fame, the announcement of his leaving Keystone started confused rumors within the industry reaching right across the Atlantic. The rumors suggested Sennett and Mabel were also moving on. On March 5, Keystone's UK distributors, the Western Export Company, issued a statement to *Bioscope* magazine: "We wish to contradict, in the most explicit manner, the statement widely advertised in the trade papers last week that 'practically the whole Keystone Company' has been engaged by another producing organization. The statement in question has naturally led a large number of our customers to imagine that the Keystone films in future will appear without any of the artists who have become so popular with the British public, whereas in fact only one prominent artiste has left the Keystone Company, and the organization will continue as before...."

Whether Sterling's alleged pay demands bore any relationship to what he envisaged the Universal deal would realize—or perhaps had been suggested to him—is questionable. If Sterling's salary at Keystone was correct, then he wasn't going for an increase, but Balshofer, in a very bighearted manner, planned to give both men a cut of the profits later. Granted they were the other two shareholders, but Balshofer covers that by saying this was not part of his original deal. Sterling must have considered the Sterling Studios deal the better offer; and who wouldn't when you are going to be part owner of a film studio, with a major company offering to distribute your movies. Whether it was for money, freedom to make his own films in a studio bearing his name, a chance to break from Keystone and the restraints the company imposed, or to have some control over the company he was working for he took the plunge. As for the freedom to make his own films, he seems to have pretty much had that at Keystone already as the style didn't change.

What is irrefutable is that Ford Sterling took Balshofer's, Laemmle's, or whoever's offer and, after codirecting *Across the Hall* with Sennett (released on March 23, 1914, after Sterling had left the company), said farewell to Keystone and moved over to Universal. He formed a partnership with Henry "Pathé" Lehrman and Fred Balshofer, and the three of them incorporated the Sterling Motion Picture Company. Unfortunately, like Fred Mace before him, the move spelled disaster for Sterling. Balshofer claimed in his book that, in February 1914, the Sterling Film Company was incorporated with himself as sole owner and a guaranteed distribution through a major company, Universal. He stated that he had the freedom to make any decisions he wanted without having to consult a partner. He seems to have been in for a surprise. They may have been silent comedians, but Sterling and Lehrman don't appear to have been silent partners.

For the Sterling Studio Balshofer said he bought the vacant Nestor Studio from David Horsley for the sum of $11,000. The buildings were used as offices, dressing rooms, and a processing laboratory; the activities of daily movie making took place on the open studio at the back. The Nestor studio had originally been the Old Blondeau's Tavern, situated at the corner of Sunset Boulevard and Gower Street. But by the time Balshofer was interested in it, the property didn't belong to David Horsley anymore. Balshofer must have forgotten that Horsley no longer owned the studio, and Horsley would have been quite surprised if he had received $11,000 from Balshofer. The studio had been taken over in 1912 by Carl Leammle as part of the Universal Manufacturing Company so that Universal could start production on the West Coast. It would seem natural for the new company to use the Nestor studio if they were making movies to be released through Universal.

On the face of it, the teaming of Sterling and Lehrman looked promising. They had regularly worked together at Keystone, producing good work, and there was a chemistry between the two men on-screen. For the new company Sterling adopted Snookee as the name for his Dutch character and his Keystone Kop became Sergeant Hofmeyer. Emma Clifton and Peggy Pearce filled the female roles and Lehrman acted as well as directed. The studio's output of Sterling vehicles was initially quite prolific, with six one-reelers and one two-reeler released within the first two months.

The date of Sterling's actual departure from Keystone and the start of his tenure with Sterling Comedies is a little vague. The second reel of the first Sterling film, *Love and Vengeance* (1914), was built round the Grand Prix auto races and Vanderbilt Cup held at Santa Monica between February 26 and 28, 1914. Sterling had obviously left Keystone before this date, maybe by a couple of weeks, if the first reel was shot prior to the races. With the April 23 release date, the studio still would have had time to shoot the reels in reverse order had he left at the end of February.

Ironically, Mabel Normand was also filming at the race track; she was directing *Mabel at the Wheel* (1914), a film in which Charles Chaplin impersonated Ford Sterling as per Sennett's instructions. In the first reel of *Love and Vengeance* Lehrman again played Sterling's nemesis; whether or not it was a jibe at Chaplin playing Ford in Mabel's film, he was impersonating Charlie. This is almost certainly the first Chaplin impersonation on film. The new company's first offering was its only two-reeler and starred Sterling with Emma Clifton, Paul "Little Billy" Jacobs, Henry "Pathé" Lehrman, who also directed, and Frank B. Good, who was involved either as cameraman or cinematographer. *Sergeant Hofmeyer*, the third Sterling Comedy to be released, could easily be mistaken for Sterling's Keystone Chief Teheezal. Hofmeyer was a very Keystone Kop–like beat officer among a band of equally Keystone Kop–looking policemen. His characterization remained the same, his fellow "Kops" behaving in the Sennett style with the exception of the chief, who was played straight. Unfortunately, there are too few surviving examples of Sterling Comedies to be able to judge the real quality of the product. Universal was not very farsighted in the preservation of its films and at present there are only three known surviving Sterling titles: *Snookee's Flirtation*, *Love and Vengeance*, and *Sergeant Hofmeyer*.

It is possible, as with many films, to get an idea of the plotlines for missing titles from publications of the day, and from reviews we are given tantalizing hints of what we are missing. *Universal Weekly* was one of the better sources in this case and it shared detailed synopses of the Universal movie plots. For example, the cast list given for *At Three O'Clock*, an August 13 release, reads: Himself — Ford Sterling; His Sweetheart — Peggy Pearce; Gangster — Arthur Tavares; Man-Killer — David Anderson. It also outlines the story over four paragraphs opening with: "When his girl turns against him, Ford decides to die and hires a professional 'killer' to do the trick. It's a scream from start to finish." Universal may have disposed of the actual material, but at least they have left the legacy of their stories for future generations.

In *At Three O'Clock*, Ford's sweetheart has been flirting with a gangster and she finally decides to turn Ford down for him. Devastated at the loss of his love, Ford is bent on suicide, although when it comes down to it he doesn't have the nerve to carry out his intentions. A convenient Professor A. A. Sassan offers Ford his services; he would be only too pleased to remove him from this vale of tears. They set the time for Sterling's death at three o'clock. Meanwhile, Ford's sweetheart tires of the domineering gangster and, feeling her love for Sterling returning, goes in search of him. Overjoyed at the reunion, Ford forgets his three o'clock appointment with the man-killer. Time for the planned act is drawing near and Professor A. A. Sassan drinks his killer liquid, which puts him in shape to do the deed, but when Ford fails to show up the professor starts hunting down his man. As Ford and his sweetheart approach the place where the planned execution is to take place, Ford is reminded of the appointment. Suddenly observing the professor approaching, Sterling grabs his sweetheart and runs.

Meanwhile, the gangster is also making plans for Ford's demise. He gets his gang together to find his rival and they give chase. By this time the professor and his undertakers are on Sterling's trail as well. Ford and his sweetheart run into the professor's laboratory which, unknown to them, is filled with explosives of all kinds. The gangster and his gang arrive hot on his tail, but Ford and his sweetheart manage to escape. The place explodes just as the professor and his undertakers arrive, blowing them and the gangsters to smithereens. Ford and his sweetheart have their happy reunion.

Moving Picture World of June 1914 tells us what we are going to do when we see another one of the Sterling Studio's products, *The Flirt* (June 22, 1914): "You will smile first, then snicker and before you know it, you will be laughing out loud at the hilariously funny situations." Unfortunately, nothing is mentioned about the cast, plot, or gags. There is a little bit more about *The Crash* (July 2, 1914): *Moving Picture World* boasted that "the last third of this comic picture is so unusually speedy that it hardly fails to take strongly with the gallery and downstairs too. It uses an old situation but goes its predecessor's one better in startling incidents at the close and is truly laughable." Sterling Studios has a full-page advertisement for the film with this enticing teaser: "Without a question of doubt it's one of the biggest and most spectacular comedy productions ever attempted. In addition to other big features you will see a terrific explosion, the blowing up of a house and barn, a real auto going over a cliff, immediately afterwards a motorcycle is madly chasing the auto and ends up landing in the middle of the auto wreckage at the bottom of the cliff." Looks like this might be a one-reeler worth searching for.

Then there was *Troublesome Pets* (July 30, 1914). Although *Moving Picture World* did not find this offering as amusing as *The Crash*, they certainly didn't slight it: "The master of the house, tired of the monkey and parrot kept by his wife, puts one in the pantry and the other down the well. The parrot's cries for help rouse the neighborhood. There are no extremely laughable places in this but it is lightly amusing throughout."

A certain report, which could be construed as odd, might indicate that there was some sort of problem at the studio in July. The article informs the public that "the Sterling Studio is guarded like a jail by a burley policeman at the gate who turns away the applicants for extra work." That in and of itself might be worth reporting, as it could intimate the studio was not employing the extras it previously had. The reporter went on to say that he had gone to the studio again later that week, taking a camera with him. This time, another policeman was on guard and when his eagle eye lit on the camera he refused to allow the reporter in. The reporter claimed that "no amount of explanation would do, so a message sent through a screened window of Fred Balshofer's office, which brought him out in a hurry and the zealous representative of justice was made to 'see.' After that he has been as nice as pie." This all seems a little peculiar, especially as it goes on to say that "at no studio do they let visitors bring cameras in." If this rule was the norm, what made this event so instantly newsworthy, unless there was something going on that merited reporting? Maybe nothing, just an overeager reporter looking for that exclusive story. Maybe.

5

Roaring Lions and Wedding Bells

It had been noted by Sennett and Balshofer that Sterling became increasingly argumentative with Lehrman and unreliable in his appearances on the set. He was supposedly working his schedule around his social plans rather than the studio's requirements. Sterling's output throughout the first six months at the studio does not support this; he was making a short an average of one every one or two weeks. This would indicate that if there were films being made and released by Sterling throughout this time there is a strong probability that he was turning up at the studio regularly. The studio hadn't been in business long enough for there to be sufficient material to make this quantity of varied films from outtakes while Ford frolicked. It is not likely that he would want to put his finances at risk, either.

That there were difficulties between Sterling and Lehrman toward the end of Lehrman's association with the studio seems pretty certain if Sennett and Balshofer are to be believed; but again the facts are hazy and conflicting. Perhaps it was between Lehrman and Balshofer, or even Sterling and Balshofer, that the real conflict lay, or perhaps it was more financial than artistic. There could be some accuracy in Sennett's biographies surrounding the making of *Hearts and Swords*, the sixth one-reeler made by Sterling's new company and released in May 1914. His account clashes with Balshofer's later claim of paying the two men a bonus and the two men going on spending sprees. As Sennett tells it, Lehrman was directing *Hearts and Swords* and it was facing financial problems; the need for an extra day of shooting would jeopardize the profits. Lehrman was said to have made a 7:00 a.m. call, but Sterling didn't show up until noon, looking exhausted. Lehrman was furious and threatened to quit, and Sterling and Balshofer decided they could do without him. So Balshofer fired Lehrman. But neither man could have fired Lehrman from the company he partly owned. He could have been bought out, which is likely, or he could have remained a silent partner who was not allowed to direct if the other partners so decided.

It is possible Lehrman did leave around this time, as there are no other directing credits listed for him for Sterling Pictures after *Hearts and Swords*; and a new director was brought in as well. *Moving Picture World* notes in the June 27 issue that George Nichols, formerly of Keystone, was to start directing the next week. Balshofer again had a different slant on matters than Sennett. He stated that everything had gone so rosy that four months after they started shooting the first picture (which

5—Roaring Lions and Wedding Bells

would have been around mid–June), he declared a dividend, with Sterling getting $1,200 and Lehrman getting $1,000. This was presumably their share of the profits rather than a generous gift from Balshofer. According to Balshofer, both men promptly let the cash go to their heads. Sterling went off to Charles Levi and Sons, one of the best tailors in town, ordered several suits and topcoats, and as soon as they were ready requested a couple of weeks off to go to New York. Once there he booked in at the Astor Hotel, taking everyone he knew in New York up to his room to show them his new wardrobe. Lehrman stayed on the West Coast, spending his money and his nights at Baron Long's Vernon Country Club. Sterling returned to the fold after three weeks, flat broke; Lehrman was in a similar financial situation when he returned.

Again, for Sterling allegedly having taken so much time off, it is interesting how his output at the studio continued at the same rigorous rate of three to four one-reelers being released every month. The *New York Clipper* did have a brief mention of Sterling traveling on October 24, 1914: it shared — after noting that Mabel Normand, the Keystone girl, was on a short visit to New York — that Ford Sterling of the Sterling Universal Comedy Company was also on a short visit to New York. The *Los Angeles Times* reported Sterling's return, referring to it as a "flying business trip." Was this Balshofer's trip that supposedly took place in June? Perhaps the reason for Sterling's trip out East was to visit the family of a certain New York native he was involved with. Sterling also bought his first house: prior to this, he had been living with his mother in a rented property in Venice, California. His new address: 5636 Carlton Way,[1] Los Angeles, just off Sunset Boulevard; Ford would remain in this house until 1934.

On January 2, 1915, Sterling took a break from filmmaking and went on a trip to San Diego. There he married nineteen-year-old Teddy Sampson, a pretty brunette. That is the date Miss Sampson cites, but the actual date of the nuptials could have been at least a month earlier, because magazines were referring to her as Mrs. Ford Sterling in December 1914. Teddy Sampson was born Nora Sampson in New York on August 8, 1895. Teddy was a seasoned veteran: she started out in vaudeville with Gus Edwards and made her first film, *Home Sweet Home*, in which she played a maid, for D. W. Griffith in 1914. Teddy worked for various companies as an actress and comedienne; she appeared in some dramas, but she also worked with Al Christie Comedies and possibly with Sennett. The marriage survived their separation in April 1917 and an aborted divorce for desertion in 1928; their reconciliation in 1932 was to last until Ford's death. Teddy was to outlive Sterling by thirty-one years, succumbing to cancer on November 24, 1970, in Woodland Hills, California.

Something does seem to have happened at the Sterling Studio around the time of the January 1915 trip. On October 22, 1914, the last short listing Sterling, *Secret Service Snitz*, was released. The next release was on October 26: *Snookee's Day Off* featured Bobby Gould and Gus Erdman. (In future shorts, Snitz was played by John E. Brennan.) With a final release date in the last week of October, Sterling may not have set foot in the studio to work since mid–September or even late August. Another indication that something may have happened around this time is that, in early September 1914, Max Asher — also famed for his Dutch makeup — was drafted from

Joker. Even after Max Asher joined the company, Sterling Studios was still releasing one-reelers with the same frequency until the last one noted in October. However, these could have been shot well before the release dates, or they could have theoretically been a compilation of Sterling outtakes and Asher or Jeske footage, or they could have been all original Sterling material.

Balshofer remembered that work continued as before, but that near the end of 1914, when their success had gone to Sterling and Lehrman's heads, it was difficult getting work out of either of them. It probably would have been very difficult to get work out of Lehrman if, as Balshofer claimed earlier, he and Sterling fired Lehrman in May 1914. If this incident occurred toward the end of the year, where are the films, or at least records of them, made between May and the end of the year? What happened to all these Sterling-starring shorts that Lehrman supposedly directed during this period? As productions were being released at the usual rate, but without Lehrman listed as director and with Sterling roles being played by others, it would have to mean that the Sterling/Lehrman products if they existed, were being squirreled away and never released.

Teddy Sampson (Mrs. Ford Sterling), June 1921. Screen News Service photograph by Evans.

It is worth remembering that Lehrman and Sterling had worked together for the previous three years, chose to work together for Balshofer, and would work together after the demise of the Sterling Studio. They were used to each other's ways, likely remained acquaintances, and probably knew all the right buttons to push. If the two had experienced such problems working together, it seems unlikely that Lehrman would have directed Sterling at Fox Sunshine later. Balshofer claims Sterling and Lehrman hated each other and would argue over scenes to the extent that the crew would have to stand around for hours waiting. The argument came down to tit-for-tat squabbling, with Sterling taking offense at Lehrman telling him what time to be on the set and Lehrman then arriving much later to spite Sterling when he turned up early. Filmmaking got so behind schedule that at this point the firing of Lehrman by Balshofer took place. Balshofer took over directing Sterling himself, a task he claims he did not enjoy. Predictably, there are no listings in the remaining Sterling Studio records of Balshofer directing Sterling, or anyone else, for that matter. There is little concrete evidence that Sterling and Lehrman were enemies: if anything, their work record together shows friendship, not animosity. Balshofer was unable to fire Sterling, though, because he was the basis of his agreement for Universal to release his films. Was Lehrman really fired or did he walk out unaided? Lehrman had a habit of suddenly leaving a company to go after a better-looking prospect; he had done so with Sennett, Universal, Fox, and First National. By January 1915, he had his first LK-O (Lehrman Knock-Out) release. Maybe he had left voluntarily to start his own company, but what had he been doing since directing *Hearts and Swords* in May? By the first week in August 1914, he had already made arrangements with Universal's New York office to release comedies in Hollywood under the LK-O banner.[2] As the new company obviously wasn't formed overnight he had had to have set the wheels in motion far in advance. May, or earlier, would make perfect sense.

It is pretty safe to assume Ford did not make any pictures for Sterling Studios after *Secret Service Snitz*. At the end of the year there were more problems for Balshofer concerning Sterling's resuming work. Sterling became ill. The *New York Clipper* on December 19, 1914, wrote that "Ford Sterling, of the Sterling Comedy Co., is very sick indeed, and unable to attend the studios." It didn't cite the nature of the illness; on December 26, 1914, the *Clipper* updated that "Ford Sterling continued seriously ill, and his condition has caused his wife and mother considerable concern." Balshofer said that someone tipped him off to this mysterious illness of Sterling's. He was spending his nights at Baron Long's Night Club whooping it up. No wonder Teddy Sampson and his mother were reported greatly worried; Teddy and Ford hadn't been married that long—that is, of course, presuming Teddy and Ford weren't at Baron Long's together. *Moving Picture World* did have a medical diagnosis in their report on the first annual ball held by the Screen Club of San Francisco. According to the report, Ford was absent from the festivities because he had been taken ill with pneumonia.[3] It wasn't just pneumonia he was fighting. Tough as that was to recover from in the days before antibiotics, he had had a far more serious illness. Two more reports tell a more life-threatening tale: he had been diagnosed with typhoid pneumonia.[4] No wonder he wasn't turning up for work and his wife and mother were so worried. Typhoid pneumonia, as its name suggests, is a complication of typhoid, something still a threat in the early decades of the twentieth century. Sterling could easily have contracted it from drinking water while out on location or visiting an area outside of the cities' treated water supply. With Sterling having been so seriously ill, it makes it all the more malicious that Balshofer should have claimed Sterling was painting the town red as a reason to remove him from the studio when he was, in reality, at death's door.

Balshofer claimed he decided Sterling would have to go, although to remove him would cost Balshofer his distributor according to the contractual agreement with Laemmle. As with Lehrman's departure, there were uncertainties. Did Ford leave of his own volition, or did Balshofer really fire him at the risk of losing his contract with Universal? Maybe Balshofer gambled that by implying a breach of contract on Ford's part, Laemmle would understand and not negate the Universal contract, allowing Balshofer to save face and his distributor. Balshofer claims there was enough material for the company to run into early 1915, long after Sterling had been let go.

Snookee shorts continued to be released, he said, utilizing the unused scenes and cutouts stored in the vaults, with George Jeske filling in for Sterling as required. Unless one of these shorts is rediscovered, we'll probably never know: Sterling was not listed as being in any of the company's releases after *Secret Service Snitz* with the exception of *His Smashing Career*, released in April 1915 (a good three months after his return to Sennett). Either it had been shelved or reissued under a different title, or it was one of Balshofer's compilations.

Ford seems to have kept up a front that all was well at the studio, or maybe he believed it would be. In December 1914, an interview with Sterling was published in *Moving Picture Magazine*: it told a very optimistic little story, but there was no indication of when the interview was given. Sterling spoke of having his own company and making great plans for the future, which he hoped would appeal to the audience. What dated this interview as being pre–December was that he was apparently not married when the article was written; it also spoke of him happily pottering around his garden indulging in one of his hobbies, gardening — not really a December pastime in California. He was living with his mother in a bungalow at 427 Lake, in Venice, California,[5] and the interviewer did state that "there was no Mrs. Ford Sterling when [she] saw him, but who knew what had happened since."

Everything was all over, bar the shouting, by the time the article reached the presses. Although shorts were still being released by the studio until August 1915 without Sterling, on January 23, 1915, *Moving Picture World* reported that "The Sterling Company had ceased production, Ford Sterling had severed his connections with it and all the employees given two weeks notice." Ford Sterling had severed his connections with it? A different story to Balshofer's firing. In fact, to date no records have come to light showing Sterling had been fired. Neither have there been any reports that Sterling was spotted in nightclubs while he was supposed to be working, only reports that he was seriously ill. Someone with such a recognizable face would have piqued the interest of at least one gossip columnist or reporter if he had been out and about as claimed. More to the point, wouldn't this have made other studios think twice about employing someone so difficult and unreliable? The studios certainly weren't put off: Sterling continued working, and next he was back with Sennett no less, his workload full.

There seems little real evidence that Sterling was as difficult, moody, and unreliable to work with as Balshofer made out. Balshofer had an ax to grind and Ford was not the only artist to fall fowl of his viperous tongue. In addition, Lehrman and Sennett were not the only people to habitually reuse Sterling in their productions. Later in Sterling's career, Mal St. Clair, Robert North, B. P. Schulberg, Nat Levine, Marshall Neilan, and John Francis Dillon all used him multiple times. Surely they were not all masochists looking for a difficult and expensive time with their actors; neither were they charity workers handing out jobs to a poor, unemployable has-been. Sterling was also used by several studios again and again — Universal, First National, Goldwyn and MGM, Columbia, Famous Players, Fox, and Paramount. Sterling wasn't a big enough star for them to tolerate tantrums from him. Singer and actress June MacCloy worked with Sterling in an educational short called *Foolish Forties* in 1931.

She remembers him as being charming, sophisticated, professional, and a gentleman. When it was suggested he could be awkward and difficult to work with she was appalled at the thought. "Absolutely not. He was charming and a pro."[6] Even Chaplin singled out, as he put it, "'the great Ford Sterling' as being immensely popular with the public and with everyone at the studio, they would surround his set and laugh at him eagerly."[7]

6

Out and In

Sterling's decision to return to Keystone may not have been immediate, or even his first choice, after departing from the Sterling Studios and its subsequent demise. There was talk that he wanted to return to the stage and was taking up an Orpheum tour. However, *Variety* reported on January 16, 1915, that any knowledge of the tour had been denied by the New York Orpheum offices. The "Frisco Orpheum office may have opened negotiations," they went on to say, "but no official OK had been announced."[1] There was also a similar report in the *Chicago Daily Tribune* which said that, instead of "vaudevilling," Ford Sterling would be returning to Keystone.[2] More than two months after Sterling had returned to Keystone, the vaudeville tour was mentioned again in *Variety* on April 9; it also gave some insight into the new agreement between Keystone and Sterling. "Sterling returns at loss," was the heading: "Ford Sterling went away from the Keystone some time ago to join the Universal, but is now back. Sterling has just affixed his John Hancock to a two-year contract with Keystone and has given up all intentions of playing any vaudeville dates."[3]

The article also alluded to what might have been, had Sterling stayed at Keystone: "Incidentally, Sterling could have had a nice, fat contract when he proposed jumping from the Keystone, but he jumped. He's back at considerably less than offered him at that time, it is said."

So, did Sennett's version of his offer to Ford have some accuracy, after all? Not much fanfare was made about Sterling's return to the Keystone Studio; certainly *Variety* had no idea of it when they were writing about the prospective vaudeville tour. Sterling was almost certainly back at Keystone by then, otherwise *Reel Life* could not have reported Sterling's return to Keystone in their February 6 issue and his having already made *That Little Band of Gold*, which was released on March 15, 1915.

From a production point of view, though, it was as if Sterling had never been away. After a cameo appearance with Mack Swain in one of Charlie Murray's Hogan series of single reelers (*Hogan's Romance Upset*, released February 13, 1915), he reteamed with Roscoe Arbuckle and Mabel Normand in *That Little Band of Gold*. It was like old times.

In the film, Arbuckle is again Sterling's rival, married to upper-class Normand, who has an ever-present mother, Alice Davenport. Sterling has two lady friends. One he desperately desires to have as his girlfriend; the other, well, he's not all that sure

Released December 26, 1915, *The Hunt*. Triangle-Keystone. L–R: Guy Woodward, unidentified actor, Ford Sterling, Polly Moran. This two-reel short was directed by Sterling. Dot Hagart, who was also in the cast, fractured both her wrists during a horse-riding scene when she fell from her mount.

why he brought her. Neither lady appears to be aware of her intended place in Sterling's heart nor all that enamored by his variable attentions.

Arbuckle and Sterling, two old friends, accompany their respective pairs of ladies to the grand opera and find themselves sitting in opposite boxes. Sterling behaves despicably toward the reject, flirting constantly with the other young lady, who continuously rebuffs his advances. He outrageously gesticulates his intentions toward her right across the auditorium to Arbuckle. It doesn't take long before the two men become bored with the opera and, by way of winks and gestures that go unnoticed or are politely ignored by the remainder of the audience, hatch a plan. They decide to double-date Sterling's two young ladies and take them to a restaurant adjacent to the theater. The two men leave Arbuckle's mother-in-law and wife watching the opera.

Sterling's poor rejected lady friend continues to get short shrift from him. On arriving at the restaurant the desired one quite correctly gives Sterling her coat to take to the cloakroom. On seeing Arbuckle heading off with her, Sterling unceremoniously throws both her coat and his on top of the rejected lady and dashes off after the couple in an attempt to reach the vacant seat next to Arbuckle's new partner for the evening. Unfortunately, Arbuckle also finds Sterling's prospective young lady rather attractive and is under the misapprehension that he is to be her escort for the evening. Before Sterling gets a chance to sit next to her, Arbuckle has taken the only other available seat, forcing Sterling to sit at the next table with the unwanted one.

Charley Chase, seen here in the 1926 Hal Roach comedy, *Bromo and Juliet*, spent his early days with Mack Sennett as a comedian and fledgling director. Sterling was given Chase as his assistant director on films such as *He Wouldn't Stay Down*, and he was the sole director for Sterling's *A Desperate Scoundrel*. Later Chase went to the Roach Studio as director and actor and directed under the name Charles Parrott. He went on to direct the Three Stooges and other notables during the sound era.

Sterling's vengeful side then kicks in, he wants that woman and he isn't about to let Arbuckle have her. The solution is simple: he anonymously telephones Mabel in her theater box and informs her that her husband is drinking with another woman. That does it. Mabel and mother soon arrive to remove Arbuckle, but not before he has whopped Sterling, sending him reeling backward into the gathering crowd of onlookers.

At this point in his career, Ford Sterling was given future Roach Studio director, writer, and comedy star Charley Chase, for his assistant director. The twenty-one-year-old, Baltimore-born Chase also costarred in their first teaming, *He Wouldn't Stay Down*, with a cast that included pretty Minta Durfee. They continued to work together frequently at Keystone, with Chase directing or acting as codirector with Sterling in several of his 1915 films, including *Our Dare Devil Chief*, *Only a Messenger Boy*, and *Courthouse Crooks*. It is quite possible that Chase directed Sterling in *Dirty Work in a Laundry*, as well. Chase had joined Keystone in 1914 from Christie after a brief spell in vaudeville. His first documented appearance for the Sennett outfit was in *Across the Hall* (March 23, 1914), which is unavailable; his first surviving film is *The Knockout* (June 11, 1914). Until Sterling's return to the studio Chase worked under the direction of Roscoe Arbuckle, Charlie Chaplin, Charles Avery, and Nick Cogley. While Sterling was away from the studio, it seems Sennett had decided Charley Chase should be another to "act like Ford." He can be seen imitating him in *Peanuts and Bullets* (January 1915), costarring and directed by Nick Cogley, *A Colored Villainy* (1915), and *Rent Jumpers* (1915). It's all there — face, gestures, mannerisms; the only thing missing is the costume and makeup. Once Sterling was back in harness — he was back at the studio by the time *Rent Jumpers* was made — Chase was able to work on his own character and drop the Sterling gestures.

At the end of 1916 Chase left Keystone and was put in charge of directing the new Fox comedies; he later spent time with King Bee and Bull's Eye studios as both actor and director in the comedies starring Chaplin imitator Billy West. While with King Bee, Charley Chase worked for the first time with Oliver Hardy, with whom he would later work again under Hal Roach. In 1921 Chase was directing comedian Lloyd Hamilton, on whom he would base his future screen character. Chase's logic behind this was that you pick the comedian bearing the least resemblance to you, play the scene in his manner, and thus produce something unique and original. Next, Chase joined the Roach Studio, where he would have his greatest success as both the director general and an actor. As director, he reverted to his given name of Charles Parrott, and the credits for the Charley Chase Comedies in which he starred often had Charles Parrott billed as the director. When sound came along, Chase was able to include a song in his comedies (he had a very good voice), and these are always entertaining on their own merit. Chase also directed Laurel and Hardy sound films and some of the Three Stooges films in the 1930s. Chase himself, although given the opportunity, never made it in features and died of a heart attack in 1940 after a long fight with alcoholism.

Another future comedy star, Harold Lloyd, worked on *Courthouse Crooks* (July 1915) with Chase and Sterling. It was one of his early roles for Sennett, and he remembered the useful information Sterling gave him. Lloyd reported to the *Los Angeles Times* in 1925[4] that, although few people knew it, when he was with Sennett's Keystone (and their comedies were at the height of their appeal) he was one of the celebrated cops. Sterling, at that time one of the most popular men on the screen, took a liking to Lloyd and frequently talked over his prospects in the business. One day Lloyd told Sterling that he was quitting Keystone, as he had been offered a job with Hal Roach playing comedy leads.

Aghast, Sterling had other advice for the young comedian: "Oh, Harold, don't do that." He continued, "I wouldn't monkey around this comedy game. Unless you get to the very top there is nothing in it for a fellow. What you ought to be doing is dramatic work. You should go over and see D. W. Griffith and try to land with him."

Lloyd thought it was nice of Sterling and he appreciated his interest in him, but about that same time Lloyd became more convinced than ever that he would like to be a comedian and not the dramatic actor Sterling envisioned him as.

Courthouse Crooks was the third time Chase and Sterling had worked together; now Chase was sole director, although Sterling probably did have some directorial input and advice to give to his protégé. Sterling stars as a district attorney working in the offices of the local judge and is having an affair with the judge's wife, Minta Durfee. It is the second wedding anniversary of the judge and his wife, which the judge has forgotten. When reminded by Minta, he hands her a roll of bills and tells her to buy a little something for herself. "No," she says, "you must get something for me."

Before Harold Lloyd discovered his "glasses character" he appeared with Sterling at Keystone in *Courthouse Crooks*. At one point Sterling suggested Lloyd give up comedy and join D. W. Griffith as a serious actor.

When the judge arrives at work, he finds Sterling on the phone with a young lady obviously making a date to meet her; the judge winks at him knowingly as the embarrassed Sterling hangs up the phone. Little does the judge know the root of Sterling's embarrassment: it is with the judge's own wife that Sterling is making arrangements for a clandestine meeting. The judge goes out to a nearby jeweler to buy Minta's gift. He selects a necklace for her and unfortunately he drops it in the street as he is trying to put it and its box into his pocket. The first person to spot the box with its precious contents, actually tripping over it, is Sterling, who is now on his way to meet Minta at a soda fountain. He picks it up, opens it, and seeing the necklace inside decides it would be a perfect gift for Minta. He takes it out and throws the box over a fence where it lands on the newspaper that a young man, Harold Lloyd, is innocently reading. Sterling meets Minta and they order sodas; he then gives her the necklace, which, with great delight, she puts on.

Meanwhile, the judge realizes his loss and rushes back out of his office to retrace his steps. Just as he passes the place where the necklace was dropped, Lloyd walks out from behind a fence examining the empty box. The judge recognizes it, makes the assumption that Lloyd has stolen the necklace, and immediately calls to two policemen who are just down the street. They chase Lloyd into the tenement where he lives with his mother and young sister and arrest him.

Lloyd comes up before the judge. His worried family, convinced of his innocence, is in court for the hearing. Sterling is doing his job as prosecuting district attorney. The judge hands Ford the box and immediately Sterling realizes this is the very one the purloined necklace came from. How to get out of this? Easy: convict Lloyd. Obviously he has to be the criminal if he was caught with evidence on him and it was the presiding judge who caught him! With Lloyd's mother and sister's pleas for justice rudely brushed aside by Sterling, Lloyd is taken to the jail. In no time, though, Lloyd escapes and makes his way toward his home, which just happens to be opposite the judge's house.

Sterling, knowing he will be in deep trouble if the necklace is discovered by the judge, is fully aware that Minta would be bound to spill the beans if questioned. Ford decides to pay a visit to his lover's home to recover the jewels; Minta is in the bathroom about to take a bath when she hears noises in the house. Sterling runs upstairs, calling out to Minta to ask her where the necklace is. She doesn't want to come out of the bathroom as she is not suitably dressed. Just then they hear the judge coming home. He also calls out to Minta. Sterling hides in her bedroom closet just in time. Meanwhile, the police have caught up with Lloyd, who climbs a ladder into the judge's house and also ends up hiding in Minta's bedroom closet. Sterling makes a deal with Lloyd that if he Lloyd gives himself up Sterling will make sure he is set free. Lloyd agrees, but once he has given himself up and been reincarcerated it still leaves Sterling with the problem of getting out of the house — and without the incriminating necklace. The only way out is via the upper-story clothesline hanging between the judge's house and Lloyd's apartment. Sterling just manages to tightrope walk across but then has problems getting into the Lloyd house due to their small dog wanting to eat him. Lloyd's mother calls the dog off and helps Sterling through the window but only after he swears that he will let her son go.

Back in court, Sterling naturally reneges on his promise, realizing that if no one is convicted the case will be reinvestigated. Sterling puts on a show for Lloyd's family that he will let him go but it is all a sham. Lloyd's little sister, aware of the D.A.'s trickery, gets an idea. She leaves the courtroom, taking a mirror and cake of soap with her. On the mirror she writes *"Brother, Dist-attorney fixed"* and shines its reflection on the courtroom wall for all to read. Just to add icing to the cake, Minta arrives bedecked in all her finery — including the necklace. The judge immediately recognizes it and asks her who bought it. Just as Ford had predicted, she confesses to her indiscretions and the truth is out. Sterling is dragged out from his hiding place under the judge's bench, and thrown into jail. Lloyd, now free, is reunited with his family and the judge forgives his wife for her transgression.

How much did the comedy and directorial tutelage of Sterling, Arbuckle, Chaplin, Avery, and Cogley influence the young Chase? As far as Sterling goes, Chase understood his character and worked well with him in front of and behind the camera; they also remained friends until Sterling's untimely death. In fact, Chase was one of his last visitors before he died. Both were members of the Masquers Club, a men-only establishment for actors, which was founded in Los Angeles in May 1925. They appeared in Masquers benefit productions that featured cast lists including Chester Conklin, Lloyd Hamilton, Lionel Barrymore, and King Baggot. Sterling regularly appeared in these events from at least 1926, when he was part of the program in a variety benefit. The club also made its own short-subject films released through RKO; Sterling was in the first of them, *Stout Hearts and Willing Hands,* released in 1931. He reprised his role as a cop with fellow ex–Keystone regulars Chester Conklin, James Finlayson, and Mack Swain. In a surviving clip, they are seen breaking into a sawmill to save the hero, who had been tied to the bed of a large circular saw; Lew Cody appears to be playing the villain in top hat and tails. *Stout Hearts and Willing Hands* won the Academy Award for Best Short Subject in 1936.

Sterling, a lifelong member of the Masquers, was also a member of another club that preceded the Masquers by thirteen years and was also connected with the movie industry. Founded on December 12, 1912, the short-lived Photoplayers Club was based on a similar establishment in New York for stage actors. Ford was a charter member of what was at first known as the Reel Club. Its name was changed because the members felt they might be confused with a fisherman's club. Mr. and Mrs. Ford Sterling were photographed at one of the Grand Balls held on March 6, 1915; the annual Valentine's Day ball was a huge event in Hollywood.

Between March and August only seven Sterling shorts were released, on the face of it, a far cry from the pre–Sterling Comedies days. These, though, were bigger productions taking longer to make and, with the exception of *He Wouldn't Stay Down*, they ran two reels. That year, 1915 (the last before Sennett's Keystone ceased to be), saw the release of two of Sterling's more available and funnier films for Keystone, *Dirty Work in a Laundry* and *Our Dare Devil Chief*.

In *Our Dare Devil Chief*, Minta Durfee once again teams with Sterling, this time as Chief Teheezal's girlfriend and the daughter of the mayor. The mayor (Harry Bernard) is less than impressed with Teheezal and the budding romance, which he finds far from desirable. The mayor demonstrates his contempt for the inept chief when he comes upon Miss Durfee looking lovingly at a photo of Teheezal. She gives the image a little Teheezal salute. The mayor chides her for her misplaced admiration, snatches away the photo, and tears it in two, throwing it in disgust onto the small table from whence it had been picked up. The mayor's views of Teheezal are confirmed when he arrives at his office, which happens to be in the police station, and finds Teheezal and his men asleep — Teheezal at his desk, his men draped over various chairs and benches. The motley crew is disturbed by the mayor's entrance; Teheezal wakes last, frantically saluting when he realizes he has been caught napping again. Teheezal doesn't improve the situation when he befriends the chief crook (Eddie Cline), who has been plotting against the mayor right in the police station under the mayor's nose. The gullible Teheezal swallows Cline's overtures hook, line, and sinker, and even fails to notice Cline deftly exchanging Teheezal's pocket watch for the mayor's, which he stole earlier.

Having been sent out on the street to hunt down the same crooks, Teheezal happens upon Miss Durfee carrying an armful of boxes home. Naturally he offers his assistance. This triggers a chain of events that further alienates Teheezal from the mayor. Once back at the mayor's house, Miss Durfee offers Teheezal, who complains of feeling hot and thirsty, a glass of wine, which he takes as his cue to make himself at home. He takes off his belt and billy club, puts them on the kitchen table, and loosens his jacket. Then he helps Miss Durfee take the boxes, one of which contains a nightdress that he finds quite fascinating, to the hall closet. Teheezal suggests they play hide-and-seek, a ploy to secretly return to the kitchen and the wine decanter.

6—Out and In

He hides first, but it doesn't take Minta long to discover him taking a long swig straight out of the decanter. She scolds him and takes her turn to hide. Teheezal covers his eyes and counts while she hides in the clothes closet. He runs around the house looking for her but isn't fooled anymore when he hears her opening the door to peep out. He throws open the door and steps into the closet.

Meanwhile, Cline and Al St. John, a second crook, have been breaking into the house. St. John, who had seen the two go into the closet, creeps up behind the door and slams it shut, locking it so that the two crooks can ransack the house in peace. Miss Durfee, quite understandably, is a bit upset and becomes quite vocal; Teheezal flaps his arms at her in an attempt to quiet her, but he appears decidedly bothered by the situation too. The mayor chooses this time to phone home and is somewhat concerned when St. John not only answers the phone but also starts playing the family piano. Brave Teheezal, by this time hiding *behind* Minta, pushes her forward, suggesting that she look through the keyhole to see what is going on. Cline, now on the other side of the door with a perfume atomizer in his hand, chooses this moment to squirt some of its contents through the keyhole and consequently straight into Minta's eye. After hopping back wet and surprised, she tells Teheezal to have a look; foolish Teheezal obliges and predictably gets the same treatment.

Ford Sterling publicity photograph ca. 1925.

The mayor dashes home concerned, the sound of his arrival scaring off the crooks, who climb out the window with their loot. On entering the kitchen, the mayor sees Teheezal's belt and billy club laying on the table, sending him off around the house on a suspicious, angry search for the elusive chief and his daughter. A noisy cascade of hat boxes from inside the closet alerts the mayor to the pair's whereabouts. The mayor opens the door and Minta explodes from inside, propelled by Teheezal's well-placed foot on her behind while he continues to hide behind one of her petticoats that hangs from the dress rail. The mayor asks where Teheezal is but she won't say, not that she needs to: Teheezal quickly gives himself away by opening the closet door and trying to creep out. He soon dives back inside when he sees the mayor heading toward him, and he is not going to come out in a hurry, that is, until the mayor shoots through the door. The mayor drags Teheezal and Minta back to the kitchen for an explanation. "She dragged me in," is the chief's cowardly reply as he points accusingly at Miss Durfee. Furiously, and deservedly, she slaps him clean through the window into the arms of Cline.

The mayor gives an ultimatum: unless Teheezal finds the crooks and gets the mayor's possessions back, it's off to jail for the chief. This leads to a climactic chase; well, not exactly a chase — yo-yo would be more accurate. Teheezal sends an optimistic note, "Please give back the loot," to the crooks via a policeman whom he has tied himself to with a rope for some reason. The crooks won't have anything to do with the letter or the policeman, whom they threaten with a gun. Fearing for his life, the terrified policeman jumps out of the upstairs window. As the policeman descends, the Teheezal counterweight bounces up the stairs to the crooks' lair, where Teheezal, too, is threatened with the gun. After running around a beam in the center of the room, he also jumps out of the window, thus sending the policeman back up again. Down leaps the policeman and up goes Teheezal. This is enough for the policeman. He throws off the rope, which lassoes itself round the mayor's ankle. (The mayor has just arrived with his daughter.) Now the mayor is at the other end of the counterweight system and takes his turn zooming up and down with Teheezal. Teheezal does inadvertently save the day, though; on one of his descents he drops through the storm doors into the cellar. Frightened, he starts firing his gun all around him just as the crooks make their decent in the dumbwaiter in a bid to escape. Instead, with hands up, they are marched into the arms of the waiting police by their heroic police chief.

Keystone was having problems of its own. In June 1915 news came that as of July 1 all production was to halt. The New York Motion Picture Company's contract with Mutual, which released all their films, expired on September 1 and was not being renegotiated. By July there would be a sufficient backlog of unreleased shorts to fulfill Mutual's September contractual requirements. The company was forced into a hiatus. The two-reeler *Only a Messenger Boy* was the last Keystone/Sennett release to feature Sterling.

Only a Messenger Boy opens in a telegraph office with Ford, holding the jug of beer he has just bought, surrounded by expectant fellow employees. The members of a local ladies' reform group come in and are horrified by the contents of Ford's jug and at the very idea that alcohol might be imbibed anywhere at all, let alone in a telegraph office. In disbelief the ladies have to sample the liquid to make sure it really is beer and find their fears are indeed true. Curiously, some of the ladies decide to sample it more than once *just to make sure*; by the time the jug is returned to the men it is empty. A pretty young lady, the only attractive one in the ladies' reform group, stays back and talks to Ford so sweetly and gently about his need for help that he is in tears, with his head on her chest, by the time a particularly hatchet-faced woman returns to retrieve her young compatriot. Ford is besotted and totally convinced the lovely young lady is in love with him.

Meanwhile, two "political crooks" are visiting the mayor in his office; they want to do a deal with him that would require the exchange of signed documents for money, and where better to accomplish this than the local park. As soon as the crooks leave, an advance guard from the ladies' group arrive at the mayor's office to complain about the disgraceful state of the messenger boys, with their drinking, gaming, and frequenting of pool halls. Some of the group enter the office, while the rest wait in the reception room, but with the deal on his mind the mayor doesn't have time for fussy women and tries to dismiss them, that is until one of the ladies, who happens to be his wife, decides it is her turn to deal with the situation and in she goes for a little discussion. Surprise, surprise—the mayor's wife is the very same woman who had spoken so sweetly to Ford. Time moves on and the mayor needs to be in the park for his illicit dealings; what better excuse to visit the park than to take her with him on the pretense of enjoying a nice lunchtime walk with his wife?

The mayor sees the crooks and leaves his wife sitting on a park bench while he goes to make the exchange, but it takes a long time and she falls asleep while waiting, her left arm draped along the back of the bench. Ford has also decided to spend his lunch hour in the park and looks around for somewhere to sit. He sees the charming young lady from the women's group and decides to coyly sit with her as there is plenty of space on the bench. Pretending not to take any notice of her, Ford plants himself on the other end and proceeds to eat his lunch. As he eats his sandwich he moves a little nearer to the mayor's wife; she does nothing; he turns and looks at her and realizes she is asleep. What an opportunity, thinks Ford, and he moves so close to her that he is practically in her lap. In her sleep the mayor's wife lets her arm fall onto Ford's shoulder; next she starts to stroke his arm and his face. Is she faking her sleep? Ford doesn't care. He rather likes the attention as he carries on trying to eat his sandwich, rapidly becoming more and more enthralled at the idea of the young lady's attraction to him.

The mayor has almost made his exchange, but who should interrupt him but the busybody women's group, who has seen his wife apparently acting inappropriately with Ford! The mayor is horrified and pulls out a gun. He runs to where he has left his wife and what he sees convinces him the women were telling the truth. The mayor confronts Ford who, unaware of the identity of the person sitting next to him on the bench, hushes the mayor and tells him not to wake his "lady friend." The mayor points out that it is his wife and holds a gun to Ford's nose. The mayor's wife awakes and realizes Ford is not the mayor, or whoever she was dreaming of, and shoves him away. Ford jumps up and runs off in panic as the Mayor fires shot after shot at the fleeing Ford.

The mayor needs to get the money he received from the crooks to a safe place, so he gives it to his wife, telling her to take it home and guard it. Meanwhile, he goes off to buy some flowers for his wife as a peace offering over his mistaken notion that she was messing about with Ford. Ford wasn't far, though, lurking out of sight, still oblivious that she had been asleep, still mired in the belief she really was fooling about with him. As soon as the mayor's wife leaves, he follows her to her house.

What neither Sterling nor the mayor's wife knows is that the crooks have called up the rest of the gang and they are already lying in wait at the house to steal back the money. (The reel change occurs at this point; footage was missing from the viewed print, making some of the subsequent action and events unclear.) There is a struggle in the house as the mayor's wife fights off the crooks. Ford is suddenly in the house and he hits one of the crooks (who is holding the mayor's wife) with a large vase, then attacks the other one, allowing the mayor's wife to escape. Unbeknownst to

Ford, the mayor's wife has called her husband to tell him of the crooks' presence in their house and he is now on his way home with a band of policemen.

Meanwhile, Ford has gone upstairs and is hiding in a bed in the mayoral couple's room! The mayor's wife hears some more commotion and runs up into the bedroom. Ford sits up just as the mayor and the police arrive outside the bedroom door. The mayor's wife is terrified that her husband will now find her in their bedroom with Ford, and locks the door. The mayor and his party crash down the door to find the room empty — until the mayor pulls back the bedclothes to reveal his wife in bed with Ford. Ford leaps out of the window, knocking two of the crooks off the balcony onto another crook, knocking him out. Ford tries to climb down the fire escape but is shot at by the crooks, so he leaps through a downstairs room and hides in the open safe. The mayor's wife, who has not seen Ford, throws the money into the safe and slams the door shut, locking it.

Now come the chases. The crooks steal the safe (with Ford and the money inside) and put it on the back of a truck. Off they go, with the mayor and his men in pursuit. The safe falls off the truck and rolls down the road. The crooks, in hot pursuit, eventually catch up with the safe and hurriedly decide to push it off a cliff to open it. They push it over the cliff but are unaware that some demolition men have just laid sticks of dynamite to blow up part of the cliff in the very place the safe will land. BOOM! Sterling and safe are sent straight up into the air. The explosion has freed Ford, who pushes open the now unlocked door to see that he is flying through the air toward who knows where. The crooks, meanwhile, are back in their truck chasing the flying safe; they, in turn, are being chased by the mayor in his car and some Kops, alerted to the situation, on railway handcarts. Up ahead is a river and the only way across is a cantilever bridge. A message is relayed to the bridge keeper. "Open it!" is the order. Up goes the bridge and off into the river go the crooks. The safe lands, too — straight in the river — and begins filling up with water, Ford trapped inside.

Now that the Mutual contract was no longer feasible and there was no distribution company interested in releasing the NYMPC films, something had to be done to stop the whole enterprise from collapsing. Harry Aitken, with Kessel and Bauman, who still owned the controlling shares of the NYMPC, had something up their sleeves to save their product. Kessel and Bauman were going in with Aitken to form their own distribution company, with Aitken in charge. Harry Aitken was very familiar with the NYMPC, as well as with Kessel and Bauman, having been the guiding light at Mutual. Aitken was a promoter from Wisconsin who, with his brother Roy, had bought several Midwest film exchanges in the first decade of the 1900s. These exchanges had been sufficiently lucrative to allow the brothers to open an overseas branch in London. Harry went on to organize the Majestic Film Company in 1911, for which he lured Mary Pickford and Owen Moore away from Carl Laemmle's IMP. Carl Laemmle was furious to have his dainty feminine star poached from under his nose. In revenge, Laemmle's Motion Picture and Sales Company, which released the Majestic product, doubled the distribution percentage Majestic had to pay them.

6—Out and In

Aitken promptly founded his own company, the Film Supply Company of America, taking the product of ten other companies with him from Laemmle. On the strength of his business reputation, for his next venture Aitken was able to get funding from Wall Street. With partner John R. Freuler he started the Mutual Film Corporation, which announced trade in March 1912. It was to Mutual that Kessel and Bauman elected to move their distribution, becoming one of the ten companies removing their product from Laemmle. In return, they sold their four Empire Exchanges and their stocks for the Carlton Motion Picture Laboratories (which also ran Reliance Pictures) to Aitken and Mutual. As in the past with his partners, it wasn't long before Aitken and Freuler were in disagreement. Things went from bad to worse. In May 1915, the Mutual board, with Mutual's seven hundred shareholders on their side, voted against Aitken, who promptly stormed out of the company.

This coincided with Kessel and Bauman's problems with Mutual and when the offer was made to join Aitken, they were only too happy to be part of the new enterprise, the Triangle Film Corporation. With the promise of being able to sign D. W. Griffith to release through Triangle, Aitken managed to finagle the huge amount of capital required to form Triangle. He managed to do this with promises of great things for the company's future, offering the financiers who had invested in his other projects good returns on their investments. They were obviously impressed and bought stock far in excess of the company's worth. Financially overstretching itself would soon prove to be the downfall of Triangle.

With Aitken and Triangle, Kessel and Bauman could now make *and* distribute their products as a package. They also planned to improve the quality and quantity of their output. Thus, on July 20, 1915, the Triangle Film Corporation was born. Keystone Comedies became Triangle Keystone Comedies; no longer was Sennett working for the NYMPC and Kessel and Bauman, but directly for Aitken, and money was being spent on the operation. Down came the old studios and offices that had grown piecemeal around Keystone since their arrival in California. New facilities boasting twelve concrete studios went up, allowing twelve separate films to be in production at any one time. Production methods changed concurrently. Triangle required two double-reel comedies per week, and they were not to be made in the haphazard way the old Keystoners were used to. Working scripts were required; more people were employed in all departments and everyone received better salaries than before. Triangle Keystone was brought up to the same standard as the other large companies of the day. The formula appeared to work. By March 1916, Triangle Keystone had fifteen units making comedies on the lot. Sterling found steady work in them.

During this period Sterling appeared in and codirected eight two-reelers, including *His Pride and Shame* (released on February 6, 1916, another directorial teaming with Charley Chase); *His Wild Oats* (June 25, 1916, codirected by Clarence Badger), and *His Lying Heart* (August 20, 1916, in which Sterling shared the director's chair with Charles Avery). By now, Aitkin's monetary deceptions were coming home to haunt him: Triangle was in deep financial trouble and to get out of it Aitken was trying to form a merger with Paramount. After that failed Triangle was doomed to bankruptcy. Gaps in Triangle's distribution were occurring because of violations by

Paramount of their block booking agreements with distributors, and by February 1917 the company's very shaky financial foundations were beginning to crumble. As things stood, Sennett would have been unable to form another studio using the guaranteed selling names of Mack Sennett or Keystone, as he had signed them away in the previous contract; Triangle now owned the rights to the name Mack Sennett and to the Keystone trademark. Sterling, as usual, was busy at the studio, releasing four shorts between February 18 and May 13. But he was nearing the end of his second tenure with Keystone. Later, in June 1917, after much discussion, Sennett struck a deal with Triangle. He managed to retain his name and cast, sold his stocks in Triangle at the current market value, and received a $180,000 cash bonus as well as the title to the Edendale studio. He didn't get the name Keystone, but without the name Sennett behind it, it proved to be worthless. By September 30, 1917, Sennett had worked out the deal Aitken had failed to close, and signed with Paramount. He kept the staff he wanted and carried on making his films as if nothing had happened. Adolph Zukor was only too pleased to announce that Mack Sennett, the foremost comedy director, would be associated with Paramount now. However, by that time Sterling was on sabbatical again.

Publicity portrait of Ford Sterling by Hartsook for the Triangle-Keystone Film Company, ca. 1915–18.

Sterling's two-year contract, signed in 1915, expired around the time that Triangle Keystone looked about to collapse. Sterling did the sensible thing, considering the uncertain prospects of his old studio's survival, and left with a contract for the second time. This time he joined Fox Sunshine Comedies for a reteaming with Fox director Henry Lehrman. Sterling was having personal troubles as well: his marriage was collapsing. He confided to fellow Dutch comedian Sam Bernard that his wife had double-crossed him. Teddy Sampson left him on April 2, after just two years of marriage. She was still referred to as Mrs. Ford Sterling in mid–April 1916 and reported as traveling from New York to Los Angeles with her friend Mabel Normand.[5] Again, in January 1917, in a list of who's married to whom in the *Washington Post*, Ford and Teddy were included as husband and wife,[6] although they had been estranged for nearly a year.

7

His Wild Oats

In addition to dropping in and out of other studios, it is likely that between 1916 and 1918 Sterling was appearing in (and codirecting with Sennett) the Mabel Normand vehicle *Oh, Mabel Behave*, which was eventually released in 1922. Viewing its remains gives a poor impression of a film that got good reviews on its release. In the currently preserved footage there is no recognizable plot and Sterling spends most of the time wildly gesticulating in front of the camera. The majority of the film stars Sterling, to the extent that out of the forty-three minutes of surviving footage, Mabel appears in only eight. The extended time in which the film was made gave rise to the need for the use of doubles to fill in for actors who were no longer available for work on the project. For example, there was a big duel between Owen Moore and Sterling and many of the shots of Moore have his face conspicuously hidden, which usually indicates a body double.

Moving Picture World described *Oh, Mabel Behave* as being well made and finely photographed, with a lot of humorous situations and laughs as well as clever and witty subtitles by Joe Farnham. The article goes on to say that "The film is a delightful burlesque on romantic love stories of the revolutionary period portrayed by four of the leading stars of today."[1] It mentions that Sterling, as the irascible Squire Peachem, carries the biggest share of the comedy and gets away with it in great shape. Sennett also gets a good review for his dense and ignorant valet and inseparable henchman to the Squire, Blaa Blaa; Owen Moore (Randolph) and Mabel Normand (an innkeeper's daughter), as the young lovers, are also described as giving a good account of themselves. The plot sounds like a generic melodrama, with Squire Peachem using the mortgage he holds on the innkeeper's property as leverage to win his daughter. Mabel, of course, is in love with Randolph and rebuffs the Squire's advances. The Squire, with Blaa Blaa's assistance, tries to cause trouble with the pair but, of course, all comes out well in the end. Unfortunately, as it stands today, *Oh, Mabel Behave* really does look like a salvage job, maybe as more pieces of the puzzle are found and restored the whole may make for better viewing.

There was a reason for the drawn-out form of film making. Mabel and Sennett's long-standing affair came to an end in 1916, after Mabel found Mack in a compromising situation with fellow Keystone player Mae Busch. Sennett, still in love with Mabel, tried to keep her nearby by forming a unit specifically to make Mabel

Normand features. This did not hold her for long, as in 1918 she signed a five-year contract with Goldwyn. Unfortunately, Mabel had become increasingly unreliable and unpredictable, nor was she particularly suited to the new material she was being given by Goldwyn. Sennett, convinced that only he could make a good film with her, came to a loan-out agreement with Goldwyn in 1922, allowing Sennett to put Mabel in his new feature, which had already been offered to Mary Pickford, *Molly O'*.

Sterling, meanwhile, was off working with (and being directed by) "Pathé" Lehrman on the first offering from the newly formed Fox Sunshine Comedies. This was the second series of comedies produced by the Fox studio, the first series arriving on the screens at the beginning of 1917 under the name of Foxfilms. Another Keystone veteran and friend of Ford was directing these — none other than Charley Chase. Unfortunately, the records for titles, including cast and the date of release, are virtually nil. Neither does much Sunshine material survive, due to one of those all too common events that occurred in the age of nitrate — a vault fire. This is a shame, because when Lehrman had a budget, as he did with the Fox Sunshines, the results could be quite excellent. Of titles featuring Sterling there seems to be but one currently known, *Moonshine,* released in October 1918. Sadly, Sterling's work for Foxfilms probably will never be available for reappraisal.

Between the time Lehrman left — or was removed from — the Sterling Studios and went to work for Fox, he had formed his own company, which also released through Universal. L-KO stood for Lehrman Knock-out, and Lehrman had set himself up for direct but poor competition with Keystone, much to the irritation of Sennett. The British comedian and ex–Karno player, Billie Ritchie,[2] was employed as a Chaplin imitator. Ritchie always claimed that it was from *him* that Chaplin got his Tramp character, rather than the other way around. There is some evidence to support that Chaplin may have borrowed some of Ritchie's act, which Ritchie proclaimed (with some exaggeration) he had been performing since 1887; both had worked for Karno and knew each other well. From contemporary reviews and the few films that are accessible, the L-KO product seems to have been a pale rip-off of the originals. L-KO gained a bad reputation in the industry, fueled by Lehrman's demands for more and more dangerous stunts from his actors. Before long, the nickname "Pathé" was replaced by "Suicide" Lehrman. Lehrman maintained control of the studio until things began to change, culminating in a huge row with Universal. Lehrman walked — straight over to Fox and Sunshine. L-KO continued for a while, too, until it was taken over by Laemmle's nephews, Julius and Abe Stern.

Sterling did the opposite of Lehrman after making the Fox Sunshines. He went to work for L-KO under the auspices of the Stern brothers. The studio by now had a worse reputation than when Lehrman was running it, and it wasn't because of injuries. Its own slogan, "L-KO Comedies are not to be laughed at," didn't really help its case. There are five known titles released between July 1, 1918, and January 19, 1919: *Her Screen Idol* (July 1918), *Summer Girls* (August 1918), *Beware of Boarders* (October 1918), *Rough on Husbands* (November 1918), and *Fools and Duels* (January 1919), the latter directed by Lehrman. *Fools and Duels* may have been a held release,

Ford Sterling with Charlotte Mineau (L) and unidentified players in *Love, Honor, and Behave*. Released November 11, 1920. Associated First National Pictures; Paramount Sennett.

with Lehrman not having worked at L-KO for two years, or it could simply be a mislabeled Fox Sunshine.

During 1918 the United States had more to be concerned with than World War I. The Spanish Influenza epidemic of 1918 was impinging on business. It affected the movie industry, not only by closing down the theaters, but also by dictating when and which studios could open, making it not unusual for actors to moonlight from studio to studio. If someone working at one of the studios came down with the disease the whole place was closed and quarantined. Therefore, Sterling was far from alone in his hopping back and forth from studio to studio to find work during this time. After his brief sabbatical from Sennett, Sterling returned to what was now Paramount Sennett for a busy schedule at the end of 1918. It started with the short *East Lynne with Variations*, released on February 24, 1919. *Hearts and Flowers* (March/April 1919) was the next to be released and Sterling, wearing his pencil-thin mustache, gave one of his more elegant and subtle performances. Under the direction of Eddie Cline,[3] *Hearts and Flowers* has a real pre–Keystone feel about Sterling's performance.

As the film begins, a large hotel orchestra is awaiting the arrival of its sophisticated leader. Suave Sterling walks onto the stage in tails, graciously acknowledging the approval of the audience seated around tables and, after flicking a piece of dust from his white gloves, proceeds to conduct the opening number. One of the more ill-mannered guests produces a peashooter and proceeds to sting Sterling with peas; Sterling does his best to ignore him while singing to the orchestra's accompaniment. So good is Sterling's rendition that an Airedale dog nearby simply has to join in. Sterling side-glances around the orchestra to see where this strange noise is coming from to no avail, but there are no attacks, no wild gesticulations from him. In the next number, Sterling performs a little dance, which the hotel's lowly flower girl (Louise Fazenda) comes in to watch, totally enamored by the elegant orchestral conductor.

One of the lady guests, a prune magnate's daughter (Phyllis Haver), is also rather taken with Sterling. She has brought a bouquet which she intends to throw to him; her nobleman boyfriend (Billy Armstrong) is not impressed and liberally sprinkles pepper over it while she is lovingly looking at Sterling. She throws the bouquet. Sterling catches it, smells it, and sneezes genteelly. He shows the bouquet to a musician, who does likewise, so Sterling hurls the offending item back at Phyllis, missing and hitting Louise in the face. Phyllis wants to join Sterling in his dance and they perform a very elegant fox-trot together, Armstrong angrily leaving the scene.

It is time for Sterling to take a break and he goes and sits with Phyllis. At the next table sits Louise, determined to win the adored Sterling for herself. He is far from interested in someone so cheap, and when she becomes too irksome he informs her that she has "the grace of a hippopotamus but lack[s] its charm." This does not dissuade her, so he has her thrown out of the dining room. Even on the way out she can't resist giving him a kiss on the cheek.

Sterling and Phyllis dance together, this time on the dance floor, but while they are away from their table Armstrong returns with a telegram, which he drops by Sterling's chair. On returning to their table Sterling sees the paper, picks it up, and is very interested to read that the flower girl's uncle has just died and left her $2,000,000 in his will. Something must be done. He excuses himself from Phyllis and goes out into the lobby to find Louise. She is with her boyfriend, Jack Ackroyd, whom Sterling dispenses by suggesting that he "Go and tell a policeman you're lost." Sterling then turns toward Louise, lifts his left leg behind him, plants his foot squarely on Ackroyd's behind, and shoves him clean across the foyer. Louise wants to play chase with Sterling — not the sort of thing he is used to at all, far too common — but for $2,000,000 he isn't about to let that bother him. Phyllis comes out to see where he is and catches them; Louise pushes her out of the way. Phyllis wonders what is going on and decides that two can play at this game, and she plays it with a twist. Phyllis goes up to her room and changes into men's clothing. On returning to the dining room, she starts to flirt with Louise to make Sterling jealous. Phyllis leads Louise into the foyer, where she kisses her.

Sterling decides it might be a good idea to take Louise out for a walk away from this other man, so they head for the park. Sterling drops his cane and, bending over to pick it up, knocks Louise down the adjacent hill. Maybe, thinks Ford, she would be safer at the beach, so they head there instead. Who should be there, much to Ford's enjoyment, but the Sennett Bathing Beauties, who are playing ball. With them is none other than Phyllis in her swimsuit. She comes over to speak to the couple, still trying to figure out what is going on. Sterling is very impressed with the (for 1919) scantily clad lady and tells her he is "working on their future." She returns to play ball with the other girls and Sterling returns to his flirting with Louise — with one eye on the ladies as they frolic — and they kiss.

It is the day of the wedding; Sterling hasn't met Louise's family yet, and has a distinctly uncomfortable feeling when her mom and three brothers turn up. He finds out the terrifying truth: Pop's in jail and the brothers fight with each other at the drop of a hat. Louise and mom don't think twice about joining in, either, and it

Louise Fazenda appeared with Sterling at the Sennett studios and later went on to team up with him in both sound and silent features.

is mom who is the only one tough enough to bring the unruly troupe to heel. The minister and Sterling come out from their place of hiding and the ceremony begins. Louise asks brother Kala Pasha for the ring; he goes through his pockets producing blackjack, mask, and iron bar, but no ring. One of the other brothers (Edgar Kennedy) brings out a bag and produces a handful of rings from it. "I got these the other day," he tells Sterling, who is becoming less impressed with the whole thing by the minute.

Then Armstrong comes in with a newspaper and shows Sterling an article headed, "Joke on prominent musician." The truth is out. Sterling has been conned. He makes a bolt for it. The brothers will have none of this: he is going to marry their sister whether he wants to or not. While they are out chasing Sterling, Louise is busy marrying Ackroyd, her true love. The brothers chase Sterling around the hotel, cornering him in his bedroom. Sterling, they decide, makes the perfect baseball; with Pasha pitching, he is thrown across the room, past the door, where the batsman Kennedy repeatedly swings and misses, to the catcher Kennedy and back.

After Sterling's return to Sennett there was a definite change in the look of his characters from those in the Keystone Triangle or Sterling Studio products. Ford had returned to his pre–Keystone technique, never really reverting to the early Sennett style again even when playing the Teheezal character in sound films. Looking at sur-

Great Scott! Released August 15, 1920. Paramount Sennett. Director: Charles Murray. Front row, L–R: Fanny Kelly, Ford Sterling, George O'Hara, Harriett Hammond, Charlie Murray, Eva Thatcher.

viving footage and stills from the Paramount Sennett films, with the exception of *Yankee Doodle in Berlin* (a character role), Sterling seems to be favoring his own thin mustache and the more sophisticated man-about-town look and demeanor; as such, he cuts quite a handsome figure. However, he is still not beyond throwing himself around, giving in to slapstick or being battered and humiliated by those he has cheated. Sterling had been occasionally playing this rather sophisticated ladies' man from the early days, but now the character took on a more rounded and stylish appearance and was soon to replace his Dutch persona in popularity, although the latter would not be forgotten.

Fresh from the City (May 1920) is another pencil-thin-mustache role for Sterling. It begins with heartbreak: "It's all off for the present," Virginia Fox informs would-be bridegroom Ford Sterling when Eddie Gribbon, her boyfriend just out of jail on probation, arrives at their wedding in the nick of time to disrupt the ceremonies. Sterling, with heart bowed down, leaves to seek forgetfulness in the country. Here he meets Marie Prevost, a country belle, whose fresh charms banish Virginia from his memory. Marie is the daughter of the owner of the local outdated general merchandise store (Pat Kelly); the store is heavily mortgaged to the evil Bert Roach.

7—His Wild Oats 73

"Ford Sterling amiably bestowed between two dancing girls [unidentified] while Billy Bevan and Billy Armstrong, as pianist and violinist, give a hickville version of Cabaret Jazz." From *Mack Sennett Weekly*, volume 2, number 5, May 3, 1920, p. 1, promotion for *Fresh from the City*.

Roach has a son (Lewis Gordon), who is also in love with Marie; she, however, prefers city-boy Sterling. Sterling quarrels with the country lover and ejects him from the store. Roach, to avenge his son, threatens to foreclose the mortgage. Sterling, however, discovers there are only thirty days left to run on it. To keep the place going and to drum up a bit of business, he renovates the place, installs a cabaret and participates, with dainty Marie, in the entertainment.

This angers Roach more and, still bent on revenge, he salts a worthless piece of land with oil (shades of *The Gusher* here). Sterling discovers the oil and falls for the fraud; thinking it a wonderful opportunity for the family, he induces Kelly into buying it. Gordon, who doesn't know of the scam, or that his father merely poured oil into holes in the ground, arrives in time to prevent Kelly from getting the land his father is selling. Sterling is determined to win the prize for Marie and her father and doubles the original offer, which, after father and son have come to an understanding, is accepted. The fraud is soon discovered and Sterling devises a plan by which he doubles the fraud of old man Roach, reselling him the same property at a greatly increased price. Teddy, the faithful Sennett Great Dane, plays a part in saving the day, too. When Roach discovers he has been duped, he starts after his son — who has just left with the money to pay for the land — to stop him from completing the purchase. The dutiful son thinks his father's yelling and gesticulations are to try to hasten him to his goal, so he runs all the faster and the first chase begins.

After the money changes hands, it is put into the safe by Kelly. Gribbon, who

Fresh from the City, Paramount Sennett, 1920. L–R: Kala Pasha in drag, Billy Bevan, Ford Sterling, Virginia Fox, Marie Prevost, Billy Armstrong, and Pat Kelly. This was a publicity still featured in the *Mack Sennett Weekly*, volume 2 number 5, for Monday, May 3, 1920.

has been informed by Sterling's near-bride Virginia about the goings on and where the money is, makes haste to the country to crack the safe. Gordon discovers Gribbon at work and later, when Roach, sore at being caught in his own trap, comes to recover his coins, Gordon sees him but doesn't recognize him as his dad under the mask. This triggers another wild chase in which the town constables take part, arriving just as the explosion set by Gribbon goes off. In the scramble Marie (who is on a rooftop chasing after one of the thieves) falls but is rescued by the heroic Sterling. The cops recover from the shock of the explosion and round up the crooks, then set about rescuing the now-stuck-on-the-roof Sterling. They hold a sheet for him to drop into from his perilous perch after his rescue of Marie. Of course the wedding bells chime for Marie and her friend who is "fresh from the city." A side note: the female bouncer of the village cabaret is none other than Kala Pasha in drag.

During the First World War, the Sennett Studio set to work on a film intended to uplift morale by poking fun at the Kaiser, his family, and the Prussian army. *Yankee Doodle in Berlin* is another character role for Sterling, in which he plays the dysfunctional, clumsy, womanizing Prussian Kaiser in this comedy. The war ended before the film's release in 1919, but it still gave returning troops and their families plenty to laugh about.

7—His Wild Oats

In the film, an American airman (Bothwell Browne, a top female impersonator of the day) is sent to Berlin to steal war documents. His disguise, naturally, is glamorous drag and a jolly good job he does of it, too. The motley crew who make up the Prussian Guard go through their paces and demonstrate their ineptness. They trip, fall, wander off in different directions, kick each other as they goose step, and manage to shoot the Kaiser in the rear end (defiant shades of the Keystone Kops here). He remarks, "If they are soldiers, then I'm an acrobat." The soldiers rush off thinking the sound of their own rifles is an attack by the allies; the Kaiser hobbles off, holding his backside, to get the buckshot removed, accompanied by his son—the crown prince—and the chief of his army, Von Hindenburg.

In the war room, the Kaiser shows his total lack of comprehension and worldliness as he explains to Von Hindenburg how he is going to divide up the Western world: "I'll take Europe, the crown prince the Orient; my other boys can use America for golf links." And he waves his hands over a map on the table showing how simple his plan is. Von Hindenburg grumbles, "If it's so easy, do it yourself." Next, the Kaiser demonstrates equal ineptness at playing croquet; his minions applaud him, ignoring his errors and his cheating. The game is interrupted by news from the front: "We are withdrawing by day and retreating by night. Outwitting the Allies successfully. We will be with you soon." Bob arrives on the scene, now dressed as an elegant woman. He was discovered by Von Hindenburg, who thought he would make a desirable croquet partner but then was purloined by the crown prince, who has brought Bob in. The game resumes with Bob joining in, much to the Kaiser's delight. Bob manages to bean the Kaiser on the head with a well-placed croquet ball, as if poleaxed, the Kaiser falls flat onto the ground. Bob goes to his aid and, just as he is sitting on the floor with the Kaiser, an arm around his shoulder, in walks the Kaiser's wife. She is unimpressed and proceeds to throttle the Kaiser, who points out that they are not alone, as his guards are all around. She steps back and pats him on the head, gently stroking his cheek, but he manages to politely decline a kiss. Now feeling safe, the Kaiser dismisses his guard. "Now, we are alone," says his wife. She promptly sets into him, knocking him backward over benches and slamming various items over his head, including a guitar, a vase, and a randomly aimed barrage of crockery that knocks out the guard one by one where they are hiding behind bushes. The Kaiser ends up reeling backward through a table, landing in a heap. His wife marches up to the sitting man and hits him over the head with a bottle just as Hindenburg enters. "He's had a bad spell," she tells Hindenburg.

Bob is now staying in the castle, where he entertains the royal company by dancing in Eastern attire. This causes a contest between the Kaiser and the crown prince (who are completely fooled) for Bob's affections. The crown prince goes into Bob's suite of rooms and, when he hears a noise outside, hides under the bed. The noise is, of course, the Kaiser coming to pay a visit on Bob, too, with the hopes of a little seduction. Bob flirts with the Kaiser, who compliments him on his wonderful dancing. The Kaiser tries to do the dance, too, but is rudely interrupted when a guard, with the same idea in mind as the crown prince and the Kaiser, marches in and stabs the Kaiser in the rearend with his bayonet. The Kaiser smartly marches the guard back out again and, calling two other guards, stands them outside the bedroom door with instructions to let no one past on pain of death. Bob knows there is only one way to achieve his errand and get the papers. He dances for the Kaiser, who playfully chases Bob round and round the bed, rolling over it on each pass. The Kaiser, thinking he has won Bob's affection, shows him the papers with the plans, then tucks them back into his pants top. Of course, the next person to arrive at the bedroom door is general Von Hindenburg, who demands to be let in. Calling for help to a large officer, who soundly beats the guards into a pulp, he then enters the bedroom just as the Kaiser is lying on the floor with Bob. The Kaiser soon scuttles under the bed, where he finds the crown prince. Father ejects both son and Von Hindenburg. Once they are alone, Bob goes into action. He pulls out a cloth covered in chloroform, uses it on the Kaiser to knock him out, retrieves the plans of war, and beats a hasty retreat to the Allies' lines.

Yankee Doodle in Berlin. Released March 20, 1919. Paramount Sennett. Ford Sterling as the Kaiser.

This was not Sterling's only effort to support the Allies. The November 4, 1917, *Los Angeles Times* article, "Stars Lend Talent for National Defense," reported the upcoming program to be put on for the National League of Defense to be held at Clune's Auditorium.[4] It was full of talent: Charlie Murray was the chairman and the cast included Henry B. Walthall, Roscoe Arbuckle, Ford Sterling, Hughie Mack, and the Three Keatons. This may well have been the last time the Three Keatons were seen together as an act; Buster had by that time already begun his film career with Arbuckle.

After Sennett finished making *Married Life* in June 1920, he began work on a new five-reel feature that he modestly alluded to as being "a super-comedy."[5] In

7—His Wild Oats 77

His Last False Step. **Released November 9, 1919. Paramount Sennett. L–R: Bert Roach, Phyllis Haver, Ford Sterling.**

the cast were Ben Turpin, Phyllis Haver, Marie Prevost, and Ford as a baseball pitcher, thus bringing two of Sterling's talents together. Unfortunately, this feature was never made. Sterling announced in mid–May that in a few weeks he was going to embark on a world tour to study film conditions abroad, with a view to producing and marketing. That trip obviously didn't take place, as six more Sennett Paramounts followed; the last, *His Last False Step,* was released in 1921 after Sterling left Sennett in October[6] for a different studio and another business venture.

Toward the end of 1920, Special Pictures Corporation approached Sterling with a deal to act in a series of shorts under the direction of Reggie Morris. It was announced on November 14 that Sterling had signed a contract to make ten Cosmograph Comedies. The intention was that Sterling would make a series of comedies yearly to be released as comedy superspecials by the Los Angeles company. Special Pictures had started a policy of securing big comedy stars for their productions; they had already signed Chester Conklin and Reggie Morris from Sennett; Morris would soon sign Louise Fazenda away from Sennett, too. General sales manager H. J. Roberts announced that by October 1 they would be releasing eight pictures a week.[7]

Special Pictures Corporation had their offices in New York and California[8] as

Great Scott! Released August 15, 1920. Paramount Sennett. Director Charles Murray. L–R: Ford Sterling, Charles Murray, Eva Thatcher, Harriett Hammond.

well as their studios; they used the Hampton Studios on Santa Monica near La Brea in Los Angeles.[9] They had great vision, and by November plans were in the works to expand the studio to nine units.[10] Also in November the company signed a contract with the Kokusai Film Corporation from Tokyo, Japan, securing them the Oriental rights to the entire Special Pictures output for a year, including the Sterlings.[11] Reggie Morris produced some of these comedies, including the Sterlings, under his own company, Reggie Morris Productions, Inc., whose offices were at 5828 Santa Monica Blvd., Hollywood. Reggie Morris was the president and Frank H. Marshall, general manager and vice president; the aim of the company was to imitate United Artists. As with United Artists, the Morris players were also the stockholders in the company. Along with Sterling, this included Neely Edwards, Charlotte Merriam, Margaret Cullingham, Jack Duffy, and Eddie Baker. Eddie Baker said Reggie Morris had the idea that if D. W. Griffith, Charlie Chaplin, Mary Pickford, and Douglas Fairbanks could do it — creating United Artists Corporation — then they could too. When the plan collapsed, all the investments were lost,[12] but this was in the future, albeit not that far into the future.

7—His Wild Oats

Production on Sterling's films didn't begin immediately, although it was announced that Sterling had left the Sennett Studio by October 9[13] due to another commitment. Sterling started out on a tour of the United States and Canada in the second week of October 1920. He had been given the honor of being appointed a roving oral publicity agent by the mayor of Los Angeles to boost Los Angeles and its motion picture industry.[14] It was a personal appearance tour but none of the appearances were to be on the stage; they were at dinners, luncheons, and other events put on in Sterling's honor by local chambers of commerce. He attended a cinema convention in San Francisco, then went on to Salt Lake City, Denver, Kansas City, Minneapolis, St. Louis, Chicago, Indianapolis, Cleveland, Cincinnati, Pittsburgh, Detroit, Buffalo, and New York City, returning via Atlanta, Savannah, Charlotte, Dallas, and El Paso. This was quite some journey by rail in the 1920s. Sterling was certainly back by December 10; he was playing golf with Leo Diegel (the golf pro) and Scotty Chisholm on the San Gabriel golf course. Diegel turned in a card of seventy-six and Ford of seventy-eight; the next afternoon Sterling was playing a private game on the Wilshire course on its inaugural day.

It is unlikely that any of the ten films were ever made under the Cosmograph banner. There was at least one short and possibly as many as four with Sterling in them, released by Special Pictures. These were ComiClassic Productions' *A Pyjama Marriage* (October 17, 1920); *Watch Your Husbands* (November 14, 1920), with Charlotte Merriam; *A Seminary Scandal* (1921) and *A Ballroom Romeo* (1921), all directed by Reggie Morris. Shortly thereafter, Special Pictures collapsed. The first reel of *A Ballroom Romeo* does still survive and is an interesting little short that gives a glimpse of what could have been a promising series. We get to see Sterling riding a horse in this one, something he did with style and elegance, even if his character was no good at it in this two-reeler and fell all over the place. Special Pictures was about to overreach itself, as far as financing went. The company was planning on extensively increasing the production schedules for 1921, but in order to do that they had to turn over their distribution to the Federal Film Exchanges of America and eliminate their own exchange system. With the money the company would now be saving (which it had been using to maintain their distribution organization), Special Pictures felt it could more than double the productivity of the studio. The plan was now to release a ComiClassic every week rather than every other week, with Reggie Morris heading his cast of Ford Sterling, Neely Edwards, Charlotte Merriam, Stan Laurel, and Eddie Baker.

In the spring of 1921 Ford and Teddy got back together, for a while at least. The *Atlanta Constitution* informed its readers that Ford Sterling and Teddy Sampson were in Europe on a pleasure jaunt after becoming reconciled.[15] But it was not to last.

8

Peeping Pete

Even during Sterling's heyday few people were aware of an apparently well-kept secret: He was an internationally renowned photographer and a recognized expert in the bromoil photographic process. Creating a comic strip, "The Sterling Kids," for the *Chicago American* was just one outlet for his talents. In the early days before entering the hectic world of Mack Sennett and the movies, Sterling worked and studied in other art forms. Sculpting and painting were his main loves, and during his years on the stage he continued his studies wherever and whenever possible.

Once Sterling joined the Keystone Studio, however, he had little time to spend on so time-consuming a hobby and he decided to turn his creative attention to photography,[1] something he had retained avid interest in since childhood.[2] He also felt, after beginning his screen career, that the arts of painting and sculpture were too widely separated from his work, so he concentrated on artistic photography.[3] Sterling had a good eye for composition; not only did this allow him to instinctively know where to stand in front of the movie camera for best effect, it also spilled over into the films he directed for the Keystone Studio. The ones that remain are beautifully framed and balanced; he used a variety of close to long shots, intercut to punctuate the action.

The complex bromoil process in which Sterling decided to specialize is a tricky technique requiring much care and precision — and it is time consuming. The technique had been formulated in 1907 by Englishman E. J. Wall; the instructions were published later in the year by C. Welborn Piper. Piper described the process as "the latest printing process; a remarkable method of turning Bromide prints and enlargements into oil-pigment prints."[4] The idea behind the process was to make a good bromide print, bleach it in a solution to produce an image in different hardening gelatin, and finally apply oil-based pigment with a brush to form an image. To get the best image, it was best to use good-quality bromide paper, hard, durable, well-sized, and thickly coated with an emulsion rich in silver. This was an extremely complex and painstaking procedure,[5] and there were some pretty serious chemicals used in the process that needed great care in handling and storage, including chromic and hydrochloric acids. Once the print was dry, Sterling would apply the thick, greasy inks with several fitch-hair brushes that had been cut at an angle. He used various application techniques to give different textured effects to the finished picture. There

"The Firefly." A study in bromoil by Ford Sterling. This was one of a set of bromoil photographs exhibited in London in 1919 that won him a prize for his work. Some examples were later printed in the July 1919 edition of *Motion Picture* magazine.

are many steps to the process from negative to finished bromoil, and plenty of chemicals involved, allowing for an abundant scope for disaster; even temperature and humidity play a role in the success of the finished article.[6]

In the early part of the century, serious photography required a fair amount of space, a lot of equipment, and an array of chemicals that would make a modern-day hazardous materials officer cordon off the area in a heartbeat. Sterling had a studio and laboratory in his home, as well as a darkroom that was noted to have been a credit to any high-class portrait photographer. Many guests would see the inside of his perfectly appointed Hollywood home, but few saw the backyard where there stood a complete photographic studio and laboratory. Between pictures, Sterling concentrated on his prints with multiple gums, bromide, and bromoil transfers as his medium.[7] For many years he experimented with different cameras, subjects, and photographic processes. Among his favorite subjects were the California desert and mountain regions, where he spent a good deal of his time between film projects with his portable outfit, seeking locations of pictorial beauty to photograph.[8] Sterling also liked to take photographs of beautiful women and some of these elegant compositions would win him international recognition and awards in exhibitions on both sides of the Atlantic.

Sterling decided on the style he wanted to adopt and soon joined the Camera Pictorialists of Los Angeles. Their ranks boasted the likes of cofounders Edward Weston and his wife Flora, and Louis Fleckenstein, among other notables. Weston had come to California soon after the San Francisco earthquake and fire of 1906 to work as a surveyor for the San Pedro, Los Angeles, and Salt Lake Railroad; in 1909, he married Flora Chandler, a photographer of note in her own right. Weston had his own portrait studio in Tropico, California, and soon began having articles published. It was in 1914 that he cofounded the Camera Pictorialists of Los Angeles. By the 1920s, however, Weston had renounced pictorialism and began one of his periods of transition. He was a charter member of Group f/64, started in 1932; its members included Ansel Adams, Imogene Cunningham, and Consuelo Kanaga. (Weston died at home in 1958.)

Cofounder and director of the Pictorialists, Louis Fleckenstein, with a colleague, had earlier organized the Salon Club of America, devoted to the nationwide promotion of the various regional pictorialist photographers' clubs. By the time he moved from Montana to Los Angeles, where he opened a portrait studio in 1907, Fleckenstein had exhibited at the Royal Photographic Society in London and become an internationally renowned photographer. He later moved to Long Beach, California, where he worked as the city's first art commissioner, while still continuing to exhibit and publish his work.

Another eminent member was Arthur F. Kales, who was born in the Arizona Territory but chose to move west to study law at the University of California, Berkeley, in 1903. He was living in the San Francisco area when he became interested in the burgeoning pictorialist movement that flourished there. Soon Kales moved to Los Angeles to work in advertising and, although he returned San Francisco in 1917, he still joined the prestigious Camera Pictorialists of Los Angeles the following year.

Kales' specialty involved nude models. (Sterling may have expanded his knowledge of how he photographed his own models by studying Kales.) From 1922 to 1936 Kales wrote about pictorialist photography in western America for the journal *Photograms of the Year*.

By 1921, the Camera Pictorialists of Los Angeles was a self-supporting, internationally respected organization, considered second in excellence only to the Royal Photographic Society of London. The advertised endeavor of the club, and the salon they held annually, was for purely educational purposes and no member was allowed to join who had anything other than a pictorial interest in photography. This was presumably a disclaimer of sorts to satisfy the moralists of the day, particularly when taking into account the attire (or lack thereof) of some of the models depicted in the photographs. To judge the genuineness of prospective members and to determine admittance, twelve photographic prints had to be exhibited and those had to be passed unanimously by a selective committee. Sterling served on this committee for several years. Meetings were held the first Monday of each month at the Fleckenstein Studio in the Walker Auditorium. Classes were offered to its members and the club boasted four darkrooms, a studio, and two enlarging rooms, as well as photographic equipment that was available for the members' use. This was an important resource for most photographers: not everyone had the means to buy the sort of equipment that Sterling boasted of in his home, or the space to set it up in.

"A Study." This bromoil study of a young lady was exhibited in London in 1919 where it, along with Sterling's other offerings, won prizes.

Sterling's work was deemed good enough for public display and he was given his first chance to show off his talent in a major exhibition at the Los Angeles International Photographers Salon. This ran from January 3–31, 1919, and Antony Anderson of the *Los Angeles Times* had this to say of his efforts: "'Mae Murray' by Ford Sterling, who seems to be as fine an artist in pictorial photography as he is in motion pictures, judging from his portrait, which has the strength, simplicity and delicacy of a Holbein drawing. Other notable things by Sterling are 'Via Crucis' and 'The Ballet.'"9

"Behind the Scenes" is a composed studio photograph. A young dancer is backstage, presumably waiting to make her entrance. She is standing *en pointe* with one hand

"The Ballet." One of a collection of bromoil prints Sterling exhibited at the London Exhibition in 1919.

resting lightly on the back of a stage flat while she holds the hem of her ballet dress with the other; she is looking wistfully over her shoulder. In contrast, there is a charming photograph of Alice Lake taken in the open air, using Sterling's front porch as the set and his front door as the back drop. Miss Lake is seen in a very natural pose sitting across the front step and leaning against one of the columns that held up the porch. This study shows how well Sterling used natural light and a convenient location. In both cases, Sterling has caught his models as if they were apparently unaware they were being photographed. Obviously, he must have made the ladies feel comfortable and at ease for them to appear oblivious of the camera. Using the plate cameras of the day, Sterling wouldn't have been able to take several photographs in quick succession; the camera had to be reloaded for each image and this took time. Ideally, only one shot was needed to get the desired composition.

Around this time Sterling was honored with another first — his bromoils being seen in other countries. From January 13 to October 11, his work was being shown at the International Exhibition of London Salon of Photographers, held at the Royal Society of Painters in Watercolour in London, England. Later in the year he had examples of his work in the International Exhibition of Photographers in Toronto, Canada, and the Pittsburg Salon of Photography. In 1920, Sterling's photographs were seen in other parts of the world, including Denmark and Scotland, as well as around the United States.

The year 1921 brought Sterling his greatest honors. On December 12, the *Los Angeles Times* ran an article on the Camera Pictorialists of Los Angeles entitled

Study of silent film actress Alice Lake. This was photographed on Sterling's front porch on Carlton Way, Los Angeles.

"Behind the Scenes." Part of the collection of bromoil images Sterling exhibited in London in 1919.

"World's Best Pictorial Artists Exhibit Here," which emphasized Sterling's international standings in the photographic world. "Mr. Fleckenstein and Edward Weston," the article read, "the last of whom was formally a member of the Camera Pictorialists of Los Angeles, but whose residence outside of the city permits him to take a less active part in the pictorialistic problems than formerly, have the reputation of being the two finest portrait Pictorialists in America, while Arthur Kales is considered superior to anyone in the country as a photographer of the nude. In the London Salon there are thirty-six acting members that are those whose pictures merit entrance into the highest class. The three Pictorialists mentioned above, together with Ford Sterling, well known local cinema comedian, and W. J. Poterfield of Buffalo, are the only members from this country honored by admission to the British Organization."[10] Sterling's work was also featured in the *American Journal of Photography* in June of that year. Perhaps, though, the highlight of Sterling's venture into photography was when twenty-six of his original photographic studies were hung in the Louvre, Paris: Ford Sterling was the first person ever to be given this honor.[11]

There was a six-year gap before Sterling's next exhibition, his only one in 1928. Again for the Los Angeles Salon, it was also his last recorded showing, although he continued to follow his hobby well into the 1930s. Had Sterling failed in his film career he could well have had a very lucrative livelihood as a photographer. In fact, in 1933, Sterling was still being heralded as one of America's leading amateur photographers and had won prizes for his work in many European competitions.[12] The photographs that are available for viewing, some of Sterling's portraits of women, are charming and elegant. Perhaps one of the best is the simple image of a nude posing in front of a black background. She is holding the center of a long flowing piece of fabric against her chest and the composition is subtly lit, delicately picking out the model's curves, giving the hint of what is behind the fabric. In 1927, Sterling boasted of owning eight cameras. Although it appears he was no longer exhibiting, Sterling admitted to spending almost all the time he was away from the studio in taking pictures.[13] One hundred and forty of his prints hung in British salons, forty in one-man exhibitions in France, and fifty in Germany. His laboratory was cluttered with prizes and awards his photographs had won.

9

Day of Faith

Ford Sterling realized it was time to consciously change the direction of his career for the better. Working for Sennett in two-reel comedies, even starring in them, was darned hard work, and not nearly as prestigious or stretching for an actor as playing supporting roles in what were considered legitimate movies. So lowly were these comedies considered by some actors — far too demeaning to have on a serious performer's resume, in fact — that once they made their name they refused to acknowledge appearing in them. The change from slapstick to features could be compared to moving from the brusqueness of burlesque up the ladder to Broadway, with its genteel comedies, musicals, and dramas. This was the direction in which Sterling was heading.

All through his career he had continued to learn, update, and improve his acting skills. He was a regular theatergoer, studying the actors' performances. However, a unique feature of his attendance at such shows was to stuff cotton wool into his ears so he could study the visual aspects solely. If the pantomime was good, he gathered in its finer points. If he found the performance weak, he said that he benefited from building it up in his mind. Comedy, Sterling explained, was constantly changing, and the successful actor had to study continuously to keep abreast and improve. Sterling's observation of changing comedy styles during the 1920s also gave an insight into how he viewed comedy. He said that when he started out at Biograph comedy was confined to slapstick, which required no mental effort, just a long period of pie throwing. Suddenly slapstick dropped away and by the twenties the best comedy was becoming more and more subtle.[1]

In June 1924, two years after Sterling began working legitimate features, the *Los Angeles Times* ran "[Sterling] Forsakes Two Reel Comedies,"[2] an article which gave his view on why he decided to go into features. The *Times* felt that two-reel comedies had lost one of their most brilliant comedians when Sterling went over into features. During the ten years he had been associated with two-reelers, he had gained an estimable reputation for sending audiences into spasms of laughter at his antics. It wasn't surprising that a cry of dismay sounded when Sterling announced his intention to enter feature-length film. Of course, he had made a few features before, including *Yankee Doodle in Berlin* for Keystone, but apparently these didn't count. Even though he was deserting the two-reel he did not forsake his comedy roles, which was

There is not much doubt as to how Sterling and his fellow jurors feel about having *The Woman on the Jury*. First National, 1924. Standing, L–R: Arthur Lubin, Leo White, Fred Warren, Kewpie King, Sylvia Breamer, Frank Mayo, unidentified, and Arthur S. Hull. Seated, L–R: Stanton Heck, Jean Hersholt, Edward Davis, and Ford Sterling.

where Sterling had honed his skills over the years and what people expected when they saw him. In all the features in which he has appeared he took a comedy relief role. And, as the *Los Angeles Times* noted, "His acting, as a result of his years of comedy training, is that much richer and holds a note of greater sincerity."

When he was asked if he intended to remain in features, Sterling answered in the affirmative. Some of the studios were trying to negotiate with him for his return to two-reelers at the same time the *Los Angeles Times* was doing its interview. But he said it was decidedly doubtful that he would go back (and he didn't until after sound came along). Sterling had also just signed with Victor Sjostrom for the principal comedy part in his next picture for Goldwyn, *He Who Gets Slapped*, starring Lon Chaney. Sterling had been offered parts in several other productions, so it obviously would have been a senseless step backward to have returned to two-reelers.

Sterling felt it was much easier to play in these features than in the two-reelers; he felt he could do better work, too. Much of the comedy action in a two-reeler was of the obvious sort, determined by the character; in drama, however, the humor could be of a more subtle nature. Sterling knew that for the type of features he was in, the more suggestive and less apparent the humor the better. Sterling went on to give an example: "Nero may be striding majestically forward, thousands below thun-

The Woman on the Jury. Released April 20, 1924. Associated First National Pictures; Paramount Pictures. Standing, L–R: Hobart Bosworth, Bessie Love, and Ford Sterling. The seated players are not identifiable except for Roy Stewart, third from left.

The Chicago City Censorship Board initially refused a permit for *The Woman on the Jury* because of concerns that a woman juror had had an affair with a principal in a murder trial that she was called upon to decide. Circuit judge Ira D. Ryner overturned the board's decision on May 2, 1924. ("Ryner Decision Today on Film," *Chicago Daily News*, May 12, 1924, p. 19.)

dering their greeting to the Emperor. Suddenly he trips, catches himself, regains his dignity and stalks on as though nothing has happened. The illustration may be rather of the obvious nature of humor, but the meaning is there. A red nose and make-up are not necessary for every type of comedy."

Sterling claimed that the ease of appearing in features also enabled him to play in as many as three productions at one time. If he was to go back to comedies, he insisted that he would want to produce his own, which did not necessarily enthrall him. He pointed out that it would mean he would have no peace of mind, no time to himself should he want it. All day he would be hard at work in the same studio and on the same sets, trying to figure out gags; he would have to work until five or later, spend an hour or so in the projection room watching the rushes, grab a bite to eat, and spend half the night planning the next day's work. After the completion of one picture he would have to start on another, with the same nerve-racking grind.

Sterling had found that by remaining in features and going from one studio to another he lived in a totally different atmosphere with an altogether different flavor of life. He was meeting more people from more walks of life, and enjoyed himself thoroughly. He had time to play two of his favorite sports, golf and tennis, as well as go swimming and devote time to his photographic hobby. Also, if he didn't feel like working for a while, he didn't have to, until he was actually contracted to a studio.

There was no chance of Sterling returning to two-reelers at that time, regardless of the rumor of his returning to Sennett back in August.[3] Sterling, with a number of the old stars, including Louise Fazenda and Charlie Murray, were reported soon to be returning to the fold that had given them their fame. This was yet another pesky tale. Ford continued with his new career. Although no longer working for him, Sterling did help out Mack Sennett in May 1922 by using his expertise for picking a pretty face. Ford was asked to stand in for Sennett by his friend and old boss as one of the five judges for the *Times*' First Beauty Quest competition.[4] The other four judges were portrait painter John Rich, art critic Antony Anderson, sculptor Maud Daggett, and Albert Witzel, the famous portrait photographer to the stars. Sennett said he designated Ford, as he had been the principal beauty picker of the Sennett Studio for years, and for the competition he was billed as "moving picture beauty expert."

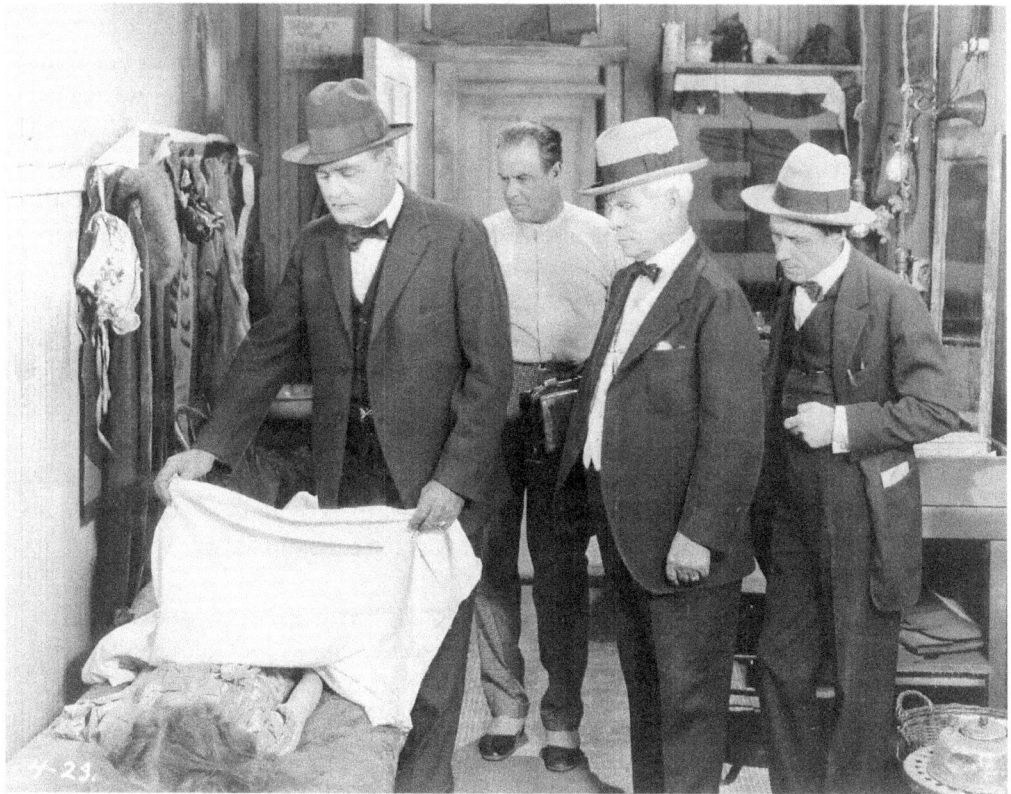

The melodrama *The Day of Faith* (1923, Goldwyn Pictures), directed by Tod Browning, has Sterling in a serious role, that of gangster Montreal Sammy. L–R: unidentified actress, Tyrone Power, Sr., Ford Sterling, and two other unidentified players.

Not all of Sterling's new cinematic roles were comic relief, although that is what audiences expected. Some of the thirteen movies Sterling made between December 1922 and May 1925 had parts for him that were in a dramatic vein, although there were also roles that had a hint of comedy about them. Tod Browning, who directed *The Day of Faith,* signed both Sterling and Sennett regular, Chester Conklin, for dramatic roles in the feature[5] and they were well accepted playing it straight. It would have been interesting to see the audience reaction to these slapstick comedians playing serious roles. Such a role also served to show the range of Sterling's acting skills and that he wasn't confined to being funny. Six of the productions made during this period were for Goldwyn/MGM with major directors like Tod Browning, King Vidor, and Victor Sjöström. Sterling was not being given bit parts either; he was playing good-sized supporting roles to leading actors of the time and, judging by the surviving movies, the reviews, and the work he was getting, he made the transition to these more serious roles quickly and successfully. With his reputation in the business and maybe the recommendation of friends, Sterling very soon found himself in significant roles in important pictures.

There was a serial, too, although Sterling didn't make it as such. Sections of one of the 1923 features Sterling made appears to have been used, along with three other films, to make up a ten-part serial.[6] It was not unheard of at the time to use component parts of several films owned by the same company and reedit them in this fashion. They were known as "cut and paste serials."[7] This particular serial was called *Marked Men* and was released as an All-Star Picture Play in 1928,[8] presumably when the originals were sufficiently at the back of cinemagoers' minds not to be too recognizable. It featured Noah Beery, Ford Sterling, George Walsh, Walter McGrail, George Nichols, and Leah Baird, among others. *Marked Men* was most likely made up from the features *Destroying Angel* (1923), *Is Divorce a Failure?* (1923), *The Miracle Maker* (1923), and *When the Devil Drives* (1922). As a group, these had the appropriate players appearing in at least one of the films.[9] All the films had similarities, too: they were produced by Arthur C. Beck and distributed through Associated Exhibitors. The ten-part serial *Marked Men* was manufactured by Plaza Pictures, Inc., and released through the Oxford Film Company in 1928, five years after the last of the component films was released. How much of a release *Marked Men* had is debatable. Until 2004, *Marked Men* was not known to exist and only came to light after a glass slide advertising the screening of part ten came up for sale with a group of other slides.

Of the films made during this period, of note is Sterling's first engagement after setting out in this new direction. It was *The Stranger's Banquet* for Goldwyn, released on December 31, 1922, and directed by Marshal Neilan. It boasted a cast of Hobart Boswell, Claire Windsor, Nigel Barrie, and Rockliffe Fellowes.

This was an earlier melodrama, something Sterling was no stranger to, and was set in a shipyard that has been left to Derith Keogh (Claire Windsor) by her father. It is not easy for the young woman to gain the respect needed to maintain control of the men, which results in considerable difficulties managing the shipyard's labor problems. Her brother (Nigel Barrie) is no help; he is away in pursuit of an Adven-

Will Rogers (L) and Charley Chase pose together outside the Roach Studios in the 1920s.

tist. Derith is in more trouble when her superintendent, Angus Campbell (Rockliffe Fellowes), resigns, exasperated at the labor situation, and leaves her alone. With no support, she is forced to consent to the unreasonable demands of an anarchistic labor agitator, John Trevelyan (Thomas Holding), but Angus, reconsidering his actions, returns to help. Derith persuades Trevelyan to settle the strike, which he manages despite being shot by one of his own men.

Sterling naturally has the comedy relief role and did it well: *Variety* seemed to like the picture, and Sterling too, saying it "was another mark for Neilan and a credit for Ulson (co-director). Not forgetting Ford Sterling, splendid in the role of a chap who never takes anything seriously."

In 1923 Sterling teamed up again with Keystone comedienne Louise Fazenda — something they would do time and again — for *The Spoilers* (August 1923). This was an MGM Maurice Tourneur production, with Milton Sills, Anna Q. Nilsson, Noah Beery, Sam De Grasse, Kate Price, Rockliffe Fellowes, and Ford Sterling as Slapjack Simms, foreman of the Midas mine in Nome. The film was a remake of the first great feature of its kind, shot in 1915 and released under the same name. Reviewers wondered if the celebrated fight scene in the original could ever be surpassed and they decided the Beery/Sills fight had done so. The scenario comprises a crooked political plot involving gold mines in Alaska, where the local judge and his partner rob mine owners by jumping their claims. Sterling and Fazenda have a good amount of screen time between them as the comic relief. *Variety* noted that "Ford Sterling is still funny. In the midst of the serious situation, when he moves there is a laugh. He did a peach of a comic bit in trying to piece up a broken sluice way with the water pouring over him." The *Los Angeles Times* reviewer, though, did not seem quite so impressed, only mentioning that from the comedy work of Ford Sterling to the saturnine villainy of Robert McKim, the people in the cast handled their parts in a workman-like manner.[10]

Sterling had a more serious role as gangster Montreal Sammy in Tod Browning's *The Day of Faith* (October 1923), a lost film. His old pal from the Sennett days, Chester Conklin, was signed for his first dramatic role too, that of Yegg Darby. This Goldwyn Cosmopolitan with Eleanor Boardman and Raymond Griffith is filled with gangsters, intrigue, and down-and-outs and revolves around a young lady's calling to start a mission. Stills of the production show Sterling in a very serious vein, unkempt with several days of beard growth and collar turned up as he peers out broodingly from under the brim of his battered hat. He certainly doesn't look like the jolly slapstick comedian as he glares at Eleanor Boardman after he has been arrested and is in the grasp of a rather sizable police officer. *Variety* said this of Sterling's performance: "Ford Sterling turned in an excellent bit of character work as Montreal Sammy."[11] These were well-deserved words: he had worked hard both night and day on the New York street set at the Culver City Studios with Eleanor Boardman, Wallace MacDonald, and the four and five hundred extras required.[12]

A demonstration of Sterling's continued popularity and the fact that he was still remembered as Keystone's chief of police, was given by Will Rogers, the kingpin wise-cracker, film and Follies star, and satirical after-dinner speaker. He honored Ford with a parody in his two-reeler *Big Moments from Little Pictures*, made in late 1923. Rogers did a wonderful and somewhat wicked job of impersonating Rudolph Valentino, Tom Mix, William S. Hart, Douglas Fairbanks, Sr., and Ford Sterling as Chief Teheezal. "As Ford Sterling," Rogers explained with his humorous twinkle, "I stopped my first pie yesterday."[13] Rogers remains the most accurate imitator of anyone who made the attempt to impersonate Sterling; he is side-splittingly funny.

*Top: **The Day of Faith**.* Released October 21, 1923. Goldwyn Pictures. "Montreal" (Sterling) gets another beating at checkers. With Jane Mercer. *Bottom:* A scene from Will Rogers' 1924 short, ***Big Moments from Little Pictures**.* In this sequence Rogers (center) does one of the best impersonations of Sterling seen on film. Other victims of Rogers' wit in this gem of a film were Rudolph Valentino and Douglas Fairbanks, Sr.

A feature was shot in late 1923 and released in January 1924 that gave Sterling the opportunity to play a complex role demonstrating the range of his acting skills: King Vidor's moody *Wild Oranges*. Sterling plays Paul Halvard, the cook, first mate, and only crew member on a sailing cruiser. This is a well-written dramatic role, which gave Sterling a character he could work with and give depth too. It could be presumed that, once again, he was going to be the comic relief, but in fact he certainly was not. Sterling played Halvard as straight as he would play Tricaud the clown in *He Who Gets Slapped* later in the year. He was realistic, with none of the expected mugging to the camera, his character exhibiting the joy of life when it is appropriate. This was not the comedian here, but an accomplished straight actor. He had two minor gags in the whole film that gave the appearance of being thrown in to keep audience expectations up. First, he was squirted with water from the faucet on a water tank; later he slipped off the boat into the water. Such business was minimal and underplayed.

Wild Oranges is a tale of the attempts of a man, John Woolfolk (Frank Mayo), to escape from personal tragedy. He is the owner and skipper of a seagoing boat, he and Halvard (Sterling), his first mate, cook, and friend, have been sailing coastal waters for three years together since the tragic death of Woolfolk's young wife in an accident. They need to go ashore to replenish their water supply and so drop anchor on the land side of a sandbar where the swamps of the south meet the sea on the Georgia coast. Woolfolk goes ashore, leaving Halvard in charge of the boat while he investigates the crumbling colonial house that's surrounded by wild orange trees and hanging moss. Woolfolk sees the young woman of the house, Nellie Stope (Virginia Valli); she is afraid of the stranger but attracted to him. He tells her why they are there and she replies that he can have as much of their drinking water as he wants. Woolfolk returns to the ship to send Halvard back with the water barrel. Halvard has to go around to the back of the house to fill the barrel from the family's supply tank; as he is returning to the dingy with the full barrel an ominous looking man, Nicholas (Charles A. Post), appears through the bushes. He threatens Halvard with a knife and knocks the barrel out of his hands, stamping on it to destroy it, thus demonstrating his views of strangers on their land. Halvard backs off, realizing he is outmatched, and rows back to the ship to tell Woolfolk what has happened. Woolfolk, angered, returns to confront this man whom we later discover is a wanted murderer who has been terrorizing Nellie and her grandfather (Nigel De Brulier).

Nellie and Woolfolk (predictably) fall in love, and he is determined to rescue her and her grandfather from the clutches of Nicholas. In part he fails. When the Stopes are about to make their escape to the meeting point where Woolfolk has a dingy to take them to the ship, Nicholas catches them and knocks down Litchfield Stopes, killing him. Woolfolk, concerned that the two are an hour overdue at the meeting place, leaves Halvard to wait with the boat in case they arrive while he's away. When Woolfolk gets to the house to investigate, he finds Nellie tied to the bed with Nicholas looming over her in a threatening manner. An extremely well-staged fight between Woolfolk and Nicholas ensues, resulting in a lamp thrown by Nicholas setting the house on fire. Nellie manages to free herself while they are fighting, and

Wild Oranges. Released January 20, 1924. Goldwyn Picture Corporation. Directed by King Vidor. L–R: Frank Mayo, Virginia Valli, Ford Sterling.

Woolfolk sends her to the dingy to wait with Halvard. Woolfolk manages to escape Nicholas and join the others at the dingy; they row back to the ship to make their way out to sea across the sandbar. Nicholas is shooting at the boat; Halvard, while pulling up the sails, is shot in the head (not an iota of overacting) as he carries on with his duties to get the boat out to sea. Halvard's injury is superficial, thankfully, not life-threatening, but it is enough to cause him problems as he carries on setting the rigging and steering the boat. He finally collapses. Nicholas gets his just desserts when the family dog breaks its chain and rushes at the man, savaging him by the throat until he is dead. All ends happily for the remaining people. Halvard lounges on the deck recovering, and the two lovers linger, arms around each other, as they sail into the sunset. Well, it may be sunset — hard to tell in black and white.

Wild Oranges was shot on location in Georgia.[14] The company of five actors, director, and twenty technical staff left on August 2, 1923, to make their headquarters in Jacksonville, Georgia. From there they traveled daily to their locations in the mosquito-infested swamps of Georgia. Shooting this film was not the most comfortable experience of Sterling's life. Georgia in August is rife with biting insects; it is hot and humid, and there was no air conditioning. The onboard ship scenes were shot aboard a large private yacht in the San Francisco Bay in late September, a much more pleasant prospect. Finally, the company returned to the studio in Los Angeles for the remaining indoor shots.[15]

The year continued well for Sterling, with substantial roles in prestigious productions. A nice little aspect to one of these — *He Who Gets Slapped* (September 1924) starring Lon Chaney directed by Victor Sjöström — was seeing Sterling return to his pre-feature days. Not only did he play a circus clown but he also helped Lon Chaney, the master makeup artist, put on his clown makeup for the character HE. It would be nice to know if the clown makeup Sterling wore in the film bore any resemblance to that which he wore in the circus. Lon Chaney plays inventor Paul Beaumont, betrayed by his wife and his patron; the patron claims the work as his own and makes a fool out of Beaumont in front of an audience of scientists. Beaumont decides to make a career out of acting the part of the clown his wife and the patron have made him. After changing his name to the anonymous HE, he becomes that clown, whose act consists of being slapped by all the other clowns led by Tricaud (Sterling). There is not a bit of humor in Sterling's totally straight portrayal, a role one would expect to be steeped in slapstick. In fact, when he is in the circus ring he underplays: his face remains blank and expressionless and his movements are stiff and mechanical. One reviewer made a point of noting Sterling's excellent characterization.[16] It makes a very interesting contrast between the reality and the presumed.

Sterling's circus experience must have been a pleasant one and he must have continued to feel a part of the circus family. He couldn't keep away, and certainly in the early days he was drawn back to visit the big top when the circus came to town. As the *New York Clipper* put it in June 1913[17]: "Ford Sterling was once known as 'Keno, the Boy Clown,' and the smell of sawdust and the noise of the band heading 'the grand free outdoor pageant' down the main street still retain their old charm for the well known comic. Recently, a small 'one-ringer' struck town and held forth for three days on the local grounds. The Keystone force were working overtime at the studios, finishing up a film in which Ford played the lead, but Sterling was nowhere to be found. A search was started, which finally ended on the circus lot, where the erstwhile boy clown was found, coat and hat off, striving to teach the white face comedian of the show some of his old laugh-getters."

In March 1924, announcements were made that Carl Laemmle, president of Universal, had decided to make *We Are French*[18] as the new Rupert Julian production. Madge Bellamy was borrowed from Ince for the leading lady role, and as leading man, World War I French army veteran Charles De Roche was borrowed from Lasky. De Roche had been wounded in the war and decorated for his bravery, very fitting for the war hero he was to portray. Sterling, referred to in the *Los Angeles Times* as one of the most famous character comedians of the screen, was signed to play Emile Pompaneau.[19] The film was based on an original story by Perley Poore Sheehan and Robert Davis, and is a strong drama woven around the people of a peasant village in the south of France. The film was released under the title *Love and Glory* in December 1924. The Sterling Studio fiasco apparently hadn't soured Carl Laemmle's opinion of Sterling, as he was not adverse to employing him again in a Universal production.

10

He Who Gets Slapped

Sterling's career was going well, but his personal life was due for a turn for the worse. The title of his next film — but unfortunately not the plot — proved to be prophetic. *The Trouble with Wives*, starring Florence Vidor and Tom Moore as happily married Grace and William Hyatt, owners of an exclusive bootery, has a happy ending, unlike Sterling's real-life drama.

In the film, the Hyatts are content in their marriage until Al Hennessey (Sterling) inadvertently tells Grace that Will has been seen dining with pretty Parisian designer Dagmar (Esther Ralston). As with all comedies of error there are the inevitable misunderstandings. Will sorts the problem out with Grace just fine, until Hennessey tells Grace that he and Will have been visiting Dagmar in her apartment. This was a business trip, but Grace believes Will has been unfaithful so in return she goes about making his life hell. Will eventually beats a retreat to a summer hotel and Grace follows him. Surprise! Dagmar is there too, but this time it is fine with Grace because Dagmar is there to marry Hennessey. Equilibrium returns once again to the Moore household.

This was not the case with the Sterling-Sampson marriage, and the irony was touched with a sad consequence. Shortly before Sterling made *The Trouble with Wives*, he was having on-again, off-again troubles with his own estranged wife of nine years, Teddy Sampson. Things escalated. Teddy had left the marital home in 1917,[1] returned in 1921, and left again. In February 1924, Sterling decided to start divorce proceedings for desertion. Teddy did not appear at the proceedings. In fact, Ford wasn't able to find where she was staying at that time and the case was heard without her.[2] Sterling's mother, though, was there to support her son when he gave his evidence. Unfortunately, the trauma of the events proved to be too much for the older Mrs. Stich. On September 13, 1924, in their section On the Set and Off, *Movie World* reported some devastating news: "While listening to her son on the witness stand in his divorce hearing as he testified about his wife's disappearance Ford's mother, Mary Stich, collapsed in the court room suffering a stroke. She never recovered and died a few hours later in a Los Angeles hospital." This put an end to the proceedings. Teddy herself would take up the divorce torch, ironically for the same charge, in 1928.

Sterling's marriage to Teddy Sampson obviously gave him pause for thought as

So Big. Released December 28, 1924. Associated First National Pictures.

to the attributes[3] he would like in a wife. Paramount sent out a press release in the mid–1920s entitled "What I Want My Wife to Be Like," by Ford Sterling. His requirements were as follows: "My wife has to have one big qualification — she has to laugh at my jokes.

"I'm a comedian. I make my living, earn my salary and pattern my life on my ability to make people laugh. Now I ask you — how could I be happy if I came home from the studio with a good gag and my wife would respond to it with a 'dead pan'? Where would my self esteem go?" He went on to ask how a comedian could be comic if he didn't think himself funny. And then he wondered how he could be funny if his wife were constantly putting the damper on his humor. So the first requisite was that his wife had to have a sense of humor.[4]

Sterling also wanted his wife to be a nonprofessional. Even though he thought it might seem queer to say this after spending his whole life on the stage and screen, Sterling wanted his wife to be devoted entirely to their home. He wasn't that particular what she looked like, either, whether she be tall or short, slim or fat, blonde or brunette. Above all, he insisted she had to be a home-loving wife with a sense of humor. This, and Sterling's comment about wanting a wife who wasn't in "the profession," poses the question of whether Teddy's career was one of the problems in the marriage. Did he consider her away from home too much, not willing to run the home, or both? Chaplin, in his biography, does allude to infidelities on her part.[5]

Sterling needed a diversion — to bury himself in his work. The Painted Desert of Arizona formed the glorious setting for Sterling's next western film location. Perhaps the beauty and peace of the locale gave Ford some solace from his recent loss. He may have taken the opportunity to bury himself in his photographic hobby when not on the set, as Sterling compiled an album of desert pictures, which was a favorite subject of his.[6] Reginald Barker directed the western, *The Great Divide,* in this most beautiful of natural kaleidoscopic vistas.[7] Released in March 1925, this much sought-after lost film also boasted Conway Tearle, Alice Terry, Wallace Beery, and ZaSu Pitts in the cast.

The plot is far from peaceful or as beautiful as its location. According to the American Film Institute, the film begins with heroine Ruth Jordan living alone in the wilderness, where she "is discovered by three drunken brutes who begin to barter for her." Terrified, she throws herself on the mercy of the one member of the trio who she thinks might have a shred of decency: Stephen Ghent. She vows to be his if he will save her. He agrees, knocking out one man and buying off the other and carrying Ruth away to be his bride. But she repents of the deal and seeks rescue, which is soon provided by her brother. Ghent, who has fallen in love, rides back after her, intending to bring her back to his goldmine. Ruth, however, is pregnant and ill. "Ghent does something good for once in his life," says the *AFI Catalog*: "he rides to a distant village to get a doctor; on the way back, the doctor's horse falls and is injured so Ghent gives him his mount, placing himself in danger. Ruth delivers a son, after hearing of Ghent's heroism she sees him in a new light and realizes she is in love with him, they are reconciled."[8]

Still on the down side of life, it seemed that Sterling had a very philosophical view on prison life. Not that he was jailed in reality; he was arrested, however, in a raid at a prominent cafe in the 1925 film, *Steppin' Out*, a farce set in the (then) modern jazz age. Sterling's character, John Durant, was taken to the police station by Prohibition officers and lodged in a cell with two underworld characters. Ford told the *Los Angeles Times*, "I never thought of it before, but it appears to me that jail is one

L–R: Ford Sterling, Dorothy Revier, Tom Ricketts, and Cissy Fitzgerald seem to be having a less than jolly evening out in Columbia Pictures' 1926 film *Steppin' Out*. Published in *Film Fun*, February 1926.

place where all men are equal. Once you get in, you might as well resign yourself to fate and let things take their own course. Your cell mate can't complain that you have more freedom than he has and the fact that you have lots of money doesn't mean a thing—you can't buy anything."[9] Both *Steppin' Out* and Sterling got good reviews; his prison scenes were universally thought of as hilariously funny by the critics.

Working with ex–Keystone players seems to have been difficult to avoid for Ford. In the Famous Players production *Stage Struck* (1925), directed by Allan Dwan, he appeared with ex–Sennett bathing beauty Gloria Swanson. The film opened with a lovely Salome-type musical number. *Stage Struck*, like the slightly later *American Venus*, was shot using the two-strip Technicolor process,[10] an expensive process at the time that was reserved only for important pictures.

In the film, Jennie Hagen (Gloria Swanson) is a stagestruck diner waitress who is in love with the cook, Orme (Lawrence Gray). He naturally has a weakness for something else: actresses. When a showboat arrives—The Water Queen, run by Waldo Buck (Sterling)—Orme pays the show a visit and falls in love with the leading lady, Lillian Lyons (Gertrude Astor). Jennie, not wanting to be outdone, takes a correspondence course in acting to try to win him back. Buck, who has taken a liking to the girl, gives her a chance by letting her have a spot in the show, billing her as The Masked Marvel in a boxing fight with Lillian. It does not have the results Jennie had anticipated: Orme is horrified by the exhibition, and in despair Jennie jumps overboard. Orme heroically dives in to save her and all works out well. They reconcile and later open a diner of their own.

Stage Struck. Released November 16, 1925. Paramount. Lawrence Gray (L) with Ford Sterling.

Gloria Swanson remembered Sterling's good rapport with children and she wrote about an event that took place while she, Gertrude Astor, and Sterling were in New Martinsville, West Virginia, for the filming of *Stage Struck*.[11] Sterling, she reminisced, who played the manager of the showboat company, enchanted the kids wherever he went. The shooting had been scheduled to coincide with the local fair and carnival and the company created so much excitement among the locals that they drew bigger crowds than the freak show.

On the strength of Sterling's performances in *The Trouble with Wives*, he was sent to New York in mid–August 1925 to sign a long-term contract with Paramount.[12] He had made several films for Lasky, but now he was wanted as a contract player. Jesse Lasky considered Sterling's performance in *The Trouble with Wives* as "one of the finest examples of polished comedy I have ever seen."[13] On Sterling's return to Hollywood, Lasky wanted him to immediately start work on the Bebe Daniels–starring vehicle, *Miss Brewster's Millions*[14] (released March 22, 1926), at the Lasky Studio. The studio gave him a good report: "Ford Sterling is getting his second wind and it's better than his first. That's what they're saying in Hollywood of the fun maker who a few years back was rated as the screen's leading comedian, then practically went into retirement and now is at the top of his form playing a leading comedy role."[15] Sterling had won his place in 1920s feature films with his splendid work in *The Trouble with Wives*, *Stage Struck*, and *The American Venus*.

Although made after *Miss Brewster's Millions*, *The American Venus* was released

Ford Sterling in full theatrical pose in the 1925 Paramount feature *Stage Struck*, staring Gloria Swanson.

first (January 31, 1926). It is a beauty pageant comedy set around the 1925 Miss America contest which, according to the *Variety* review, gave a good excuse to show nudity. How nude these ladies were we can only imagine as the film is lost, although a trailer for the film was found in Australia in the late 1990s. The beauty pageant is shot in two-strip Technicolor, but the *Variety* reviewer wasn't that impressed, only considering some of the pageant scenes well done, the others rather garish. *The American Venus* did prove popular when it was released, and continued to be seen around the United States for nearly two years.

There was a special effect in the film that initially proved difficult to obtain.[16] In the picture, human figures walk out of a magazine. This in and of itself was not a problem: to obtain this illusion, a huge book, big enough for the girls to walk through, was constructed and put on a desktop built to the same proportions. The problem Fred Waller, the guiding light behind the Paramount model department, had was having Sterling turn the pages of the magazine and the actresses appear, suddenly come to life, and step off the page. This sequence was eventually achieved by having the scale between the actual magazine and the enormous one so accurately gauged in front of the camera that the apparently small figures seemed to step right off the page under Sterling's eyes.

Stage Struck. 1925, Paramount Pictures. Directed by Alan Dwan. Sterling played the manager of the riverboat company. Gloria Swanson played Jennie Hagen, a diner waitress who joins the riverboat crew just to make a point to her boyfriend.

(Like most prominent performers, Sterling was not immune from being approached by would-be starlets. An extra, a girl of generous proportions, approached him while he was seated on the sidelines during the making of *Miss Brewster's Millions*. "I'm going to confine myself to the drama in my future productions," she said to Sterling. "I feel it is the only profitable end of the game and I know I must have a capable manager to handle me. Whom would you suggest, Mr. Sterling?" Ford took one look at her and said, "Gig Rooney."[17] For the uninitiated, Gig Rooney was the manager of several heavyweight boxers of the day.)

Sterling played Hugo Niles, a cosmetic manufacturer, with Edna May Oliver as his wife, Esther Ralston, and, in a small early role as Miss Bayport, Louise Brooks. Sterling would work with Brooks again in *The Show Off*, where she had a supporting role. A *Variety* review gives the story outline: "The plot concerns two rival beauty cream factories out west. A son of one proprietor is engaged to marry the daughter of the other. A publicity man annexes himself to the minor plant and almost puts over the plant's daughter as 'The American Venus.' The plan was to have her endorse a cold cream and, on that basis, sell millions of jars, thus putting the other man out of business. But the girl's father became ill and she was called back home, going to Atlantic City the second time, but arriving too late for the final. Her friend, 'Miss Alabama,' wins. Although the heroine has had an accident and is confined to her room, the winner endorses her father's cold cream gratis." Of Sterling's performance,

Ford Sterling visits the set of *We're in the Navy Now*. At the time, he was filming *Stranded in Paris*, with Bebe Daniels. L–R seated: Sterling, Raymond Halton, Wallace Beery. Standing: Chester Conklin, Edward Sutherland, and Tom Kennedy.

the review stated, "Some comedy because of Ford Sterling and Edna May Oliver. Sterling plays the wealthy cold cream magnate, and Miss Oliver is his wife — one of the types who hot-foots it behind her husband."[18]

Then there was *Good and Naughty*, starring the legendary vamp, Pola Negri. Of this, the *Washington Post* says that Sterling steps in and steals a good bit of the movie from the "erstwhile Emotional One."[19] Other reviews for *Good and Naughty* gave Sterling laurels similar to those they had given him for *The American Venus*, but to a slightly lesser degree due to, they claimed, the smaller amount of film footage given to Sterling. "There was not a scene in which he appeared but what he stole the interest away from the other players."[20]

Sterling was now considered to be "a comedian as well established in the motion-picture realm as a camera." The result was that he could not fill a fraction of his proffered engagements, with a king's ransom as a salary.[21] Sterling was doing so well that on October 31, 1926, he, along with Wallace Beery and Pauline Fredericks, bought a brand-new Lincoln automobile.[22] Sterling had been an avid motorist and gadget collector for years. Back in 1915, a list of some of his "toys" was included in an interview. "Fond of motoring and possessing motor cars," it noted of Ford, "but he does not let his possession of machinery end there as he explained to a friend the other day. He says he has a limousine, touring car, a special roadster and a racing car, a

Betty Bronson, Raymond Hitchcock, and Ford Sterling in *Everybody's Acting*. Paramount, 1926. Courtesy of Bruce Calvert.

plain town machine, a Singer sewing machine, a Victrola, a washing machine, a projecting machine and an adding machine."[23] While Sterling was making *The Show Off* (1926), in which he played the featured role, it was said of him that he had put his slapstick methods behind him and blossomed forth as an expert pantomimist in full-length comedies. The *Los Angeles Times* wrote in August 1926 that "If Ford Sterling isn't careful he'll soon be topping all the comedians. His performances for years have seen rare ventures into the realm of comedy—but recently he has been scoring such knockouts that his popularity has increased a thousand fold."

It was considered that in *The Show Off* Sterling was perfectly cast in the title role of Aubrey Piper—the windbag nobody loves but his wife. In fact, it was felt by the *Los Angeles Times* critic when he reviewed the film that Sterling "gave so excellent a representation of Aubrey Piper that he seemed to actually live the role. Every expression on his face, every tilt of his head, every action spelled audience laughs, laughs which what were Harold Lloyd terms 'belly laughs,' or the spectators were that a master hand at the art of comedy was entertaining them."[24] The *Chicago Daily Tribune* gave Sterling an equally rave review, the headline tells it all: "Ford Sterling, Almost a Perfect, Bumptious Bombastic Show Off."[25]

The Show Off was the high point of Sterling's silent features; he was the featured star. This was another Famous Players production, released on August 16, 1926. It was directed by Mal St. Clair and alongside Sterling the cast boasted Lois Wilson, Louise Brooks, and Gregory Kelly. One of the joys of this film is that it was shot on location in Philadelphia. We are shown some of the historic sights of the city in the opening montage, which pauses on a statue of William Penn just before the opening title tells us that "Around the feet of William Penn now swarm the commercial giants of the modern age, among them is Aubrey Piper — our Mr. Piper of the Pennsylvania Railroad, in his own mind, the most important man in that great organization."

We cut to Aubrey Piper emerging from a subway station nattily dressed in a checkered suit, carnation in his button hole, all topped off with a straw boater. Aubrey falls in behind a man in top hat and morning suit; they walk into the Pennsylvania Railroad building where Piper raises his hat to the gentleman, who, after looking at Piper oddly, walks through a door marked "Vice President in Charge of Operations." Piper goes through the opposite door labeled "Offices of the General Manager, Eastern Passenger Agents." He is late as he makes his way to his desk among the other agents. Piper sits at his desk reading the newspaper and he starts to laugh louder and louder; he is reading the funnies. The office manager, like the other occupants of the office, is not pleased and curtly instructs him to get on with his work. A young lady comes into the office selling raffle tickets for the Widows and Orphans Fund, the prize a new car. When she gets to him, Piper boasts that he wouldn't know what to do with another one, but he buys a ticket anyway.

At lunch Piper meets his girlfriend, Amy Fisher, in the park; there he proposes to her, giving her an engagement ring. She is under the impression he is a bigwig with the railroad as she is totally taken in by his performance. That evening he invites himself over to her house for supper, which appears to be a regular thing for him. Her family is less than impressed to see Aubrey as they can see right through him! Joe Fisher, Amy's brother, has his girlfriend, Clara from next door, over for supper, too; she is well aware who Aubrey is and tells Amy's parents he is nothing but a clerk in an office. Piper continues the act, telling the family he has a big business meeting that evening so won't be able to stay. But wait. He pretends to phone the vice president, canceling the meeting so he can stay for supper, after all. Everyone except Amy looks despondent at the thought of sharing any more time with the awful Aubrey.

Joe Fisher is an inventor who has created rustproof paint; he is trying to sell his invention to a major steel manufacturing corporation but needs money to finance his work. His father loans him money that has been put aside to pay the mortgage, telling Joe he can pay it back when the invention is sold.

Amy is so taken in by Piper that she marries him, but she soon finds herself living in a one-room apartment, waiting on Aubrey hand and foot. Promises of a cottage with roses growing round the door fade very fast. Aubrey would rather buy a new suit than pay the rent, and they end up losing the apartment and moving in with her parents. Things are not good; her father is taken ill and dies.

Back at the office, Aubrey wins the raffle for the car. He calls home to ask Amy if she has heard the news: his Uncle George Stitch (Sterling's real name), has left him some shares in an automobile factory and he's cashed them in for a beautiful new car. Amy's mother wants to know what he has bought the car with. Piper picks up the car from the dealer, boasting to the salesman that he can drive marvelously and that he used to drive in the Vanderbilt Cup Race. It is not surprising that he has some problems sorting out the controls and, predictably, he zooms off backward into the car showroom. The trip home is full of obstacles for the new driver, mainly other cars and the occasional policeman. He chases an officer over the sidewalk and across a courtyard and finally pins him to some railings. He gets a ticket. (Instead of the studio employing a double, Sterling did his own driving for these scenes.) Aubrey arrives home, car being towed and bandage around his head. He spins a yarn about avoiding a young child and crashing, thus saving her life. He is not believed except by Amy.

The case comes to court and, because of Aubrey's boasting in the courtroom, the judge keeps compounding his punishment, from $500 or three months in jail to $1,000 or six month's hard labor. Aubrey cannot pay and is just about to go to jail when Joe, rather than have his sister's husband in jail, pays the fine with the money his father gave him. Now he will not be able to make the money back when he sells his invention. Aubrey, realizing what damage his actions have caused the family, goes out to right the wrong. He uses his skills as a show-off to sell Joe's invention for a good deal of money. He arrives home with an advance check, just in time to give it to a man from the bank who has come to foreclose on the house. Aubrey really is a hero, now.

Carella Black Cat cigarette card featuring Ford Sterling. Paramount Stars #24, ca. 1927, British. It states Sterling was "5'11" with dark hair and eyes."

This film shows that Sterling could carry the leading role in a major picture and it is a shame he was not given more such parts to play.

Sterling was busy during the last few months of 1926. *Casey at the Bat* (1927) is a farce based on Ernest Thayer's legendary verses of the same name. It opens in turn of the century Centerville, where Casey (Wallace Beery) is a junk dealer, hardest hitter in the village ball club, and, next to the town barber Putnam, the most persistent suitor of Camille (ZaSu Pitts). O'Dowd (Sterling), supposedly a big-league scout, arrives in town and at Putnam's suggestion signs Casey with the New York Giants. Once the party arrives in New York they do just that, *party*; Spec (Spec O'Donnell) convinces Casey he has been hoaxed. At the game, when he comes to bat, O'Dowd throws the pitcher a trick ball and Casey strikes out. The conspirators are captured and the manager exonerates Casey.

This film not only gave Sterling the opportunity to show his baseball acumen, but he also got to drive the beautiful ZaSu Pitts around in a turn of the century automobile.

The automobile in question was a 1904 four-cylinder, air-cooled Franklin loaned by Ralph Hamlin. And it wasn't just any old Franklin, but the same automobile that made history in 1904 when it established a transcontinental record between San Francisco and New York. (It was driven by L. C. Whitman and C. S. Carris, who made the trip in thirty-three days.[26]) Sterling and Pitts look as if they had come straight off the pages of an Edwardian magazine.

There was discontent at Paramount in January 1927. The actors at the Long Island Studios on the East Coast had been having management problems for some time, and now it looked as if they were about to spill over onto the West Coast. Wallace Beery had resigned, complaining of being compelled to risk his life in the making of his pictures, and there were persistent rumors that Raymond Griffith, Adolphe Menjou, *and* Ford Sterling were about to follow suit. United Artists, Metro-Goldwyn-Mayer, and First National had been offering contracts to the three of them.[27] In April, Sterling chose to pack his trunk, with all the garments a well-dressed man should wear, hop a train to New York, and go make a film for First National.[28]

Sterling was only on loan to First National, however. He was there to make *For the Love of Mike*, directed by Frank Capra. Capra was excited at the thought of working with Ford Sterling, whom he considered one of the great comedians, and at the prospects of demonstrating to Harry Langdon that he could direct comedy and do it well.[29] *For the Love of Mike* was the only major film being made in New York at that time, and First National hoped to get extra publicity from that. By the end of July, Ford was back in Los Angeles on the golf course, teamed with old Sennett friend and Paramount director, Edward Sutherland. They beat the Fox team by three points, the only clean sweep of the day.[30] But that was not the first thing Sterling did on his return: immediately he was back in harness. Paramount reported that "Ford Sterling arrived back in Hollywood from New York today to appear in one of the chief supporting roles in the Bebe Daniels' new starring vehicle, *Stranded in Paris*.

Ford Sterling, *The Galloping Fish*. 1924, First National.

"The dual announcement of Sterling's

return to California and his selection for the role of a French count in the Daniels' production was made today by B. P. Schulburg.

"Three hours after his arrival in L.A., the veteran character comedian was aboard another train — a French passenger coach used in a sequence of Miss Daniels' starring picture."[31]

Sterling was soon to leave the warmth of Southern California again, this time to make *Drums of the Desert* just outside of Flagstaff, Arizona. The company consisted of director John Waters and cast members Warner Baxter (John Curry), Marietta Millner (Mary Manton), Ford Sterling (Perkins), Wallace MacDonald (Will Newton), Heinie Conklin (Hi-Lo), George Irving (Professor Elias Manton), Bernard Siegel (Chief Brave Bear), and Guy Oliver (Indian Agent). They left Hollywood for Flagstaff with their film crew during some extremely warm weather. It wasn't so bad during the day, but when night came, as Sterling said, "It was plumb cold."[32] Director John Waters, however, sent back to the trading post for a quantity of extra blankets and comforters, which improved conditions for cast and crew alike.

The making of this film and its location would prove to have great significance for Sterling. Contemporary Paramount releases help to give an insight into Sterling's character — generosity and acceptance and friendship of a people who, at the time, were considered third-class citizens at best. Ford had very fond memories of the trip; Paramount released a statement on his return to California that said "Ford Sterling, veteran of innumerable location trips, has returned from a location that he proclaims to have been the most satisfactory in his long years before motion picture cameras."[33]

So what was the location and who were the people that made such an impression on Sterling? It was the middle of Arizona's desert lands on the Navajo reservation that Paramount chose for their location, and it was the exteriors for the screen version of Zane Grey's *Drums of the Desert* were shot. Sterling raved, "I have never been on a location where we were given such marvelous treatment." He continued, "Here we were, plumb in the middle of the desert. You couldn't get any more middler no matter how hard you tried. They built us a comfortable city of tents and then imported fresh vegetables and fruit from Flagstaff every day, serving us the best meals I have ever eaten on location."[34]

It was not only the location that impressed Sterling, but also the American Navajo that he met there. Sterling struck up a friendship with the Navajo, treating them with respect and consideration, both on their reservation and back in California after the location work was finished. A group of the Navajo was brought out to California to shoot the remaining indoor scenes. The group included the chief of the Western Navajo, Chief Seginitso, who was accompanied by Nattani, He Is to Be Chief; Chissy-Begay, Son of the Apache; Tsam-Begay, The Son of Nez, known also as Teddy Nez, and medicine man Bella-Gonna, whose name signified The White Indian; his skin was apparently very much lighter than the others.[35]

One of the Paramount press releases of the time tells us something about the Navajo's trip to Los Angeles and a special event Sterling arranged for them. The occasion was a dinner that had been prepared for the visiting Navajo by the Paramount comedian in his own home. It was in the spirit of hospitality and in reciprocation for similar generosity extended toward him by the Navajo while he was on the Arizona reservation. This is what they thought of Sterling's home: "New marvels of the 'First Coyote' were discovered by Chief Seginitso and five Navajo Indians, who have never before been off their Arizona reservation, when they were entertained by the Paramount comedian Ford Sterling in his home last night."

Before they all sat down to eat, Sterling introduced them to the marvels of radio and gave them a tour of his home. The Indians were particularly awed by Sterling's trick bathroom, declaring that it must have been the work of the First Coyote, who, according to the Navajo mythology, was the supreme deity of creation and achievement. But it was the radio that impressed them the most. Sterling had one of the most complete sets of the day, which boasted a phonographic attachment. In contrast to the big outfit, he also had a smaller portable affair, and while the Navajo were being amazed at the voice coming out of the big box Sterling switched to the same radio station coming from the portable, which apparently mystified the Indians. The final spectacle came when he switched off the radio and turned on a phonograph record and from the same box came a new voice.[36]

The chief and his entourage were genuinely appreciative of Sterling's hospitality and friendship and to show it they accorded Sterling the highest tribute in the power of the Navajo Indians to bestow on anyone. After the meal, Chief Seginitso proclaimed Sterling "brother to the red men in an impassioned speech such has rarely been heard, even in the councils of the Indians themselves."[37]

Chief Seginitso arose and, with all the dignity of his station and all the dramatic intensity he could muster, addressed the gathering. In his native tongue, the only one he knew, the chief thanked Sterling for his hospitality and then, turning to his braves, pointed to the screen comedian and announced Sterling to be "a man among men, a white man who is brother to the Indian."[38] When Seginitso sat down at the end of his speech, one of the accompanying Navajo, Willie Tee, interpreted. He prefaced his interpretation by saying that he would try to convey what the chief had said but acknowledged that his own vocabulary was too inadequate to do justice to the words of Seginitso. Willie Tee said the Chief had used "big talk words" when referring to Sterling that have not been heard in Indian council for many, many years. A lot of what he had said Willie Tee admitted he couldn't translate as he didn't know the English equivalent.[39]

The burden of the chief's talk, according to what Willie Tee could translate, was based on the attitude of the white man in general, as contrasted with the wholehearted hospitality of Ford Sterling. "Look well upon this man," Seginitso said, "He is a man among men. Other men came to our land. They pat us on the back and give us cigarettes. When we come to their land, they slap us on the back and say we are good fellows. But do they take us into their homes? This man invited us into his house. He asks us to put our moccasins under his table. He treats us as a brother. He is a man among men."[40]

Chief Seginitso also gave Sterling an Indian name: "The Funny Man with the Big Heart."[41] The Navajo consider humor an important element of their culture. It shows in the Navajo language, with its frequency of humor in day-to-day conversation. The strong emphasis and value Navajo place on humor is well demonstrated in the First Laugh rite. The first time a Navajo child laughs out loud is a time for honor and celebration. Sterling's dinner with the Navajo was only the start to the evening's entertainment; next, he took them to one of the big fights in the American Legion Stadium. Here they got about as much entertainment from the excitement of the white spectators as they did from the give-and-take of the boxers.

Sterling played Perkins, the featured comedy role in *Drums of the Desert*. He is a traveling faker, ready to turn his hand at any moment to any field or activity that promises monetary return, whether it is performing "painless" dentistry or acting as an Indian guide. This is, of course, regardless of Perkins' complete ignorance concerning both.

The movie deals with the romance of the discovery of oil on an Indian reservation in the Southwest and the efforts of unscrupulous whites to rob the Native Americans of their rights. A group of men, headed by Will Newton, is trying to force the Navajo off their land so they can steal their oil rights. Chief Brave Bear and his people gather at the reservation to hold a meeting to decide what they are going to do about this problem. Perkins and Hi-Lo meet up with a party of explorers headed by Elias Manton and his daughter Mary. Perkins and Hi-Lo, looking for work, pose as desert rats, which gets them hired as guides for the explorers. The newly formed assembly encounters John Curry, a friend of the Indians, but his friendliness arouses their suspicion. Newton is concerned that the explorers will prove to be a threat to his plans, and unsuccessfully tries to dissuade them from continuing their work in the desert. Being aware of their suspicions about Curry, Newton uses their mistrust for his own purposes and casts aspersions on the innocent man. Manton is kidnapped by Newton's men, but Curry, proving to Manton which side he is really on, rescues him after a search. Newton meanwhile starts for the oil claims, but the Navajo are prepared to defend their sacred lands and rights. Curry tries unsuccessfully to placate the Indians and, failing to listen to reason, Newton shoots and wounds him. True to form, the United States Cavalry arrives just in time, and places Newton's men under arrest. Mary finally realizes that Curry has been their protector all along.

After completing *Drums of the Desert*, Sterling took another long trip to New York, returning to make *Figures Don't Lie*, which was directed by Eddie Sutherland. Sutherland (1895–1973) had quite a theatrical pedigree, born in London of American parents. His father, Al Sutherland, was a theatrical manager and producer and his mother, Julie Ring, was a vaudeville headliner. His great-grandfather, J. H. Ring, was a prominent English playwright and two of his aunts were Blanche Ring, a major American stage star, and Charlotte Greenwood, an American comedienne and eccentric dancer. One of his uncles was Thomas Meighan, the popular silent film actor.

Eddie Sutherland started out as an actor with Mack Sennett at the Keystone Studio, later working with Buster Keaton and as codirector with Charles Chaplin on *A Woman of Paris* and *Gold Rush*. Sutherland directed many sound films with great stars, including W. C. Fields in *Mississippi* (1935) and *Poppy* (1936), Eddie Cantor in *Palmy Days* (1931), Laurel and Hardy in *The Flying Deuces* (1939), and Allan Jones and

French publicity booklet cover for Paramount Pictures' 1927 release *Figures Don't Lie*.

Martha Raye in *The Boys from Syracuse* (1940). He also found a niche in television as a director. Sutherland was briefly married to silent star and sex goddess Louise Brooks.

The cast of *Figures Don't Lie* (October 1927) included Esther Ralston as Janet Wells, Richard Arlen as Bob Blewe, and Sterling as "Howdy" Jones. Janet Wells, who is "Howdy" Jones's secretary, has everything to disturb a jealous wife. She is beauti-

One of several publicity photographs for Paramount's *Figures Don't Lie* that were sent out for the 1927 French release in a publication entitled *Manuel de Publicité et d'Exploitation* (No. 51). The French knew the movie as *Mon Patron et Moi*. Esther Ralston plays Sterling's secretary, who has to deal with a jealous wife and a playboy boyfriend.

ful and an efficient worker who spends her day at the beck and call of Mr. Jones. Unfortunately, Janet finds it difficult to conduct office business because of Jones's behavior, and that of his violently jealous wife. Janet's mind is taken off this issue by the attentions of the new sales manager, Bob Blewe. She does consider him to be a bit too fresh, however, and when she refuses his invitation to the office picnic by the sea, Bob takes Dolores, the office's pretty but empty-headed stenographer. Taking a leaf out of Mrs. Jones's book, Janet demonstrates she can be jealous, too. She decides to play up to Mr. Jones at the picnic, but when she goes for a swim she gets tangled up in seaweed and has to be rescued by Bob. Later, the enraged Mrs. Jones finds Janet and her husband in a somewhat compromising situation and decides the only solution is to shoot Janet. Bob thwarts her plans and all ends happily.

In November 1927, shortly after the release of *Figures Don't Lie*, Sterling was involved in an accident in his home which could have put an end to his career.[42] A gas furnace in the basement exploded, causing Ford to suffer burns to his hands, arms, and face. He had been due to play the important role of Mr. Jordan, sporting goods store proprietor, in the latest Richard Dix film, *Sporting Goods*, then in production. It was thought he would have to be replaced as his injuries caused him to be off work for two weeks. Initially it was feared Sterling's injuries were so severe that they would leave his face scarred, but later his physicians issued a statement reassuring the press that he would not suffer any permanent signs of the incident.[43] (From his physical appearance in later films it seems, fortunately, they were right.) As it happened, Sterling did not need to be replaced; the company shot around him, leaving his scenes the last to be made. And his face healed nicely, so nicely, in fact, that he quipped, "I shouldn't be playing comedy parts; I should be a leading man. Look at me. Don't I look twenty years younger? Why, I've got a brand-new face."[44]

It seems fortunate that Sterling was able to return to *Sporting Goods*; it was the type of role that gave him a chance to demonstrate his gift for physical comedy.

Sporting Goods is a comedy of mistaken identity. Young socialite Alice Elliott (Gertrude Olmstead) thinks that traveling sporting goods salesman and inventor of a new type of golf suit, Richard Shelby (Richard Dix), is actually millionaire Timothy Stanfield (Claude King). Shelby falls in love with Alice and, so as not to disillusion her, allows himself to be installed in an expensive California hotel. Realizing he is going to need to be able to produce at least some cash, Shelby comes up with a get-rich-quick brain wave. He persuades Jordan (Ford Sterling), who is the head of a department store and a keen golfer, to wear his golf suit made of "elasto-tweed" on the golf course. Shelby hopes that Jordan will think the suit so wonderful that he will buy a great quantity of them. At first, Jordan is suitably impressed but then it begins to rain. As the rain soaks the elasto-tweed suit it gradually stretches to the ground. Jordan, no longer impressed, cancels his order, leaving Shelby with no cash and an exorbitant hotel bill. Later, as Jordan returns to the hotel, Shelby is caught trying to sneak out. Jordan has a reason for returning and seeking out Shelby: he has heard that these golf suits are all the rage in the East and doubles his order. Stanfield, who owns the company that manufactures the suits, promotes Shelby to sales manager. This gives Shelby enough income to marry Alice Elliott.

Next came a movie that was later made legendary by Marilyn Monroe, Goldwyn's *Gentlemen Prefer Blondes* (1928). It featured Sterling as wealthy button king and fellow transatlantic traveler, Gus Eisman. The story takes place on shipboard, where two girls, gold digger Lorelei Lee (Ruth Taylor) and her friend, Dorothy Shaw (Alice White), try to capture one of America's richest bachelors, Henry Spoffard (Holmes Herbert). Spoffard is traveling to Paris to investigate reports of immoral activities of American tourists in that city. The girls don't have any money for tickets, especially not for ones in first class, where they'll need to be to snare their catch. This is solved by Lorelei, who borrows (to her way of thinking, least) money from fellow traveler Gus Eisman to finance their trip.

Other members of the cast were fellow Keystonians Mack Swain and Chester Conklin. Sterling and Swain were both praised for their performances in an otherwise average review by *Variety*.

"Opposite the two girls are Ford Sterling as the button monarch, Holmes Herbert is the wealthy bachelor whom the blonde snares into marriage. Mack Swain is the old bachelor who unknowingly bankrolls Lovelace into buying his wife's tiara. It's a heavy contrast in characters, maybe too much.

"If all that's against the picture then the assets include this s.a., the misses Taylor and White spread across the screen, the comedy is the theme, the production background and the support of Sterling and Swain."[45]

Instead of his audience going to see *him*, Sterling was soon to enter many homes in the Los Angeles area, not in person, but through a KNRC radio broadcast from the Elks Temple.[46] KNRC, Santa Monica (now the call sign of a Denver, Colorado, station), had run a remote control line to the Elks Temple in Los Angeles, where studio programs were given. One of the innovations was the Air Theater, broadcast each weekday at noon until 4:00 p.m.; after a two-hour break, the show continued from 6:00 p.m. to midnight. At 9:00 p.m., during the February 1928 inaugural program, there was a dedication ceremony for the main studio held on the patio. Some of the artists appearing in the variety show, chaired by Charlie Murray, were the Elks Band, the Hollywood Symphony, and Ford Sterling. Thus Sterling's voice was heard for the first time through the microphone. Sadly, no recording of this program survives and there is no record of the success or ratings of the broadcast.

At the end of February 1928, Sterling's marriage problem reared its ugly head again. This time, Teddy Sampson was suing him for divorce on grounds of desertion and unlike the last hearing she appeared for the proceedings. The suit was served under their real names, George and Nora Stitch. Teddy was looking for alimony — she claimed Sterling earned a salary of $5,000 per week and that they had community property worth $50,000.[47] Teddy didn't want to stay around; she stated that as soon as this troublesome problem of her divorce was settled she would head back to New York where she had been living. She had plans to leave in May for Europe and had hopes of making a career in British and French pictures.[48] She did not, though, find the success she was after. Strangely, this divorce was not finalized, and they yet again, eventually, reconciled in 1931.

With his Paramount contract ended, Sterling signed to make films with Fox. It would be with Fox that he would make his last silent films. He was to be directed by one of his first directors and coperformer from many of the two-reelers of old, Henry "Pathé" Lehrman. Now they were making a feature, teaming up for a movie version of the stage play *Mr. Romeo*, which was released under the title *Chicken a La King*. George Meeker, who was contracted to Fox, and Nancy Carroll took the romantic leads. This would prove to be the last time Sterling and Lehrman would work together. Lehrman had suffered from a grave alcohol problem for many years and had been arrested several times for drunk driving. His habit had been the cause of several car accidents, some more serious then others. One involved the maiming of a young actress he was dating; the unfortunate young woman received serious facial injuries and lost an eye,[49] which naturally resulted in the end of her chances of a career in the movies. Lehrman's reputation in Hollywood, owing to his drinking and arrests, was none too good, either, nor had it been since the early days.

Alongside Sterling, Carroll, and Meeker in the cast were Buck Taylor, Arthur Stone, and Oscar Barrows. The *Motion Picture News Booking Guide* heralded the *Chicken a La King*'s June 9, 1928, release with this plot summary: "Prosperous business man finds himself in the toils of two gold-digging chorus girls when he tires of his drab wife. Wife goes in for modern clothes and spends considerable of his cash to make herself look young again, and wins him back to the family fireside." Fortunately, Sterling's sound films appear to have been of a higher standard.

11

Stout Hearts and Willing Hands

Equity, the actor's union, was attempting to change and improve employment requirements and working conditions for movie actors in 1929. By June 5, Equity was trying to enforce the edict that actors could sign a contract only if the entire cast of a film were Equity members, and should not sign the standard contract usually offered by studios. Many actors and actresses disagreed with the union, and Sterling stood with this group. In a list published on June 21, of 164 actors and actresses who had signed standard, nonexclusive contracts rather than abide by the agreement, Ford Sterling's name was near the top.[1] Other notable actors on the list were Bela Lugosi, Roland Young, Hedda Hopper, Dot Farley, Jack Duffy, Louise Fazenda, Wheeler Oakman, Slim Summerville, and Walter Brennan.

The Actors' Equity Association had been founded in New York City in May 1913, and the Associated Actors and Artistes of America (the 4A's), had 112 founding members who committed themselves to fighting the arbitrary work rules and low wages that prevailed in the American theater at that time. In July 1919 the American Federation of Labor chartered the 4A's and Equity which, with a membership of 2,700, became its largest component. But recognition did not come easily. A major theater strike was called in August 1919 and, with the support of the musicians' and stagehands' unions, swelled Equity's ranks and won a strong five-year contract between the union and the Producing Managers Association. The strike took place in eight cities, and caused the closure of thirty-seven productions and prevented sixteen others from opening. By 1924, Equity had achieved its goal of a closed shop. Under the auspices of the 4A's, Equity-affiliated screen actors attempted to gain the same working conditions for themselves as their stage counterparts in the 1920s, but their efforts were frustrated; in 1934 the 4A's gave the jurisdiction over screen actors to the newly formed Screen Actors Guild (SAG).[2]

The idea of SAG germinated among the members of the Masquers Club in the 1930s. The Masquers Club was founded in Hollywood in 1925 and was based on the New York clubs for male stage actors and their associates. Their motto was "We Laugh to Win" and they did a lot of that. They also talked, ate, drank, smoked, and put on performances called "Revels" in their clubhouse at 1765 North Sycamore, and were to be instrumental in the founding of SAG. An effect of the stock market crash of 1929 was multiple cuts in many actors' salaries. This, combined with horrendously

Daddy's Gone A-Hunting. Released August 3, 1925. Metro-Goldwyn Picture Corporation. Percy Marmont (L) with Sterling.

long working hours (largely brought on by the time involved in making the new sound films), set the stage for revolt. An eight-week salary cut, announced by the producers in March 1933 through the Academy of Motion Picture Arts and Sciences, was the final straw. The Academy of Motion Picture Arts and Sciences was supposed to protect the actors and their contracts, but the actors felt that the Academy was in the pockets of the producers and the actors were not getting a fair deal.

A small group of Masquers met at the home of Masquer Kenneth Thomson and his wife, actress Alden Gay. Two of the group, Grant Mitchell and Ralph Morgan, had law degrees, which would prove useful. Mitchell and Morgan had been very active in Equity reforms: both were among the 185 actors sued by the Schubert organization in 1919 for their roles in the Equity strike.[3] Sterling had been affiliated with the Masquers Club from its Los Angeles inception and was close friends with many of the other members. Why he chose not to abide by the Equity edict is not mentioned. Perhaps it had to do with his having been on the other side, so to speak. He had been part owner of the Sterling Studio back in 1915 and a shareholder with Special Pictures, and there was talk of another part ownership in the air in 1929. It was announced in late February of 1929 that Mabel Normand, Roscoe Arbuckle, and Ford Sterling had formed a motion picture company among them. The company was due to start production in the beginning of March at the Universal Studios. It was billed as "the largest aggregation of film stars working together at one time in one studio in the United States."[4] For whatever reason (perhaps Normand's health) and presuming the announcement to be accurate, the Normand-Arbuckle-Sterling company never came to fruition. What comedy gems could have been produced by such a company!

Sterling's next movie to be released, *The Girl in the Show*, was filmed in a silent version, yet was also released with a Movietone sound track. This was not unusual for the transitional period between silent and sound films. Movietone differed from Warner's Vitaphone sound-on-disc system, which had been used for the first recognized sound feature, *The Jazz Singer* (1927). *The Girl in the Show* had the sound track physically on the film and not via synchronized disc.[5] Fox's all-talking feature, *Old Arizona*, released in January 1929 using the Movietone system,[6] proved so far superior to the Vitaphone system that it and other sound-on-disc systems were immediately dropped in favor of the more reliable sound-on-film.

The Girl in the Show, costarring Bessie Love, Raymond Hackett, and Jed Prouty, is a tale about a touring company of actors who have taken *Uncle Tom's Cabin* on the road. Trouble starts for the company when its manager walks out and, to save the show, Love decides to settle with Prouty, who has offered her marriage and to take care of her little sister. Hackett, though, organizes an impromptu show that raises sufficient funds to keep the company's tour going and also stops the mismatched marriage. Love and Hackett have fallen for each other and Love has now become the star of the show.

The Girl in the Show was the first film directed by Edgar Selwyn, who with his brother Archibald started the All Star Feature Film Company in 1912; from this, the Goldwyn Picture Corporation was formed in 1917, incorporating part of Selwyn's name. The Goldwyn Corporation became part of Metro-Goldwyn-Mayer in 1929. Sterling was to have a long working relationship with both Goldwyn and MGM throughout his career.

Sterling made his first all-sound film later in 1929, *The Fall of Eve*, released on June 17, 1929. It was a Columbia picture directed by Frank Strayer and starred Patsy Ruth Miller as Eve Grant, Gertrude Astor as Mrs. Ford, Ford Sterling as Mr. Mack, Jed Prouty as Tom Ford, Sr., and from the Sennett stable, Fred Kelsey and Hank Mann.

As the film begins, we learn that Tom Ford's son, Tom, Jr., has a secret: he and his father's secretary, Eve Grant, are in love. Unexpectedly, an out of town buyer, Mr. Mack, arrives with his wife, and they are expecting to be entertained by Mr. and Mrs. Ford, Sr. With his wife taking a solo vacation and wishing to make a good impression on the out-of-towners, Ford, Sr., enlists Eve's help to act as hostess. The plan is to go to a nightclub for supper and a show, but complications ensue when Mack's wife insists on joining the nightclub party. Eve inadvertently gets introduced as Mrs. Ford and things go from bad to worse. There is a radio broadcast from the nightclub and the announcement that the next dance tune has been requested by Mr.

and Mrs. Tom Ford is heard by the *real* Mrs. Tom Ford, who happens to be listening to the radio in her hotel. Meanwhile, Ford, Sr., is not having a very good time with the Macks. He calls his son to help him out of his problems with his guests and their belief that Eve is his wife. Junior agrees on one condition, that Senior consent to his marriage to Eve. The mismatched party returns to the Ford home. An intoxicated Mr. Mack and his corpulent wife are in no condition to go anywhere else, and it is decided that they will just stay the night. Before they retire for bed, it is apparent to them that the nightclub supper wasn't adequate; when Mrs. Ford returns she sees an unfamiliar figure raiding her icebox and calls the police. But all is not lost: Ford, Jr., saves the day, or the night in this case. He explains the situation to Mrs. Ford, the police, and both the Macks, and when the misunderstandings are cleared up he introduces Eve as his bride.

Although *The Fall of Eve* provided the bulk of the entertainment on the Pantages bill and the cast were lauded for their efforts, there were some complaints. These centered around the sound track, of which the *Los Angeles Times* said, "The recording of the film in several sequences, especially in the night club, sounds as if Niagara Falls were just around the corner. Other scenes were much better though."[7]

Sterling made the transition to talkies easily, thanks to his extensive stage experience and continued appearances in the "Revels" put on by the Masquers Club. He had a fine tenor voice with an impeccably timed delivery. When the character or situation required, his lines were perfectly punctuated with little guttural noises and squeaks. His accent, which he was renowned for in his vaudeville days, was flexible, ranging from a sophisticated, near-British, lyrical tenor in *A Missed Engagement* (1935) to harried Teutonic flusterings in the likes of *Keystone Hotel* (1935) and *Auto Intoxication* (RKO, 1931). Sometimes, as in *Spring Is Here*, Ford's presence and witty delivery hold a rather slow and tedious film together. Even the usual chemistry between Sterling and his screen wife, Louise Fazenda, didn't help improve that musical. Neither did such familiar songs as "Yours Sincerely," "With a Song in My Heart," and "Crying for the Carolines." Unfortunately, we do not get to hear Sterling sing in any of the currently available musicals he appeared in, that is unless you count the *three notes* he sang in the opening of RKO's *Trouble from Abroad* (1931) as he ties up his army boots. Perhaps a song will come to light one day. Sterling does do an occasional brief dance, and he always did look rather elegant in his tails, waltzing with his partner.

Throughout 1929 and 1931, Sterling's early ambitions continued to be fulfilled with a series of musicals. In *Sally*, starring Broadway leading lady Marilyn Miller in the title role, Sterling played "Pops" Shendorff (a dialect role), the owner of the Elm Tree Inn, a restaurant that offered a musical show while one dined. Directed by John Francis Dillon, the Broadway musical was adapted from a play by P.G. Wodehouse. Appearing with Miller and Sterling was a very young Joe E. Brown as the Grand Duke "Connie" Constantine of Czekosovinia, and Jack Duffy, who had specialized in playing old men in silent comedies, as the old Commodore.

Sally of the film's title is a waitress who wants to be a dancer. She has been fired from the diner where she worked because of her flirtation with one of its young patrons. Spilling soup all over a dining theatrical agent she is trying to impress doesn't help either. She manages to get another job waiting tables at the Elm Tree Inn, which "Pops" Shendorff owns. Farrell, a young rich society boy who is in love with Sally but doesn't really know her, comes across her as she is setting up a table for a bachelor party he is going to attend. He, of course, is the young man she had been flirting with at the diner. They get to talking and she tells him her life story—a tale of poverty—and her ambition to dance. Pops hears them and is "interested." Farrell tells Pops she is a great dancer down on her luck, and persuades him to let her dance the next night.

One of Pops' waiters is none other than the Grand Duke "Connie" of Czekosovinia, who is penniless, having squandered his fortune on a famous dancer. Connie and Pops have an odd relationship, because Connie is just a lowly waiter but is also the Grand Duke. Pops reluctantly salutes him and kisses the Duke's hand when it is offered out of duty to his superior employee. Pops mutters under his breath, if only he could tell him what he wanted to say.

Louise Fazenda as seen in the 1928 First National production *Heart to Heart*, in which she appeared with Mary Astor, Lloyd Hughs, and Thelma Todd.

Sally does her dance number and is naturally a great success. Pops Shendorff makes her his star act at triple the salary. (The dance sequences were originally shot in color and for that reason it was decided to use redheads, as they apparently photographed better.[8]) The agent whom Sally had spilled the food on is also at the restaurant. He is impressed and persuades Sally to impersonate the great dancer Naskarova, who has failed to turn up to perform at a society fete. Pops thinks his star has been stolen from him and goes to the fete with the police to retrieve her. When he sees Sally and Connie he blows their cover, but no one believes him and he is arrested. Sally tells them the truth and Connie, who as the Grand Duke was an invited guest, takes her home. She goes home upset because she thinks Farrell is going to marry a society girl. Sally accepts a contract offered by the agent, who saw her dance, to feature in the Ziegfeld Follies. After the show there are roses in her dressing room and she is expecting a visit from the person who sent them. It turns out to be Pops, rather than Farrell whom she had hoped for as Farrell had sent her a note asking forgiveness. The roses Pops brings for her are really from Farrell; attached is another note asking again for forgiveness. Farrell is outside as he and Pops have planned, and when they find out that Sally will forgive Farrell they exchange places when Sally goes to get out of costume. Yet another "all is well" ending.

Spring Is Here. Released April 13, 1930. First National Pictures, Inc.

In addition to working with Marilyn Miller in *Sally*, two years later Ford was playing her would-be fiancé's father in *Her Majesty Love*. Miller's screen father was played by the great W. C. Fields, who gave an exquisite performance of his juggling act at the fiancé's family banquet. Fields had been a successful juggler in vaudeville and part of his act was preserved on film in the silent *Sally in the Sawdust* (1925).

It is just as well Sterling was busy in 1929 because he was about to have a small problem with the government. On June 25, a lien was filed against him by the United States district court by the collector of Internal Revenue. Sterling, now living at 5638 Carlton Way, Los Angeles, was served for additional taxes for income made in 1928 amounting to $383.90.[9] Apparently Sterling did not pay the whole amount because he was served another lien in October 1930 for $203 in taxes also due from 1928.[10] Presuming Sterling had paid no taxes for the year 1928, and there is no proof to substantiate this, a total tax bill of $586.90 for the year shows he had had a pretty good income for the late 1920s.

Fazenda and Sterling worked together many times in their careers in both sound and silent pictures. They even appeared together in a 1930s *Screen Snapshots* short, reprising their pie-throwing days at Keystone. There was also a part in another fantasy film for Ford and Fazenda —*Alice in Wonderland* (1933), with its all-star cast and

interesting shuffling of the Alice books by Lewis Carroll. They became the White King and Queen with child actor Billy Barty as the White Pawn. They were also teamed in the tantalizingly lost film, *Bride of the Regiment* (1930), boasting a stellar cast alongside Sterling and Fazenda, including Lupino Lane, Walter Pidgeon, and Myrna Loy. *Bride of the Regiment*, a First National production, was directed by John Francis Dillon. The reviews were not generally that enthusiastic as it was referred to as "the good old Tosca plot with the single variation that there is no knitting or the exacting Scarpio."[11] The highlight of the film seems to have been Sterling, Fazenda, and Lane, as we are told that "the real entertainers of the film are those concerned with the comedy

Top: Sterling as the White King and Billy Barty as the White Pawn in Paramount Pictures' *Alice in Wonderland*. Released December 22, 1933. *Bottom:* In *Screen Snapshots*, 1931, Series 9, number 10, Sterling reprised his role as a Keystone Kop. He was aided by fellow Keystone alumna Louise Fazenda, who is seen with him here along with two unidentified players.

including Lane, Miss Fazenda and Sterling. Of the three I believe Sterling has the most consistent opportunities and is the most genuinely amusing."[12]

There was a further reunion for Sterling in 1930 with one of the actors he had worked with on the stage before joining Biograph. Sterling played Amru in *Kismet* with Otis Skinner, who was reprising the lead role that he had become famous for in the theater; another costar was seventeen-year-old Loretta Young. The film was shot in Warner Brothers Vitascope on 65mm stock to give a wide-screen image; it was also available in the standard 35mm for showing in general theaters that were not equipped with the larger format projectors.

Still in a musical vein, Sterling made *Showgirl in Hollywood* in 1930. Sterling played a movie mogul who had been brought a New York nightclub star, the star then was whisked to Hollywood by a shady producer. It was a parody of how movies were made and had some interesting and accurate behind-the-scenes footage of how silent films were made. There was also a poignant moment when silent star Blanche Sweet, playing a fading actress, sang "There's a Tear for Every Smile in Hollywood." The movie transcended the media: on Saturday, May 24, 1930, at 7:30 p.m. EST, Washington, D.C., station WRC broadcast a radio version of *Showgirl in Hollywood*, featuring the original cast. Whether this was a live broadcast or the studio was playing the Vitaphone disc sound track from the movie is not known but, considering where the broadcast took place and where the cast was generally located, it would be safe to presume the latter.

In August 1930 Sterling signed with Al Christie to make a series of Educational Comedies[13]; he had freelanced in several Christie Comedies during 1929, including *Fatal Forceps*, but now he was contracted with the company. These were to be made at the Metropolitan Sound Studios and Sterling was working practically every day. He did get time off at Christmas and made a trip to Phoenix, Arizona.[14] Unfortunately, he was taken ill with a stomach ailment in Yuma, which delayed his arrival. He was soon back in California, though, to fulfill his contract with Educational. These short films were released under the Gayety Comedies banner, one of them, *The Foolish Forties*, released in June 1931, co-starred the pretty young singer and actress, June MacCloy, who remembered Sterling fondly.

June MacCloy had just graduated from St. Joseph's Academy, Michigan, when she traveled to New York to find work as a singer. Harry Richman, who was appearing in the Broadway show *Scandals*, saw and heard June and was so impressed that he referred her to the producers of the show and they promptly signed her up to appear in it. After *Scandals* closed, Richman engaged June to sing in his chain of New York nightclubs, where the columnist, Walter Winchell, saw her and being as impressed as everyone else suggested she try her hand at pictures. This led her to making a short for Paramount on the East Coast. Back in Hollywood, Budd Schulberg saw the movie and sent for June to come out to Hollywood and sign for a series of pictures. This she did but the series never materialized. Instead she was costarred with Douglas Fairbanks in *Reaching for the Moon*. Sterling saw her in this and requested June for his leading lady in *The Foolish Forties*. Later in her career she appeared with the Marx Brothers in *Go West* (1941). Soon after that, she married an architect and retired from the stage. June MacCloy affectionately remembered working with Sterling and considered him quiet, kind, and a gentleman.[15] (Sterling certainly seems to have had quiet, gentlemanly reading habits; *Creative Art* and the French *L'Illustration* were his regular purchases at this time.[16])

In August, Sterling went back to the East Coast for a short while to make a series of two-reel[17] comedies for Al Christie and Educational, including *Twenty Horses, Walking the Dog,* and *Come to Papa,* but he had returned to Los Angeles by Christmas. There was a reunion of the Keystone Kops in December; they got together with the BPO Elks number 99 to honor the local police. The Los Angeles police provided the band and a crack pistol team, which furnished some hair-raising thrills, and Chief Roy Steckel spoke at the Elks' show.[18]

During 1931 Sterling made a few shorts for various studios, including the slightly bizarre Paramount short *Auto Intoxication*. This is another German-accent film; Sterling plays Otto Krausmeyer, a successful middle-aged business man with a wife, his own home, and money in his bank account. The short opens in a police station, where a suspected criminal stands on a rostrum. "Take him to the cells," orders a detective. Next up is a forlorn- and bewildered-looking Otto on crutches, peering at the shadowy figures in Homburgs and masks, the room full of cigarette smoke. Asks a voice, "Assault and attempt to kill. Do you know this man?" The result: "Take him down to the conference room." The interrogation begins. "You tried to kill a pal of mine." Otto tries to explain: "I caught him with my wife, we had everything, we were so happy." "We don't want to hear about a mug like you being happy." Otto continues to relate the rest of his story in flashback.

June MacCloy costarred with Sterling in *Foolish Forties* in 1931. She had nothing but fond memories for the man she described as "a professional and a gentleman."

Otto arrives home with a bundle of packages and when he enters the house he hears his wife laughing and giggling with a man in their living room. Otto, curious, goes in to investigate and finds his middle-aged wife and a young man sitting on the sofa together. His wife introduces the man as Sam, who has brought them a car. "But I don't want a car," protests Otto as he follows his wife and "Smiling Sam the Sales Man" out the door. The very next shot shows Otto back home sitting at his desk writing a check. As soon as it is signed and the car is his, Sam opens the door to let in

Aileen Cook causes Sterling some annoyance in the Paramount short *Twenty Horses*. Released April 28, 1931.

Joe, a pal of his, who just happens to be an insurance salesman. "He's a great guy to know if you are in trouble," says Sam. Joe starts his patter: he postulates a horrendous scenario, with Otto and his wife going on a pleasure trip and running someone over. "Some pleasure trip," retorts Otto. "I bet we are going on a trip to Jersey." Joe continues—supposing Otto has run over a child and the crowd attack him and pull off his arms and he has to have them surgically amputated at the elbow. "I knew it had to be Jersey," interrupts Otto, but continues that it would be OK because he would be paid $5,000 for his injuries. The policy would cost $250 for one year or $400 for two (just because "I am a pal of Sam's"). "I'll take a couple of years," says Otto. "No," replies his wife, "take one; you may not need the second."

Otto, Mrs. Krausmeyer, and Sam take the car, a brand new Celebrity 8, out so Otto can learn to drive it. The road is busy and when Sam sees a pal, he yells out to him. Otto stops the car thinking Sam is talking to him. This causes the traffic to back up behind him and Otto has great difficulty getting the car back into gear. Eventually, finding reverse, the party zip backward up the road, weaving in and out of the gridlocked traffic with the obvious results.

Otto is lying in a hospital bed, head bandaged, on the edge of consciousness. He is dreaming of cars, pedestrians, buildings, and trolleys flying past; then Sam's

Walking the Dog, 1931. Al Christie Comedy, Paramount. The lady who is apparently giving Sterling a problem is Francetta Malloy. The player at right is unidentified.

face looms in front of him, laughing as usual, and the dream becomes reality. "Where am I? What happened?" asks the befuddled Otto. His wife tells him he hit three autos, two street cars, and a policeman. Otto notices some business cards in her hand and asks her what they are; they are from pals of Sam's—a doctor and the lawyer who is handling the lawsuits brought against Otto. Otto sees another card Mrs. Krausmeyer is trying to hide and he wants to know what it is. After much protest she gives it to him. It reads, "Martingales, the friendly undertaker."

An inter-title informs us that after a few months Otto is up and about—and out of his mind. He returns to a new home (a small apartment) still on crutches. "Very nice if you like living in a piano box," is his comment. He has lost everything except his pocket watch. The lawyers now own his business, the doctors now own his house, and the insurance company now owns his car. Mrs. Krausmeyer is very pleased with the apartment, especially as they got a good deal: the manager happens to be Sam's pal. Sam comes to see how they are settling in and has brought yet another pal of his, Little Miss Sunshine (Aileen Cook), who, to cheer up Otto, dances and plays the cornet. Otto is not amused and stalks off into the bedroom. Sam follows

Twenty Horses. 1931, Al Christie Comedy, Paramount short. L–R: Jed Prouty, Aileen Cook, Ford Sterling.

him to "laugh him out of it." We hear both men laughing, a CLUNK, and then silence. Mrs. Krausmeyer and Little Miss Sunshine rush into the bedroom to find a maniacally laughing Otto kneeling over the prone Sam and placing the undertaker's card on his chest. "He's a pal of mine," snorts Otto.

Back at the police station there is no sympathy for poor Otto: "Take him down." At that moment, the alarm sounds and an immediate evacuation takes place. Everybody out and into the new Celebrity 8 police cars parked out front. They all start up but won't go anywhere except back and forth, back and forth. Sam arrives with Little Miss Sunshine — guess which pal of theirs the police department bought their new cars from. Every officer whips out a gun and chases Sam over a fence. Otto and Little Miss Sunshine hear the barrage of shots and look over the fence. They turn back and Otto removes his hat and lowers his eyes. Little Miss Sunshine takes out her cornet and plays the "Last Post."

Another slightly more standard offering from 1931 for Sterling is *Trouble from Abroad*, an early RKO short. Sterling costarred with Lucien Littlefield and this makes one wonder if there could have been an intention of teaming them for a series. The two of them play friends and army buddies who had fought together in France during World War I in Company A of the White Mule Division; Sterling plays Sgt. Joe

Widgett and Littlefield plays Captain Bill Wimble. They are staying at the Embassy Club Hotel with their wives for their company's first reunion. As it is a stag banquet, their wives are going to a bridge party also being held in the hotel.

While they are getting ready for the banquet, Bill decides to let Joe in on a little secret he has told no one: he lifts his shirt and reveals a large dressing that covers part of his right side. "I told my wife it is a wound." But he reveals a tattoo he got in France. "I have one, too," says Joe, pulling up his shirt and displaying the same tattoo. In unison, they say "Fifi." Joe tells Bill that he managed to convince his wife it was a Greek letter fraternity, "Fi Fi," that Company A had started in France. As they continue to examine each other's tattoos, their wives walk in from the adjoining bedroom where they have been getting ready. Bill's wife sees the tattoo and asks why he had lied to her about his wound. The two men go into an elaborate explanation of Joe's story, which Bill's wife buys—sort of. The wives leave for their bridge game.

The men suddenly realize their Fifi's are one and the same Fifi, from Brest. Bill pulls rank on Joe, as he is still the senior officer when in uniform, and marches him down to the banquet. The two flank their commanding officer (none other than James Finlayson, the nemesis in many a Laurel and Hardy film). Meanwhile, the wives are sitting at their table playing bridge. The radio in the room announces it is changing from dance music to listen in to the celebrations at the White Mule's reunion banquet. The suspicious wives are interested as they listen to Finlayson begin his speech.

"The first speaker needs no introduction, a man who has served his country well and has done more to cement French and American relations than any one man!" Joe stands proudly but soon sits down again, deflated, as the major indicates Bill. "When I say French relations, perhaps I should be more specific: I mean the feminine population. The daring, heartbreaking, lovemaking Lothario, Captain Wimble was second to none."

Mrs. Wimble's face is a picture of embarrassed horror as they listen to the radio; Mrs. Widgett's is a picture of smug satisfaction, especially when Bill gets up to make his speech. "As Napoleon once said, 'a great soldier must be a great lover.' I must have been the best soldier in the late war!" Suddenly, Bill spots the microphone among some table dressing and imagines his wife's face looming out of it. "But seriously, gentlemen, it was not I but Sergeant Widgett. Casanova at the height of his glory was just a piker compared to Sergeant Widgett."

Joe stands up, just bursting with pride: "Being an honest man, I must bow to the truth. A toast to the past and present, and if they should ever meet—what a future!"

Unknown to the two comrades, although they are seconds away from finding out, Fifi herself is to appear as a surprise guest and sing to the company (having just arrived and been given Joe's room to change in). The major tells the two of the surprise; Bill splutters his excuses ("a little heart attack") and runs from the banquet hall. The major announces Fifi. The wives, still playing bridge in the other room, upon hearing her name very quickly put two and two together. "What a homecoming for Casanova," declares Mrs. Wimble. The major decides to raise the microphone so everyone can hear Fifi sing. Joe, on seeing it, spits out his drink in a great shower and rushes out, too.

Fifi has returned to Joe's room to change back into her street clothes. Meanwhile, Joe has gone to Bill's adjoining room to see what happened to him; they both make simultaneous excuses as to why they left the banquet and, strangely, remember that neither of their particular Fifi's was from Brest at all. Joe decides to return to his room to go to bed before his wife gets back, the furthest thought from his mind being that Fifi might be getting undressed in his bathroom! Fifi sees him and runs out of the bathroom wearing nothing except her step-ins and stockings. She hugs the embarrassed Joe, who quickly points out he is a married man now. She bursts into tears, but Joe has an idea and sends her into Bill's room. She sits next to Bill and puts a hand on each shoulder. He screams in fear and horror that his wife could return at any moment. He, too, announces he is a married man and then he hears a key in the door. Quickly, he picks up the protesting Fifi and puts her in the closet. Meanwhile, Joe, whose wife has also returned, has seen Fifi's dress hanging on the coatrack. Joe grabs the dress and tries to stuff it down the back of his pants.

To his horror, Bill's wife wants to put her dress in the closet. He tells her he can't go in there because he saw big mouse footprints. She squeals in disgust. He grabs the dress and rushes into the closet, closing the door behind him. He tells Fifi she must go quickly but she says she can't as she doesn't have her clothes. Bill goes over to talk to his wife, who is now sitting with her back to the connecting door at the dressing table. While he is talking, Fifi goes back into Joe's room for her dress. She sees it tucked into Joe's pants and tries to tug it out. Joe's wife, who is in the bathroom, tells him to get undressed and he turns out the light, much to his wife's astonishment at his sudden shyness. She tells him not to be silly and to turn the light on again. Fifi has meanwhile hidden inside Bill's overcoat, which is on the coatrack. This gives Joe an idea: he must return the coat to Bill. He takes coat, hanger, and Fifi back into Bill's room and then returns to his own. His wife now wants her nightdress, which is in their trunk in Bill's room. At that moment, Bill brings the trunk in! Joe suspiciously rocks the trunk, testing its weight. His suspicions are confirmed when he opens it and sees Fifi inside. He feels around for the requested nightdress and, thinking he has found it, whips out Fifi's step-ins instead. Hurriedly, he throws them back in as his wife comes to look for the nightdress herself. Fifi has by now crawled under the bed. Joe sits down exhausted, letting his hand fall down beside the bed. Fifi bites it and Joe yelps in pain. "What is the matter?" asks his wife. "It's an old ailment I contracted in France. Get a doctor." Joe's wife runs next door for help and Bill's wife sends him protesting in to Joe while the two women call for the doctor. Fifi is now dressing in the bathroom. Bill sees that the coast is clear and they hurry her out of the room to the elevator doors. The wives pick this moment to go downstairs to see if they can find the doctor! They see the trio and step back into the doorway to watch their men. Bill and Joe both kiss Fifi good-bye, which makes both men go weak at the knees. They shake hands, thinking they have gotten away with murder. Suddenly a wifely hand grabs each erring husband by the collar and yanks him backwards. Loud crashes are heard as "The End" appears on the screen.

There was also the first Masquers Club short released through RKO in 1932, *Stout Hearts and Willing Hands,* which had a Keystone Kop–type role for Sterling, was nominated as the best short comedy subject in 1933, and won. The film does not survive, but there is a tantalizing fragmented outtake held in the UCLA archives that unfortunately has no sound track. It shows Sterling and the Kops bursting through the doors of a sawmill to rescue the hero, who is tied to circular-saw bed with the spinning blade getting ever nearer to his head. Sterling had a reputation for being wonderful at showing the younger players "how to take it real big" for funnier effect. In the old Sennett days, he had coached Harold Lloyd, Chester Conklin, and Charlie Chase. A young member of the *Stout Hearts and Willing Hands* cast was Eddie Quillan, whom he remembered speaking with Sterling about some facial reactions Quillan had been making. Ford slapped him on the back and said, "You're fine, kid; you worked for Mack Sennett."[19]

Between the end of 1931 and early 1935 Sterling was mysteriously absent from the screen with the exception of the aforementioned *Stout Hearts and Willing Hands* and RKO's *Pretty Puppies, Playthings of Desire,* and *Alice in Wonderland,* made in 1933. It was even noted by the *Los Angeles Times* when Sterling signed for a lead in *The Black Sheep* in 1935, that he hadn't been seen for a long time and with no explanation.[20] But there was a perfectly good justification.

In 1933 Sterling had flown by transcontinental plane to Florida to make three films at the Kennedy City Studios in St. Petersburg.[21] The first, *Playthings of Desire,* directed by George Melford, was the only one actually made. The *St. Petersburg Times* gave what might be construed as an insight as to what Sterling thought of the experience of making films in Florida: "A portly gentleman sits aloof to one side of the Bayou Farms swimming pool.

"A moving picture is being made on the opposite side of the pool but the portly man might be in another world. His indifference borders on the superb. What matters another moving picture to him? He's seen hundreds of them made, directed dozens and played in many more.

"The man was a famous comedian, that was clear, but seeing him sitting there you would think him a profound tragedian. However, there was one feature that betrayed his woeful pose; his lower lip. It was jutting out like an angry little boy which looked funny on a grown man, but this was one of the features that makes the screen's funny man funny. The rotund fellow was wearing what were a bathing suit and robe, so new that the canvas trunks almost crinkled when he moved, which wasn't often. To top it all off, his face is peculiarly colored with makeup. He stared broodingly into the shimmering waters of the pool, oblivious to all about him, but as soon as the scene being shot on the other side of the pool was finished, the comedian rose and slaps at a mosquito."

Opposite page. Top: Sterling looking as if he means business in this publicity still from Fox Film Corporation's ***Black Sheep***. Released June 14, 1935. However determined he may have looked as the onboard detective on a passenger ship, it didn't appear to help him catch his man. **Bottom:** Buster Keaton, seen here in MGM's ***The Cameraman***, had planned to make the film ***The Fisherman*** with Sterling in Florida. After venue changes and money problems, the film was scrapped after only a few scenes were shot. It is unlikely Sterling was in any of the footage.

11—Stout Hearts and Willing Hands 133

The comedian whom these paragraphs were written about was Ford Sterling, and it was noted by the writer that he would be directing *The Tomcat* for Aubrey M. Kennedy.[22] There was, however, another film to be made before Sterling could start on *The Tomcat*. It was announced in July, not long after the completion of *Playthings of Desire*, that Sterling had been cast in Buster Keaton's new picture, *The Fisherman*, being made by the Flamingo Film Company. Sterling was to have a strong supporting role in the picture, which would have brought together these two noted comedians for the only time on film. Marshall Neilan was to direct the film originally at the Kennedy City Studio, but because the studio was not ready on time to meet the shooting schedule it was

decided to make the interior scenes in New York. The company then planned to go to Havana to make 40 percent of the picture and return to St. Petersburg to make the remainder. Buster Keaton paid a visit to Sterling in the studio when they were filming *Playthings of Desire* in early July to discuss their project.[23] As it happened, sadly, only a small amount of footage was shot before the money ran out. *The Tomcat* never got off the ground for the same reason[24] and Sterling returned to Los Angeles — and retirement.

There was but one sighting of Ford Sterling during 1934. He made no movies and it could have been thought he had dropped off the planet; that is, if it were not for one report on Christmas Day, 1934, of Sterling assisting Mrs. Tod Browning with the organization and distri-

Buster Keaton

bution of Christmas hampers to the poor for the Christmas Basket Fund run by the Assistance League of Southern California. Throughout his career Sterling had given his time to aid charitable and worthy causes. Most likely, few of them were recorded.[25]

So what was he doing during the missing year and why had he hardly worked for some time previously? Sterling had promised himself that when he made a million dollars he would retire from the screen and he had accomplished that goal. One report even claimed that he owned a villa in Nice and went to England yearly to buy the clothes that had earned him the title of Best Dressed Man in Hollywood. Since leaving home, Sterling had accumulated many interests to keep him occupied during his semiretirement. He appears to have had an alert agile mind, and he enjoyed continuing to learn, picking up miscellaneous knowledge at home, on the road (before joining the movie community), and in his European travels. Sterling liked German police dogs, Scottish terriers, and Persian cats; he could dance a professional waltz, clog, and was one of Hollywood's most gracious hosts. He spoke four languages, cried when he heard a sentimental song, and was an accomplished drawing-room conversationalist. He was different from the public's conception of the pie-throwing comedian — in a sense. Different to the extent that his was not the slapstick mind or character, although the natural humor in him was always bubbling out, on the screen or off.[26]

Sterling put his money in what he considered safe investments and property, but they proved not to be as safe as he had thought. A fall in property prices also took a sizable chunk out of his investments, and he decided there was nothing to do about it but go back to work. He also had to sell the Carlton Way house in 1934, and he bought a property at 5272 Hollywood Boulevard,[27] near his old home. As Sterling said in the *Washington Post* in April 1937, "I always looked forward to retirement when I had a certain sum and I thought about it so much that I just had to quit when I got that money. It wasn't nearly so much fun as I thought it would be. But I was determined to stay retired, to travel, to do many things pictures had kept me from doing. I can't say I was happy losing my money, but I can truthfully say I am happy to be back at work."

12

The Unhappy Finish

With the loss of his fortune, 1935 saw Sterling up and running again in featured roles. The *Los Angeles Times*[1] heralded his signing on for the feature *Black Sheep*: "Ford Sterling will be seen on the screens again in a leading role, and in a leading production. Do you recall the days, not so long ago, when he was a premier comedian?" Sterling had obviously been keeping his private life to himself, with no announcement of retirement or that he was simply busying himself with occasional projects. The writer could not understand why, when not so long ago Sterling had been the premier comedian, there was little or no explanation as to why he hadn't continued in that vein. The last major studio feature in which Sterling was cast was *Alice in Wonderland,* where he played the White King. After that, he had apparently just vanished off the face of the earth. Now Sterling was back, and signed up for *Black Sheep,* which Allan Dwan was directing. This would be the first of the three final feature films Sterling would make.

Black Sheep is set on an oceangoing liner, the SS *Southampton.* Sterling is the onboard company detective who is outwitted throughout the film by the rest of the cast, always missing what really is going on as he follows red herrings and doggedly pursues the young couple who he is convinced are up to no good. They are, but not up to whatever it is that the determined detective thinks it is. He prowls the ship's decks and public rooms—derby hat firmly on his head—looking for any sort of trouble; he is not averse to paying unannounced visits to staterooms, either. (Ironically, Jed Prouty, Sterling's longtime friend, who was to play Sterling in *Hollywood Cavalcade* because Sterling was too ill to work, had a role in *The Black Sheep* as a gambling passenger on the ship. The resemblance between the two is uncanny, making Prouty the perfect choice for the *Hollywood Cavalcade* role.)

On April 5, 1935,[2] Sterling started work on the Mascot picture *The Headline Woman*, with Heather Angel, Roger Pryor, Jack LaRue, Conway Tearle, Franklin Pangborn, Jack Mulhall, Ward Bond, and Wheeler Oakman. Here Sterling, as Hugo Meyer, returns to the police force, gradually climbing up the ranks by feeding the press with information. In return, the gentlemen of the press solve the crimes, for which Sterling gets credit. The reporters have no trouble getting the naïve police officer into the palms of their collective hands, and he willingly goes along with them

Black Sheep. 1935, Fox. Ford Sterling (R), as the passenger ship's onboard detective, is not pleased to see Tom Brown aboard the ship but shakes hands with him nonetheless as Eugene Pallette looks on.

as he enjoys his meteoric rise through the police ranks. Meyer establishes his bumbling and inept character in his first scene. In a popular but crooked gambling venue frequented by society folk as well as gangsters, a murder is committed. It is the third murder where the police suspect the victim is part of a gambling war. Meyer, who is pounding his beat just around the corner from the venue, sees the murderer running toward him, but the ever-helpful Meyer inadvertently lets the man go by, hailing a cab for him. Bob Grayson (Roger Pryor), star reporter, sees this as an opportunity to embarrass the police chief, who is having a war of his own with the newspaper's editor. The police chief refuses to give out any bulletins to the editor, so Grayson has the idea to use Meyer. They get him to feed them information on current crimes and in return the reporters start a publicity campaign to promote Meyer, who takes credit for crimes solved by the reporters. Meyer takes the credit for the solved crimes with ever-increasing pride; there are certainly little bits of Chief Teheezal body language in his portrayal.

Harrison's Report[3] enjoyed Sterling's performance, saying that his stupid detective provoked laughter.

Soon after starting production on this, Sterling was signed to make the two-reeler

Bumbling police officer Hugo Meyer (Ford Sterling, L) shakes hands with the police chief (Conway Tearle) in *The Headline Woman*. Mascot Pictures Corporation; Republic Pictures Corporation. Released May 13, 1935.

Keystone Hotel, which also included many of the old Sennett team. Sterling was back playing his old Teheezal character, Captain of the Keystone Kops. The short is full of old Sennett gags and slapstick and it is fun to hear Sterling chattering away to himself as he goes through his business, pretty much as one could imagine he did in the silent days. The little film was released as a supplementary feature; the *Washington Post*[4] noted that Sterling had put on weight and wasn't as spry jumping on and off

12—*The Unhappy Finish* 139

Sterling seems happy with his lot in this publicity photograph from *Keystone Hotel*. 1935, Warner Brothers. He is surrounded by (L–R) Sue Barstead, Virginia Myers, Barbara Hubbard, and Betty McMann.

the police wagon. They did, though, give the film a nice spread with several photos in their July 28, 1935, edition under the headline, "Back come the Keystone Cops and up goes the pie market."

The next film was Sterling's final feature, *Behind the Green Lights*. Sterling played Max Schultz, a German janitor who is a material witness to a murder and fake diamond robbery. Schultz holds the key evidence and he is prepared to stand as the star witness in the crime, but he is threatened and eventually bought out by the gang's crooked lawyer. The bright young detective and hero of the piece finds where Schultz is hiding and manages to persuade him to "do the right thing" and appear at the trial. This he does and the criminal and their shyster lawyer get their just desserts. *Behind the Green Lights* was Mascot Pictures' next-to-last feature production before the studio was reorganized as Republic. *Harrison's Report*[5] considered this to be one of the most intelligently produced melodramas, in which the brains of racketeers are pitted against those of the police. The plot was adapted from a book by retired New York homicide captain, Cornelius W. Willemse, who in his time had broken up many

Tom Moore (L) and Ford Sterling in the 1926 Pola Negri vehicle *Good and Naughty*. Paramount. Courtesy of Bruce Calvert.

gangs; the captain was also the advisor for the picture. Sterling was not the comic relief this time. Schultz was a serious man.

In May 1935, Sterling started making shorts for RKO, including *A Quiet Fourth, Bridal Grease,* and *Framing Father*,[6] the latter short focusing on the complications surrounding how to get father (Sterling) to allow his son to marry a chorus girl. During 1936 RKO had Sterling appearing in what seem to be Leon Errol scripts; they had the same director, Leigh Jason, and writers, Jean Yarborough, Leslie Goodwins, and Jack Townley. Another of them, *A Missed Engagement,* was most likely another Masquers production but this cannot be confirmed. Sterling may well have been filling in for Errol, who made only three shorts for RKO in 1936 and 1937 due to other commitments (most years he made seven appearances per annum). The two men looked similar, played the same type of characters, and were perfectly interchangeable in these roles.

There *may* have been another feature on the books for Sterling—*Human Cargo* (May 29, 1936). Ford is listed in production charts but not credited in the film or seen in any stills from the production, and until a copy of the picture or a still turns up showing Sterling in it, it will not be known if he was in the actual production or not. There were more shorts though, this time for Fox. Two of them, both from 1936, were *Framing Father* and *Bridle Grease*. In May 1937,[7] Bert Gilroy signed Sterling to make a series of featurettes for RKO, making him a contracted player with the company he had been freelancing with for the last two years. But he was only destined to make one.

Sterling's final film was the 1937 RKO release, *Many Unhappy Returns*, directed by Charles Roberts. It was the standard fare: Sterling once again played the upper-middle-class gentleman with a suspicious wife, an innocent cigar counter girl, and a collection of farce situations. This time, he ended up in a straightjacket.

By now Sterling was looking much older. He had put on weight and looked unhealthily puffy around the face. The sparkle in his eyes was still there, and he was giving the same energetic performances, but it was beginning to show that he was not in the best of health. A swelling on the right side of his neck that began to be noticeable in 1929 was conspicuously larger and harder to hide. By 1938 Ford Sterling had been forced to retire from the screen due to ill health. Although not mentioned at the time, it would later be reported that he had been suffering from heart disease and atherosclerosis.

To add to his health problems, Sterling was hospitalized with bronchial pneumonia in May of 1938. Pneumonia was something Sterling had been prone to throughout his life and usually came through just fine, including the typhoid pneumonia contracted earlier in his life. It looked as if he was going to make a full recovery this time, too; he was well on the road to recovery when a heart condition began to cause complications. His physician, Dr. E. J. Moffit, announced that Sterling had been showing some improvement over the past several days but would have to remain in the hospital for the next few weeks.[8] The weeks turned into months and Sterling remained in Good Samaritan Hospital, too sick to be discharged. He had many visitors from the old days to aid him and cheer him up, but his stay was much longer than anticipated.

Mid-February 1939 was not a good time for Sterling. On the 18th, he was reportedly seriously ill in Good Samaritan Hospital with a "circulatory ailment." Dr. Francis E. Brown, a spokesman for Good Samaritan, reported that Sterling's condition was poor and he could not predict whether the illness would be fatal or not.[9]

On February 19, 1939, a rather worrying report was printed in the *Los Angeles Times*[10] about Sterling's declining health. This was the first update on his condition since May 1938, and it was not good. The veteran Hollywood comedian had been ill with the heart ailment for nearly a year and had been confined to bed for much of the time during that year, the past few months spent in Good Samaritan Hospital. Now the doctors were reporting that he was in serious condition and facing amputation of one of his legs as a result of thrombosis. Dr. S. M. Atler, one of the physicians attending Sterling, said following a conference that his doctors agreed the operation was necessary, but not until the comedian had gained a little more strength.

Presumably, Sterling either did not regain enough strength to undergo surgery in February or, more likely, the thrombosis at that time resolved and was not as life-threatening as had been thought. It is unlikely, if Sterling had had to wait for six months to regain his strength, that he would have survived at all. It was not until August that both the *Chicago Daily Tribune* and the *New York Times* picked up a story from the Associated Press.[11] Dr. Francis Brown said a thrombosis and an infection had necessitated the amputation of Sterling's left leg several days earlier. The doctor went on to say that Sterling was resting comfortably and should make a full recovery but (once again) Sterling would need to spend several more weeks in the hospital. Sterling remained amazingly optimistic; the gallant fighting spirit that had kept him going so far continued to bolster the ailing and nearly impoverished actor against despair. Despite having been in the hospital for months (he was home for only two months between two lengthy stays) and having his left leg amputated above the knee in the hope of halting the gangrene that had now set in, his friends still found the old Sterling waiting to greet them. One friend told the AP, "Doctors say he is doing fine and may be able to walk again one of these days if all goes well. You'd think with all the hard luck he's been having, Ford would become embittered, but he's still his humorous self."[12]

Hospital bills had taken their toll. Sterling had nothing left except for his friends, including Charley Chase, who himself was not in good physical or financial health by then; Joe Kavigon, the switchboard operator at the Masquers Club, and his longtime friend Jed Prouty.[13] It was Prouty who came to Sterling's aid. Hedda Hopper put a paragraph about Ford's plight in her column in August 1939,[14] which, as well as pointing out Prouty's generosity, shone a little light onto Sterling's character.

"It ought to be known that Ford Sterling, onetime organizer of the Keystone company, has been in the hospital for two years, had one leg amputated last week. And being completely broke, wouldn't have been able to hang on but for Jed Prouty (of Jones Family fame) who has helped financially, and visits daily. Now that we know, come on fellows, do your stuff. He would."

Things were looking grim. Growing steadily weaker. Sterling was reported by mid–September as having "a less than even chance" for recovery.[15] Jed Prouty was not only supporting Sterling financially and emotionally, he was also impersonating Sterling in Darryl F. Zanuck's Technicolor production, *Hollywood Cavalcade,* a film extravaganza about the early days of silent comedy up to the coming of sound and loosely based on the life of Mack Sennett and the Keystone Studio. It included the Keystone Kops— mostly the original team playing themselves— with the exception of Sterling, who had been too sick to work on the production. Prouty was chosen to take his place and he did a good job. There was a rather unfortunate reference to Sterling in what would have been a review of a prerelease screening had the reporter managed to show up. The gentleman in question, Nelson B. Bell, was really looking forward to seeing Jed Prouty's remarkably faithful impersonation of "the late Ford Sterling," but missed it.[16] One hopes Sterling was spared seeing reports of his premature demise.

Mr. Bell must have had a premonition, because Sterling lost the fight following another heart attack on the evening of Friday, October 13, 1939. He had spent a total of sixteen months in Good Samaritan Hospital.

There were more than one hundred mourners at his funeral, including many stars of the silent screen and sports. Among those who paid their tributes were Charlie Chaplin, Mack Sennett, Douglas Fairbanks, Sr., Barney Oldfield, Baron Long, and Harold Lloyd. After an Episcopal funeral service on October 17, Ford Sterling was cremated and his ashes interred in a communal niche at the Hollywood Forever

Jed Prouty (L), whose generosity helped Sterling significantly during his final illness, impersonates Sterling in the 1939 20th Century Fox feature *Hollywood Cavalcade*. Sterling was originally wanted for the part but was too sick to work.

Cemetery (then known as Hollywood Memorial Park). His pallbearers were Douglas Fairbanks, Sr., Barney Oldfield, Marshall Neilan, Baron Long, Earle C. Anthony, and F. C. Griffin. The brief chapel service opened with the singing of "Abide with Me" and "Crossing the Bar," after which an organist played Sterling's favorite song, "Whispering."[17]

Joe Kavigon, the phone operator at the Masquers Club, was a friend of Ford's and was one of the last people to see him alive. Joe referred to this time as "The last horrible days of Ford Sterling." He visited Sterling at Good Samaritan a few days before Ford died, as Joe put it, penniless, alone, and ill.[18] The only possession Ford owned was a table fan, which he offered to give to Joe. Joe accepted it but soon threw it away. Even Sterling's last possession was broken. Ironically, the feature Jed Prouty had replaced Ford Sterling in as Chief Teheezal, *Hollywood Cavalcade*, was released the very day of Sterling's death.

Hedda Hopper said in her column, "What a pity Ford Sterling died before he saw *Hollywood Cavalcade*. The boys at the studio were arranging to show him the sequence when Jed Prouty played Ford in the old days, but Sterling passed on before they could do it. The success of *Cavalcade* is a fitting obituary for him."[19]

At the time of this writing, Ford Sterling's ashes remain in a water-damaged communal niche at Hollywood Forever Cemetery in Los Angeles, California. It is unmarked, except for the word *Dawn* on a brass plate. After so long in the hospital there was no money left to pay for a personal resting place for his ashes, so they were placed in a niche generously paid for by the Actors' Fund. It was a gesture of respect for a man who had given so much to an industry he greatly loved.

"Ford Sterling" signed in negative by someone other than Sterling. Fan photograph ca. 1925.

Ford Sterling Filmography

The films are listed chronologically by release date. All known production, cast, crew, and story information is included in each entry. Pertinent notes will follow in entries as needed.

1911

A Dutch Gold Mine
Biograph, 6/1/1911. Director: Mack Sennett.
Note: Listed in some filmographies but not confirmed as having Sterling in the cast.

Lucky Horseshoe
Biograph 9/11/1911. Director: Mack Sennett.
Note: Listed in some filmographies but not confirmed as having Sterling in the cast.

Too Many Burglars
Biograph, 10/2/1911. Director: Mack Sennett.
Note: Listed in some filmographies but not confirmed as having Sterling in the cast.

Inventor's Secret
Biograph, 10/23/1911. Director: Mack Sennett.
Note: Listed in some filmographies but not confirmed as having Sterling in the cast.

1912

The Interrupted Elopement
Biograph, 8/15/1912. Director: Mack Sennett; Scenario: S. Walter Bunting.
Cast: Ford Sterling, Mabel Normand, Edward Dillon, Elmer Booth, Charles Gorman.
Bob's sweetheart's father doesn't much care for him, so his friend (Sterling) hatches a plan for the couple to elope, with disastrous results.

Tragedy of a Dress Suit
Biograph, 8/15/1912. Director: Mack Sennett; Scenario: Mabel Normand.
Cast: Ford Sterling, Dell Henderson, Mabel Normand, Edward Dillon, Charles Avery, William Beaudine, Kate Bruce, William J. Butler, Christy Cabanne, Frank Evans, Grace Henderson, Harry Hyde.
A young man who is down on his luck makes an impression on a local heiress, who asks him to her house party. He needs an evening suit so helps himself to his landlord's (Sterling). The landlord is not impressed and goes in search of the elusive suit to retrieve it.

He Must Have a Wife
Biograph, 9/5/1912. Director: Mack Sennett; Scenario: John A. Walsh.
Cast: Gus Pixley, William J. Butler, Mabel Normand, Ford Sterling, Kathleen Butler.
In order to inherit from his eccentric uncle's will, Harry has to be happily married. Unfortunately, he is still single; his uncle is still alive (as he wants to ensure the estate is

distributed as he wishes); and there is a very short time for Harry to find a wife.

Note: Buster Keaton used a similar plot in his 1925 six reel comedy *Seven Chances*.

Stern Papa

Biograph, 9/16/1912. Director: Mack Sennett; Scenario: Edward Acker.

Cast: Ford Sterling, Mack Sennett, Edward Dillon, Gus Pixley, William Beaudine, Dell Henderson.

Papa (Sterling) is trying to get his daughter married off and tries all sorts of tactics to get her off his hands.

Cohen Collects a Debt

Keystone Film Company, 9/23/1912; split reel. Director: Mack Sennett.

Cast: Ford Sterling, Fred Mace.

The Water Nymph

Keystone Film Company, 9/28/1912; split reel. Director: Mack Sennett.

Cast: Ford Sterling, Mabel Normand, Fred Mace, Mack Sennett.

The young man is taking his girlfriend to the beach to meet his parents. His father has already met her and taken a fancy to her. The young man, finding out, hatches a plan with the girl. She goes to the beachside café where the family plans to meet and before long the boy's father arrives and sits with her. He doesn't realize who she is and knows nothing of the plot. The girl goes along with the father's flirting and when she leaves to change into a swimsuit, he does likewise. She performs several dives from a board high above the sea; the father attempts to impress her but only succeeds in falling awkwardly into the water. The young man's mother sees her husband and the young girl together and when they return to the café the father is embarrassed to find himself being introduced to the girl in front of his wife by his son, who tells him she is his girlfriend.

Riley and Schultz

Keystone Film Company, 9/30/1912; split reel. Director: Mack Sennett.

Cast: Ford Sterling, Fred Mace.

The New Neighbor

Keystone Film Company, 9/30/1912; split reel. Director: Mack Sennett.

Cast: Ford Sterling.

Stolen Glory

Keystone Film Company. 10/4/1912; one reel. Director: Mack Sennett.

Cast: Ford Sterling, Mabel Normand, Fred Mace, Henry Lehrman.

Two elderly soldiers from the Civil War are both in love with the local matron, and nothing is sacred in their fight to impress her. There is to be a parade of old soldiers in the town and one of the men is to be in it, proudly wearing his old uniform and medals. He takes his uniform jacket with its medals out to where he has been working and leaves it unattended while he goes and talks to the matron, telling her to look out for him in the parade and to pay attention to his medals. While he is talking, the other old soldier sneaks up and takes the coat, puts it on, and joins the parade, pretending the medals are his own. The coat's owner, seeing the parade approach, goes to put it on but, of course, it has gone. He runs off to find his treasures while the matron sits on the bleachers to watch the parade. The parade goes by and she waves to the old soldier with his medals, believing them to be his. The wronged soldier runs through the marchers and spies the thief. They fight among the other marchers and the owner of the coat eventually retrieves it and impresses the matron.

The Beating He Needed

Keystone Film Company. 10/7/1912; split reel. Director: Mack Sennett.

Cast: Ford Sterling, Fred Mace.

Note: The working title of this film is *The Sissy*.

Pedro's Dilemma

Keystone Film Company, 10/7/1912; split reel. Director: Mack Sennett.

Cast: Ford Sterling, Mack Sennett, Mabel Normand, Fred Mace, Victoria Forde.

Ambitious Butler
Keystone Film Company, 10/21/1912; split reel. Director: Mack Sennett.
Cast: Ford Sterling, Mack Sennett, Mabel Normand, Fred Mace.

The Flirting Husband
Keystone Film Company, 10/21/1912; split reel. Director: Mack Sennett.
Cast: Ford Sterling, Mabel Normand.

The Grocery Clerk's Romance
Keystone Film Company. 10/28/1912; split reel.
Cast: Ford Sterling, Fred Mace.

At Coney Island, aka Cohen at Coney Island
Keystone Film Company, 10/28/1912; split reel.
Cast: Ford Sterling, Mack Sennett, Mabel Normand.

Mabel's Lovers
Keystone Film Company, 11/4/1912; split reel.
Cast: Ford Sterling, Fred Mace, Mabel Normand, Alice Davenport.

At It Again
Keystone Film Company, 11/4/1912; Split reel.
Cast: Ford Sterling, Fred Mace, Mack Sennett, Mabel Normand.

The Deacon's Troubles
Keystone Film Company, 11/11/1912; Split reel.
Cast: Ford Sterling, Mabel Normand, Fred Mace.

A Temperamental Husband
Keystone Film Company, 11/11/1912; Split reel.
Cast: Ford Sterling.

The Rivals
Keystone Film Company, 11/18/1912; Split reel.
Cast: Ford Sterling, Mack Sennett, Mabel Normand.

Mr. Fix-It, aka Mr. Fixer
Keystone Film Company, 11/18/1912; Split reel.
Cast: Ford Sterling, Mack Sennett, Mabel Normand, Fred Mace.

A Bear Escape
Keystone Film Company, 11/25/1912; Split reel.
Cast: Ford Sterling, Mack Sennett, Fred Mace.

Pat's Day Off
Keystone Film Company, 12/2/1912; Split reel.
Cast: Ford Sterling, Mack Sennett, Fred Mace, Alice Davenport.

A Midnight Elopement
Keystone Film Company, 12/9/1912; split reel. Director: George Nichols.
Cast: Ford Sterling, Mabel Normand, Fred Mace.

Mabel's Adventures
Keystone Film Company, 12/16/1912; Split reel.
Cast: Mabel Normand, Ford Sterling.

Hoffmeyer's Legacy
Keystone Film Company, 12/23/1912; Split reel.
Cast: Ford Sterling.

1913

A Double Wedding
Keystone Film Company, 1/6/1913; Split reel.
Cast: Ford Sterling, Fred Mace.

Saving Mabel's Dad
Keystone Film Company, 1/6/1913; split reel. Director: Mack Sennett.

Cast: Ford Sterling, Mabel Normand, Fred Mace, George Nichols, Henry Lehrman.

The Cure That Failed

Keystone Film Company, 1/13/1913; split reel. Director: George Nichols.

Cast: Ford Sterling, Mabel Normand, Fred Mace.

A habitual drunk sits at an outside table at a cafe between two women he doesn't know. He is pixilated, flirts with them, then falls backward off his chair much to the annoyance and amusement of the patrons. He has three friends who decide to save the man from the evil of drink and hatch a plot. This entails one of them dressing up as a frumpy woman and pretending the drunk and "she" were married while he was under the influence. The drunk wakes up in bed to find the "woman" sitting in a chair next to him. Initially the drunk is horrified, until he sees men's shoes and pants legs sticking out from under the woman's ample skirt. This gives the drunk an idea. When the woman goes out to tell their other two friends how things are going, the drunk douses his shirt with red ink and then fires off a gun. The three friends rush in and are confronted by an apparently dead drunk lying on the bed. Believing the plot was all too real for the drunk, and in his horror that he committed suicide, they feel they are responsible. Their fears are confirmed when a policeman arrives, confirms the drunk is dead, and arrests them. As soon as they all leave the room the drunk jumps up and makes his escape through the window. He is discovered when the policeman marches the three friends around the same corner where the drunk is hiding.

How Hiram Won Out

Keystone Film Company, 1/13/1913; split reel.

Cast: Ford Sterling.

The Mistaken Masher

Keystone Film Company, 1/27/1913; split reel. Director: Mack Sennett.

Cast: Ford Sterling, Mabel Normand, Mack Sennett.

The Deacon Outwitted

Keystone Film Company, 1/27/1913; split reel. Director: Henry Lehrman.

Cast: Ford Sterling, Mabel Normand, Harry McCoy, Betty Schade.

Just Brown's Luck

Keystone Film Company, 2/3/1913; split reel.

Cast: Ford Sterling, Fred Mace, Mabel Normand, Alice Davenport.

The Battle of Who Run

Keystone Film Company, 2/6/1913; one reel.

Cast: Ford Sterling Mack Sennett, Mabel Normand, Fred Mace.

The Stolen Purse

Keystone Film Company, 2/10/1913; Split reel.

Cast: Ford Sterling, Mack Sennett, Fred Mace.

The Jealous Waiter

Keystone Film Company, 2/10/1913; split reel.

Cast: Ford Sterling.

The Elite Ball

Keystone Film Company, 2/13/1913; split reel.

Cast: Ford Sterling.

Heinze's Resurrection

Keystone Film Company, 2/13/1913; one reel.

Cast: Ford Sterling, Mabel Normand, Fred Mace.

Her Birthday Present

Keystone Film Company, 2/17/1913; split reel.

Cast: Ford Sterling, Fred Mace.

A Landlord's Troubles

Keystone Film Company, 2/20/1913; split reel.

Cast: Ford Sterling.

The Professor's Daughter
Keystone Film Company, 2/24/1913; split reel: Director: Mack Sennett.
Cast: Ford Sterling, Mabel Normand, Fred Mace, Evelyn Quick.

A Red Hot Romance
Keystone Film Company, 2/27/1913; split reel. Director: Mack Sennett.
Cast: Ford Sterling, Mabel Normand, Fred Mace.

A Deaf Burglar
Keystone Film Company, 3/3/1913; split reel.
Note: Includes an intercut scene of Sterling from stock footage used in another Sennett short.

The Sleuths at the Floral Parade
Keystone Film Company, 3/6/1913; split reel. Director: Mack Sennett.
Cast: Ford Sterling, Fred Mace, Mabel Normand, Mack Sennett.

The Man Next Door
Keystone Film Company, 3/7/1913; split reel.
Cast: Ford Sterling, Fred Mace.

A Strong Revenge
Keystone Film Company, 3/10/1913; one reel: Director: Mack Sennett.
Cast: Ford Sterling, Mack Sennett, Mabel Normand, Nick Cogley.
The clueless grocer and the cunning cobbler both fight for the same girl's affections. The rivalry escalates when the cobbler, knowing the grocer is going to a party to impress the girl, secretly puts Limburger cheese in the grocer's shoe, which he is mending. The grocer, suspicious as to why everyone keeps moving away from him at the party, finds the cheese and tucks it into the cobbler's trousers. Now it is the cobbler they are intent on avoiding.

The Sleuth's Last Stand
Keystone Film Company, 3/13/1913; split reel. Director: Mack Sennett.
Cast: Ford Sterling, Mack Sennett.

The Two Widows
Keystone Film Company, 3/13/1913; split reel. Director: Mack Sennett.
Cast: Ford Sterling, Mack Sennett.

Foiling Fickle Father
Keystone Film Company, 3/13/1913; split reel.
Cast: Ford Sterling.

Love and Pain
Keystone Film Company, 3/17/1913; split reel.
Cast: Ford Sterling.

A Wife Wanted
Keystone Film Company, 3/20/1913; split reel.
Cast: Ford Sterling, Dot Farley.

The Rube and the Baron
Keystone Film Company, 3/20/1913; split reel.
Cast: Ford Sterling, Mack Sennett, Fred Mace, Mabel Normand.

The Chief's Predicament
Keystone Film Company, 3/24/1913; split reel. Codirectors: George Nichols, Mack Sennett.
Cast: Ford Sterling, Nick Cogley, Edgar Kennedy, Hank Mann, Al St. John.

On His Wedding Day
Keystone Film Company, 3/31/1913; split reel.
Cast: Ford Sterling.

The Land Salesman
Keystone Film Company, 4/3/1913; split reel.
Cast: Ford Sterling.

Hide and Seek
Keystone Film Company, 4/3/1913; split reel. Director: George Nichols.
Cast: Ford Sterling, Mabel Normand, Betty Schade, Helen Holmes, Edgar Kennedy.
A woman thinks the young girl she is look-

ing after is locked in a bank safe. Police are called and after many misadventures the safe is opened but the child is found safe outside where she has been all along.
Note: This film is a spoof of the King Baggot film, *The Time Lock Safe*.

Help! Help! Hydrophobia!
Keystone Film Company, 4/3/1913; split reel.
Cast: Ford Sterling.

Those Good Old Days
Keystone Film Company, 4/7/1913; one reel. Director: Mack Sennett.
Cast: Ford Sterling, Fred Mace, Mabel Normand, Phyllis Allen.

A Game of Poker
Keystone Film Company, 4/10/1913; split reel.
Cast: Ford Sterling.

Father's Choice
Keystone Film Company, 4/10/1913; split reel. Director: George Nichols.
Cast: Ford Sterling, Mabel Normand, Fred Mace, George Nichols.

A Life in the Balance
Keystone Film Company, 4/14/1913; one reel. Director: Mack Sennett.
Cast: Ford Sterling, Dot Farley.
A man and his wife, living in a small apartment, need money, so they rent out the house they have. Inadvertently the man rents it to three anarchists who are building bombs. After the man tries to remove the gang from his house, they seek revenge by trying to blow the man and his family up, but they only succeed in blowing themselves up.

Murphy's I.O.U.
Keystone Film Company, 4/17/1913; split reel. Director: Henry Lehrman.
Cast: Ford Sterling.

A Fishy Affair
Keystone Film Company, 4/27/1913; split reel. Director: Mack Sennett.
Cast: Ford Sterling.

The New Conductor
Keystone Film Company, 4/28/1913; split reel. Director: Mack Sennett.
Cast: Ford Sterling.

His Chum the Baron
Keystone Film Company, 4/28/1913; split reel. Director: Mack Sennett.
Cast: Ford Sterling, Mabel Normand.
Man borrows a friend's (who is a Baron) clothes and identity to go to a society party. He is unmasked and a chase ensues as he tries to make his escape. Finally, he is trapped in a closet from which he eventually emerges in his underwear.

That Ragtime Band, aka The Jazz Band
Keystone Film Company, 5/1/1913; split reel. Director: Mack Sennett.
Cast: Ford Sterling, Mabel Normand, Hank Mann, Alice Davenport, Nick Cogley.
More than one member of the band is in love with the girl, and they enter an amateur contest to impress her. While they are waiting their turn in the contest, the bandleader is intent on collecting the addresses of all the girls in the other acts, except for one rather large lady. When the band start playing, their music turns out to be so bad that they are pelted with rotten fruit and vegetables by the audience. In retaliation the leader turns a fire hose on the audience to cool them off.

His Ups and Downs
Keystone Film Company, 5/5/1913; split reel. Director: Mack Sennett.
Cast: Ford Sterling.

Algy on the Force
Keystone Film Company, 5/5/1913; split reel. Director: Henry Lehrman.
Cast: Fred Mace, Ford Sterling, Hank Mann, Al St. John, Betty Schade, Nick Cogley, Dot Farley, Edgar Kennedy.

Mabel's Awful Mistake
Keystone Film Company, 5/12/1913; one reel. Director: Mack Sennett.
Cast: Ford Sterling, Mabel Normand, Mack Sennett, Edgar Kennedy.

Their First Execution
Keystone Film Company, 5/15/1913; one reel. Director: Mack Sennett.
Cast: Ford Sterling.

The Foreman of the Jury
Keystone Film Company, 5/22/1913; one reel. Director: Mack Sennett.
Cast: Ford Sterling, Mabel Normand, Fred Mace, Hank Mann, Roscoe Arbuckle.

Toplitsky and Co.
Keystone Film Company, 5/26/1913; one reel. Director: Henry Lehrman.
Cast: Ford Sterling.
Toplitsky owns a secondhand clothes and tailor shop. He believes he is happily married but he has an assistant who is after Mrs. Toplitsky, and she flirts with him as well. Toplitsky finds out, forgives his wife, but chases the assistant away. The assistant hides in a bathhouse but is chased out in nothing but a bathing suit by an escaped bear. He eventually finds a temporary safe haven under Mrs. Toplitsky's bed, where he is found by Mr. Toplitsky and his friends.

The Gangsters
Keystone Film Company, 5/29/1913; one reel. Director: Henry Lehrman.
Cast: Ford Sterling, Fred Mace, Roscoe Arbuckle.

Barney Oldfield—A Race for a Life
Keystone Film Company, 6/3/1913; one reel. Director: Mack Sennett.
Cast: Ford Sterling, Mack Sennett, Mabel Normand, Barney Oldfield, Helen Holmes, William Hauber.
The rube is happy with his girlfriend, but the villain wants her, too. She rebuffs the villain's advances, so he kidnaps her, ties her to the tracks, and hijacks a train with which to run her over. The rube finds Barney Oldfield, the famous racing driver, and they give chase, hoping to reach the girl before the train does. They do, just in the nick of time, and free her.

The Hansom Driver
Keystone Film Company, 6/9/1913; half reel. Director: Mack Sennett.
Cast: Ford Sterling, Mack Sennett, Mabel Normand.

The Speed Queen
Keystone Film Company, 6/12/1913; one reel. Director: Mack Sennett.
Cast: Ford Sterling, Mabel Normand, Nick Cogley.

The Waiters' Picnic
Keystone Film Company, 6/16/1913; one reel. Director: Mack Sennett.
Cast: Ford Sterling, Mabel Normand, Roscoe Arbuckle, Hank Mann, Al St. John.

Out and In
Keystone Film Company, 6/19/1913; half reel. Director: Henry Lehrman.
Cast: Ford Sterling.

Peeping Pete
Keystone Film Company, 6/23/1913; half reel. Director: Mack Sennett.
Cast: Ford Sterling, Mack Sennett, Roscoe Arbuckle.
The neighbor man likes to peep through a hole in the fence at his neighbor's wife. The neighbor doesn't like this so chases him around town. Eventually they decide to let bygones be bygones and become friends, leading the rest of the town on a wild chase.

His Crooked Career
Keystone Film Company, 6/26/1913; two-third reel. Director: Mack Sennett.
Cast: Ford Sterling, Mack Sennett.

For the Love of Mabel
Keystone Film Company, 6/30/1913; one reel. Director: Henry Lehrman.

Cast: Ford Sterling, Mabel Normand, Roscoe Arbuckle.

Rastus and the Game Cock
Keystone Film Company, 7/3/1913; one reel. Director: Mack Sennett.
Cast: Ford Sterling.

Safe in Jail
Keystone Film Company, 7/7/1913; one reel. Director: Mack Sennett.
Cast: Ford Sterling.

Love and Rubbish
Keystone Film Company, 7/14/1913; one reel. Director: Henry Lehrman.
Cast: Ford Sterling, Charles Avery, Paul "Little Billy" Jacobs, Alice Davenport, Roscoe Arbuckle.

Set in a park that is supposedly kept free from litter by two park keepers. To flirt with the ladies in the park, the two men trade their white park-keepers' uniforms for frock coats, which they keep hidden in garbage cans. Those frequenting the park include a woman and small boy, whom she puts in a large barrel to stop him from getting into trouble; however, he escapes. When the park superintendent comes along, one of the park keepers dives into the little boy's now vacated barrel. The barrel is knocked over and rolls down a hill into a lake; the whole population of the park have given chase in the belief the little boy is still inside. The other park keeper heroically dives in to bring the barrel to shore and save the little boy. Imagine their surprise when the top is removed and a water-squirting park keeper pops out.

The Peddler
Keystone Film Company, 7/21/1913; half reel. Director: Henry Lehrman.
Cast: Ford Sterling.

Just Kids
Keystone Film Company, 7/29/1913; one reel. Director: Henry Lehrman.
Cast: Ford Sterling, Alice Davenport, Edgar Kennedy, Paul "Little Billy" Jacobs, Jules White.

Professor Bean's Removal
Keystone Film Company, 7/31/1913; one reel. Director: Henry Lehrman.
Cast: Ford Sterling, Mabel Normand, Roscoe Arbuckle.

Cohen's Outing
Keystone Film Company, 8/4/1913; one reel. Director: Wilfred Lucas.
Cast: Ford Sterling, Charles Avery, Alice Davenport, Wilfred Lucas.

A Game of Pool
Keystone Film Company, 8/7/1913; half reel. Director: Wilfred Lucas.
Cast: Ford Sterling.

The Riot
Keystone Film Company, 8/11/1913; one reel. Director: Mack Sennett.
Cast: Ford Sterling, Roscoe Arbuckle, Mabel Normand.

The Firebugs
Keystone Film Company, 8/21/1913; two reels; Director: Mack Sennett.
Cast: Ford Sterling, Fred Mace.

Baby Day
Keystone Film Company, 8/25/1913; one reel. Director: Wilfred Lucas.
Cast: Ford Sterling, Mabel Normand.

Mabel's Dramatic Career, aka Her Dramatic Debut
Keystone Film Company, 9/8/1913; one reel. Director: Mack Sennett.
Cast: Ford Sterling, Mabel Normand, Alice Davenport, Roscoe Arbuckle, Virginia Kirtley, Mack Swain, Paul "Little Billy" Jacobs.

The Faithful Taxicab, aka Fatal Taxicab
Keystone Film Company, 9/18/1913; one reel. Director: Mack Sennett.
Cast: Ford Sterling, Mabel Normand, Roscoe Arbuckle.

When Dreams Come True
Keystone Film Company, 9/22/1913; one reel. Director: Mack Sennett.
Cast: Ford Sterling, Mabel Normand.

The Bowling Match
Keystone Film Company, 9/27/1913; one reel. Director: Mack Sennett.
Cast: Ford Sterling, Mabel Normand.
Two men pit their talents against each other at the bowling alley. They will stop at nothing to win, even rigging the pins with a machine so that they move out of the path of the opponent's ball.
Note: To move the pins around on the screen, stop-motion animation was used.

Schnitz the Tailor
Keystone Film Company, 10/9/1913; one reel. Director: Mack Sennett.
Cast: Ford Sterling.

Their Husbands
Keystone Film Company, 10/13/1913. Director: Henry Lehrman.
Cast: Ford Sterling, Jewel Carmen.

A Healthy Neighborhood
Keystone Film Company, 10/16/1913. one reel. Director: Mack Sennett.
Cast: Ford Sterling.

The Speed Kings
Keystone Film Company, 10/30/1913; one reel. Director: William Lucas.
Cast: Ford Sterling, Mabel Normand, Teddy Tezlaff, Earl Cooper.

Love Sickness at Sea
Keystone Film Company, 11/6/1913; one reel. Director: Mack Sennett.
Cast: Ford Sterling, Mabel Normand, Mack Sennett.

A Small Time Act
Keystone Film Company, 11/10/1913; half reel.
Cast: Ford Sterling.

Wine
Keystone Film Company, 11/13/1913; one reel. Director: George Nichols.
Cast: Ford Sterling, Roscoe Arbuckle, Minta Durfee.

A Bad Game
Keystone Film Company, 11/19/1913; one reel. Director: Mack Sennett.
Cast: Ford Sterling, Alice Davenport, Edgar Kennedy, Hank Mann.

A Muddy Romance, aka Muddled in Mud
Keystone Film Company, 11/20/1913; one reel. Director: Mack Sennett.
Cast: Ford Sterling, Mabel Normand, Mack Swain, Charles Avery, William Hauber.
Young man is in love with the woman next door, and believes they are about to get married. She, though, has different ideas and, although flirting with him, she is about to marry someone else. So that the young neighbor doesn't know about it the couple row into the middle of a lake with a parson to get married; the neighbor follows them and drains the lake in an attempt to get to them. The police arrive with the intention of arresting the young neighbor.
Note: Lake location: Echo Park, Los Angeles, California

Cohen Saves the Flag
Keystone Film Company, 11/27/1913; one reel. Director: Mack Sennett.
Cast: Ford Sterling, Mabel Normand, Henry Lehrman, Nick Cogley.
Set during the Civil War, two men are in love with the same woman. Both join the army, one as an officer, the other a private. The officer sends the private on a suicide mission but instead the private saves the flag and becomes a hero.

The Gusher
Keystone Film Company, 12/15/1913; one reel. Director: Mack Sennett.
Cast: Ford Sterling, Mabel Normand.
Oil wells flourish around a small town and the young man promises to marry his girl

when he strikes it rich. He buys a sham oil well from some crooks but it turns out to be a real gusher; the angry crooks get the last laugh though when, during the couple's wedding, they set fire to the gusher.

Zuzu, the Band Leader
Keystone Film Company, 12/24/1913; two reels. Director: Mack Sennett.
Cast: Ford Sterling, Mabel Normand, Charles Haggerty, Hank Mann.
The leader of the town band is in love with a local girl and so is one of the band members. They march through the street to a local hall where they are playing in a talent show that has several bad acts featuring pretty starlets. The bandleader is only interested in getting the actresses' addresses. When the band performs they are greeted with jeers and flying tomatoes by the audience.

Some Nerve
Keystone Film Company, 12/25/1913; one reel. Director: Mack Sennett.
Cast: Ford Sterling.

Ladies' Tailor
Keystone Film Company, 1913; one reel
Cast: Ford Sterling.

1914

Love and Dynamite
Keystone Film Company, 1/3/1914; one reel. Director: Mack Sennett.
Cast: Ford Sterling.

In the Clutches of the Gang
Keystone Film Company, 1/17/1914; two reels. Director: George Nichols.
Cast: Ford Sterling, Hank Mann, Roscoe Arbuckle, Rube Miller, Al St. John.

Too Many Brides, aka *The Love Chase*
Keystone Film Company, 1/19/1914; one reel. Director: Mack Sennett.
Cast: Ford Sterling.

Double Crossed
Keystone Film Company, 1/26/1914; one reel. Director: Ford Sterling.
Cast: Ford Sterling.

A Robust Romeo
Keystone Film Company, 2/12/1914; one reel. Director: George Nichols.
Cast: Ford Sterling.

Baffles, Gentleman Burglar
Keystone Film Company, 2/16/1914; two reels. Director: Henry Lehrman.
Cast: Ford Sterling.

A Thief Catcher
Keystone Film Company, 2/19/1914; one reel. Director: Ford Sterling.
Cast: Ford Sterling.

Between Showers, aka *Charlie and the Umbrella,* aka *The Flirts,* aka *In Wrong Thunder and Lightning*
Keystone Film Company, 2/28/1914. Director: Henry Lehrman.
Cast: Ford Sterling, Charles Chaplin, Emma Clifton, Chester Conklin.
It has been raining in the park but that doesn't stop two rivals from fighting over the woman of interest or an umbrella.

A Film Johnnie, aka *Charlie at the Studio,* aka *Million Dollar Job,* aka *Movie Nut*
Keystone Film Company, 3/2/1914; one reel. Director: George Nichols.
Cast: Ford Sterling, Charles Chaplin, Virginia Kitley, Minta Durfee, Roscoe Arbuckle.

A False Beauty, aka *A Faded Vampire*
Keystone Film Company, 3/5/1914; one reel. Director: Ford Sterling.
Cast: Ford Sterling, Alice Davenport.
The man has just become betrothed to the lady of his dreams. He thinks her the most beautiful woman in the world, that is, until

he sneaks around outside her bedroom window to watch her undress to go to bed. She removes her wig and teeth and scratches her bald head. From that moment on he is bent on retrieving his engagement ring.

Tango Tangles, aka Band Leader, aka Charlie's Recreation, aka Music Hall

Keystone Film Company, 3/9/1914; three-quarter reel. Director: Mack Sennett.

Cast: Ford Sterling, Charles Chaplin, Roscoe Arbuckle, Chester Conklin.

The nightclub bandleader, one of the musicians, and a drunken patron are all in love with the same woman. The bandleader tries all sorts of tricks to put off the other two men, finally ending up brawling with the drunk.

The Fatal Wedding

Sterling Motion Picture Co., Universal Manufacturing Co.; 4/13/1914; one reel. Director: Henry Lehrman.

Cast: Ford Sterling.

Love and Vengeance

Sterling Motion Picture Co., Universal Manufacturing Co., 4/23/1914; two reels; Director: Henry Lehrman.

Cast: Ford Sterling, Henry Lehrman, Emma Clifton.

Two men are in love with the same woman they meet in a park; she, though, is in love with a racing car driver.

Note: Written around the Vanderbilt Cup and Grand Prix automobile race held at Santa Monica on February 26 and 28, 1914.

Sergeant Hofmeyer

Sterling Motion Picture Co., Universal Manufacturing Co., 5/7/1914; one reel. Director: Henry Lehrman.

Cast: Ford Sterling.

Police sergeant's son wants a soapbox go-cart, a popular toy with the boys in the neighborhood. His father steals one from another boy but is seen by a toddler who tells the police. The stolen go-cart just happens to belong to the police commissioner's son.

Papa's Boy

Sterling Motion Picture Co., Universal Manufacturing Co., 5/14/1914; one reel. Director: Henry Lehrman.

Cast: Ford Sterling, Billy Jacobs.

The comedy is centered around the strife between a father and his son of four and it's a case of "like father, like son," with the son leading the race.

Note: *The Daily News*, Frederick, Maryland, 6/17/1914.

Snitz Joins the Force

Sterling Motion Picture Co., Universal Manufacturing Co., 6/4/1914. One reel.

Cast: Ford Sterling.

When Smaltz Loves

Sterling Motion Picture Co., Universal Manufacturing Co., 6/11/1914; one reel.

Cast: Ford Sterling.

The Jealous Husband

Sterling Motion Picture Co., Universal Manufacturing Co., 6/25/1914; one reel.

Cast: Ford Sterling.

Hearts and Swords

Sterling Motion Picture Co., Universal Manufacturing Co., 6/28/1914; one reel. Director: Henry Lehrman.

Cast: Ford Sterling, Peggy Pearce.

The Crash

Sterling Motion Picture Co., Universal Manufacturing Co., 7/2/1914; one reel.

Cast: Ford Sterling.

Note: This film features a terrific explosion, the blowing up of a house and barn, and a real auto going over a cliff, immediately followed by a motorcycle that is madly chasing the auto and lands in the middle of the auto wreckage at the bottom of the cliff.

Snookee's Flirtation

Sterling Motion Picture Co., Universal Manufacturing Co., 7/9/1914; one reel.

Cast: Ford Sterling.

Almost Married
Sterling Motion Picture Co., Universal Manufacturing Co., 7/13/1914; one reel.
Cast: Ford Sterling.

Troublesome Pets
Sterling Motion Picture Co., Universal Manufacturing Co., 7/30/1914; one reel.
Cast: Ford Sterling.
The master of the house, tired of the monkey and parrot kept by his wife, puts one in the pantry and the other down the well. The parrot's cries for help rouse the neighborhood.

At Three o'Clock
Sterling Motion Picture Co., Universal Manufacturing Co., 8/13/1914; one reel.
Cast: Ford Sterling, Peggy Pearce.
The man, rejected by his girlfriend in preference for a gangster, plans on suicide. He cannot do the deed himself, so he hires a hit man to do the job. When the girl decides she prefers him after all, he is overjoyed, then remembers the appointment he has with the assassin at three o'clock.

A Dramatic Mistake
Sterling Motion Picture Co.; Universal Manufacturing Co.; 8/16/1914; one reel.
Cast: Ford Sterling, June Clark, Henry Griffith, Alberta McCoy, James Dalton, Arthur Travers, John F. Dillon, Arthur Tavares.

That Minstrel Man
Keystone Film Company, 8/17/1914; Director: Roscoe Arbuckle.
Cast: Ford Sterling.
Note: This is possibly a delayed release, as it was produced by Keystone, not Sterling Pictures.

His Wife's Flirtation
Sterling Motion Picture Co., Universal Manufacturing Co., 8/20/1914; one reel.
Cast: Ford Sterling.

Snookee's Disguise
Sterling Motion Picture Co., Universal Manufacturing Co., 8/27/1914; one reel.
Cast: Ford Sterling.

A Bogus Baron
Sterling Motion Picture Co., Universal Manufacturing Co., 9/3/1914; one reel. Director: Ford Sterling.
Cast: Ford Sterling, Peggy Pearce.

An Ill Wind
Sterling Motion Picture Co., Universal Manufacturing Co., 9/11/1914; one reel.
Cast: Ford Sterling.

In and Out
Sterling Motion Picture Co., Universal Manufacturing Co., 9/21/1914, one reel.
Cast: Ford Sterling.

A Shooting Match
Sterling Motion Picture Co., Universal Manufacturing Co., 9/24/1914; one reel.
Cast: Ford Sterling.

His Smashing Career
Sterling Motion Picture Co., Universal Manufacturing Co., 10/1914; one reel.
Cast: Ford Sterling.

Hypnotic Power
Sterling Motion Picture Co., Universal Manufacturing Co., 10/8/1914; one reel.
Cast: Ford Sterling, Dave Anderson, David Kirkland.

The Close Call
Sterling Motion Picture Co., Universal Manufacturing Co., 10/12/1914; one reel.
Cast: Ford Sterling.

His New Job
Sterling Motion Picture Co., Universal Manufacturing Co., 10/12/1914; one reel.
Cast: Ford Sterling.

Heinie's Outing
Sterling Motion Picture Co., Universal Manufacturing Co., 10/15/1914; one reel.
Cast: Ford Sterling.

Carmen's Washday
Sterling Motion Picture Co., Universal Manufacturing Co., 10/19/1914; one reel.
Cast: Ford Sterling.

Secret Service Snitz
Sterling Motion Picture Co., Universal Manufacturing Co., 10/22/1914; one reel.
Cast: Ford Sterling.

Snookee's Day Off
Sterling Motion Picture Co., Universal Manufacturing Co., 10/26/1914; one reel.
Cast: Ford Sterling.

The Dog Raffles
Sterling Motion Picture Co., Universal Manufacturing Co., 11/12/1914; one reel.
Cast: Ford Sterling.

A Bear Escape
Sterling Motion Picture Co., Universal Manufacturing Co., 11/16/1914; one reel.
Cast: Ford Sterling.

Black Hands
Sterling Motion Picture Co., Universal Manufacturing Co., 11/23/1914; one reel.
Cast: Ford Sterling.

The Manicurist
Keystone Film Company, 1914; Codirectors: Ford Sterling.
Cast: Ford Sterling.

The Jury
Universal, 1914.
Cast: Ford Sterling, Frank Lloyd.
Note: Not listed as a Sterling Comedy.

Olive's Love Affair
Sterling Motion Picture Co., Universal Manufacturing Co., no release date available.
Cast: Ford Sterling.

1915

Hogan's Romance Upset
Keystone Film Company, 2/13/1915; Director: Charles Avery.
Cast: Ford Sterling (cameo), Mack Swain, Roscoe Arbuckle, Harold Lloyd.
Note: Sterling has a bit part as an audience member in this, his first film after returning to Sennett.

That Little Band of Gold, aka For Better or Worse
Keystone Film Company, 3/15/1915.
Cast: Ford Sterling, Roscoe Arbuckle, Mabel Normand, Ethel Madison, Alice Davenport.
A young man goes to the opera with his wife and her mother. Seated in the box opposite is his friend with two young ladies; his friend likes one but not the other. The two men decide to meet at the local restaurant, the young man sneaking out of the box and leaving his wife and mother-in-law to watch the opera. The husband takes a shine to one of the other man's girlfriends, the preferred one. The man is not happy, so decides to put the husband on the spot by calling up his wife at the theater. The two women arrive, catching the guilty husband.

Our Dare Devil Chief
Keystone Film Company, 5/10/1915, Director: Charles Parrott (Charley Chase).
Cast: Ford Sterling, Mack Swain, Minta Durfee, Al St. John, Harry Bernard.
The bumbling police chief is in love with the mayor's daughter; the mayor is not impressed. The mayor's house is robbed while the police chief is there, so the mayor tells the chief he has to arrest the crooks and retrieve the stolen goods or lose his job.

He Wouldn't Stay Down
Keystone Film Company, 5/30/1915. Codirectors. Ford Sterling, Charles Parrott.
Cast: Ford Sterling, Charley Chase, Minta Durfee.
The man's wife is apparently having an affair with their mutual friend. After she takes

out a life insurance policy on her husband, the friend hatches a plan to get rid of the husband. He persuades the husband to pretend to commit suicide (although the friend plans on success) in front of his wife, thus regaining her affections. The friend then plans to run off with the widow and the insurance money. The man is rescued and returns home, catching his friend and the wife.

Courthouse Crooks, aka The District Attorney

Keystone Film Company, 6/5/1915; Codirectors: Ford Sterling, Charles Parrott.

Cast: Ford Sterling, Harold Lloyd, Minta Durfee, Charles Arling.

The district attorney is in love with the judge's wife. He has a date with her and plans to meet her at an ice-cream parlor. It happens to be the judge and his wife's wedding anniversary, too, and the judge has gone to the jewelers to buy a present. He loses the gift, a necklace, on the way back to the office. The district attorney, on his way to his meeting, finds it, removes it from the box, and takes it to give to the judge's wife as his gift. A young man finds the box and is arrested for theft. When the young man goes to trial he is defended by the district attorney and judged by the judge. The judge's wife is wearing the necklace, which the judge sees and recognizes. The truth comes out.

Dirty Work in a Laundry, aka A Desperate Scoundrel

Keystone Film Company, 7/19/1915; Director: Charles Parrott.

Cast: Ford Sterling, Minta Durfee, Harry Bernard, Al St. John.

A man falls in love with a laundry girl but her fiancé objects. In retaliation, the man steals money from the laundry and inadvertently imprisons the girl, whom he ties to the belt of the laundry press. Her boyfriend comes to the rescue but has to be helped by the police and laundry employees before the man is trapped in the laundry tub.

Only a Messenger Boy

Keystone Film Company, 8/23/1915.

Cast: Ford Sterling.

The messenger boys at the telegraph office like a drop of beer now and again, but the ladies of the local Temperance Society disapprove. One happens to be the mayor's wife, who gently takes away the jug of beer from one of the messenger boys, which he mistakes for flirting. At lunchtime he goes to the park to eat and sees the girl there; he sits next to her but unbeknownst to him, she is asleep. When her arm falls on his shoulder he thinks she is really paying him attention. In fact, she has gone to the park to meet her husband, who is making a shady deal with some crooks. When the husband sees her and the boy he starts to shoot at him. The boy runs and finds himself outside the mayor's house at the same time the girl is going in. He follows her, but when caught by her husband, he hides in a safe. The safe gets stolen and blown into the air by a bomb with the boy inside; finally it ends up at the bottom of the river.

Note: Last Keystone that Sennett released.

His Father's Footsteps

Triangle-Keystone, 11/28/1915. Director: Ford Sterling.

Cast: Ford Sterling, Charley Chase.

Fatty and the Broadway Stars

Triangle-Keystone, 12/19/1915.

Cast: Ford Sterling, Roscoe Arbuckle.

The Hunt

Triangle-Keystone, 12/26/1915. Director: Ford Sterling.

Cast: Ford Sterling, Polly Moran, May Emory, Bobby Vernon, Fritz Schade, Guy Woodward, Dot Hagart.

1916

Because He Loved Her

Triangle-Keystone, 1/16/1916. Director: Dell Henderson.

Cast: Ford Sterling, Sam Bernard, Glen Cavander, Mae Busch, Harry McCoy.

His Pride and Shame
Triangle-Keystone, 2/6/1916. Codirectors: Ford Sterling, Charles Parrott.
Cast: Ford Sterling, Juanita Hansen, Bobby Vernon, Bobby Dunn, Guy Woodward.

The Snow Cure
Triangle-Keystone, 4/23/1916. Director: Arvid Gillstrom.
Cast: Ford Sterling, Fritz Schade, Alice Davenport, James Donnelly.

The flirtatious bachelor endeavors to strike up a relationship with the lady across the hall. The husband, on the other hand, has other ideas and violently inflicts them on the bachelor, then takes his wife off to their summer home in the mountains. So shaken up is the bachelor that he goes to take a course of treatment from Dr. Quack, who has a sanitarium in the same mountains. Dr. Quack has a brown bear that he uses to chase his patients, thus ensuring that they get their exercise. The bear chases the bachelor into a cabin that just happens to belong to the bachelor's neighbors. The jealous husband seizes a shotgun to slay the flirtatious friend and is only just restrained by Dr. Quack, who has followed the patient into the cabin and explains the situation.

His Wild Oats
Triangle-Keystone, 6/25/1916. Codirectors: Ford Sterling, Clarence Badger.
Cast: Ford Sterling, Mack Swain, Polly Moran, Vivian Edwards, Harry Gribbon, Joseph Swickard.

His Lying Heart
Triangle-Keystone, 8/20/1916; Codirectors, Ford Sterling, Charles Avery.
Cast: Ford Sterling.
Note: At this point, a Triangle distribution dispute caused a gap in releases.

1917

Stars and Bars
Triangle-Keystone. 2/18/1917; Director: Victor Heerman.
Cast: Ford Sterling, Harry Gribbon.

Done in Oil
Triangle-Keystone, 2/25/1917. Director: Charles Avery; Scenario: Ford Sterling, Clarence G. Badger, Hampton Del Ruth.
Cast: Reggie Morris, Clair Anderson, Patrick Kelly, Harry Depp, Charles Bennett, Ford Sterling.

Pinched in the Finish
Triangle-Keystone, 4/1/1917.
Cast: Ford Sterling, Harry Gribbon.

A Maiden's Trust
Triangle-Keystone, 4/29/1917. Director: Harry Williams.
Cast: Ford Sterling, Alice Davenport, Wayland Trask.

Her Torpedoed Love
Triangle-Keystone, 5/13/1917; Director: Frank Griffin.
Cast: Ford Sterling, Louise Fazenda, Tom Kennedy, Harry Booker, Wayland Trask.

1918

Wild Women and Tame Lions
LK-O; Universal Manufacturing Co., 6/2/1918.
Cast: Ford Sterling.

Beware of Boarders
Triangle-Keystone, 10/16/1918.
Cast: Ford Sterling.

Rough on Husbands
LK-O, Universal Manufacturing Co., 11/12/1918.
Cast: Ford Sterling.

It's a Cinch
Triangle-Keystone, 1918.
Cast: Ford Sterling.
Note: The film was finished in August 1918; the exact release date is unknown.

Moonshine
Fox Sunshine, 1918.

Cast: Ford Sterling.

Note: Most Fox Sunshine titles for this period are currently lost. Sterling made several.

1919

Fools and Duels
LK-O, Universal Manufacturing Co., 1/19/1919. Director: Henry Lehrman.
Cast: Ford Sterling.

East Lynne with Variations
Paramount Sennett, 2/23/1919. Director: Edward Cline.
Cast: Ford Sterling.

Yankee Doodle in Berlin
Paramount Sennett, 3/20/1919; five reels. Director: F. Richard Jones; Scenario: Mack Sennett.
Cast: Bothwell Browne, Ford Sterling, Malcolm St. Clair, Bert Roach, Ben Turpin, Charles Murray, Eva Thatcher, Joseph Belmont, Chester Conklin, Charles Lynn, Phyllis Haver, Jane Allen, Heinie Conklin, Bobby Dunn, James Finlayson, Eddie Foy, Harry Gribbon, Laurel Lee Hamilton, Harriet Hammond, Frank Hayes, Fanny Kelly, Edgar Kennedy, Tom Kennedy, Myrtle Lind, Kalla Pasha, Marvel Rea, Wayland Trask.
Set in World War I, with Germany ruled by an inept and bumbling Kaiser with an equally inept army. They are all bamboozled by an American airman who is not only a spy but also a female impersonator. All the men fall in love with "her," allowing the spy to remove the war plans from the Kaiser's coat pocket and whisk them back to America.
Note: This was Sennett's patriotic film made for the war effort. Boswell Brown was a well-known female impersonator of the day.

Hearts and Flowers
Paramount Sennett, March and April 1919. Director: Edward F. Cline; Writing credits: Mack Sennett.
Cast: Louise Fazenda, Ford Sterling, Phyllis Haver, Billy Armstrong, Jack Ackroyd, Charles Lynn, Harriet Hammond, Bert Roach, Kala Pasha.
The bandleader loves a girl in the audience but is pestered by the flower girl. He does everything in his power to get rid of her until he finds out she has inherited a fortune. She hasn't, however. It is a trick by his beloved's beau. The bandleader woos the flower girl and now offers marriage. On the day of the wedding, surrounded by her family of rough-looking crooks, he learns the truth that she is poor, and he tries to escape, but is chased by her brothers. Meanwhile, she marries her old boyfriend.

Among Those Present
Paramount Sennett, 4/19/1919. Codirectors: Ray Grey, Erle Kenton.
Cast: Ford Sterling, Bert Roach, Phyllis Haver, Myrtle Lind, Eddie Gribbon, Edgar Kennedy, Lois Boyd, Eva Thatcher, Fanny Kelly.

The Little Widow
Paramount Sennett, 4/22/1919. Director: Malcolm St. Clair; Scenario: Mack Sennett.
Cast: Ford Sterling, Minta Durfee.

Trying to Get Along
Paramount Sennett, 7/6/1919.
Cast: Ford Sterling, Phyllis Haver.

Treating Them Rough
Paramount Sennett, 8/3/1919.
Cast: Ford Sterling.

Salome vs. Shenandoah
Paramount Sennett, 10/1919.
Cast: Ford Sterling, Ben Turpin.

His Last False Step
Paramount Sennett, 11/9/1919.
Cast: Ford Sterling, Phyllis Haver, Bert Roach.

A Lady's Tailor
Paramount Sennett, 12/7/1919; Codirectors: Ray Grey, Erle C. Kenton.
Cast: Ford Sterling, Billy Bevan, Kathryn

McGuire, Ben Turpin, Phyllis Haver, Isabelle Keith, John Rand, Myrtle Lind, Bert Roach, Elva Diltz, Mildred June, Sibyl Trevilla.

Her Screen Idol
Paramount Sennett, 1919. Director: Edward Cline.
Cast: Ford Sterling, Louise Fazenda, Edgar Kennedy, Lillian Biron.

Summer Girls
Paramount Sennett, 1919.
Cast: Ford Sterling.

1920

Ten Dollars or Ten Days
Paramount Sennett, 2/15/1920. Director: Del Lord.
Cast: Ford Sterling, Ben Turpin, Harry Gribbon, Phyllis Haver, Jack Richardson, Bud Ross.

Fresh from the City
Paramount Sennett, 5/3/1920; Director: Walter Wright.
Cast: Ford Sterling, Marie Prevost, Pat Kelly, Bert Roach, Lewis Gordon, Virginia Fox, Eddie Gribbon, Kala Pasha, Billy Bevan, Billy Armstrong.

The city boy moves to the country to escape a broken relationship. He falls for the store owner's daughter and helps them put on a show to raise money to pay their mortgage. The man who holds the title to the store doesn't want them to pay; if they don't, the store reverts to him. He gets his son to stop the delivery of the cash, but the city boy helps to foil them and wins the storekeeper's daughter.

By Golly
Paramount Sennett, 6/6/1920.
Cast: Ford Sterling.

Married Life
Mack Sennett Special Feature Production, Associated First National Pictures, Inc., 6/14/1920; five reels. Director: Mack Sennett.

Cast: Ford Sterling, Ben Turpin, James Finlayson, Phyllis Haver, Charlotte Mineau, Charles Conklin, Kalla Pasha, Charlie Murray, Louise Fazenda, Eddie Gribbon.

A married college girl has written a play in which she stars. Her husband is jealous of the hero and when the hero is injured, the husband insists he be taken to the hospital for an operation. The doctor accidentally gives the young man "illuminating gas," which makes him float around the hospital. When the police come to arrest the doctor and the husband, the husband makes his escape in a plane but is chased by another plane and the two have a dogfight in the air.

[First National 5-reeler]
Cast: Ford Sterling.
Note: This untitled film featured the Keystone regulars and could possibly be a rerelease of *Yankee Doodle in Berlin*.

Great Scott!
Paramount Sennett, 8/15/1920. Director: Charles Murray.
Cast: Ford Sterling, Charles Murray, Eva Thatcher, Fanny Kelly, Harriet Hammond, Billy Armstrong, Virginia Fox, James Finlayson, Kathryn McGuire, Charlotte Mineau, George O'Hara, Teddy the Dog.

Don't Weaken
Paramount Sennett, 9/1920.
Cast: Ford Sterling.

His Youthful Fancy
Paramount Sennett, 10/3/1920.
Cast: Ford Sterling.

Movie Fans
Paramount Sennett, 10/31/1920.
Cast: Ford Sterling.

Fickle Fancy
Paramount Sennett. 11/14/1920.
Cast: Ford Sterling.

Watch Your Husbands
Cosmograph Comedies, Special Pictures

Corporation, 11/14/1920. Director: Reggie Morris.
Cast: Ford Sterling, Neely Edwards, Charlotte Merriam.
Note: This film is a *probable* inclusion in the Sterling filmography but it is not certain.

Love, Honor and Behave!

Paramount Sennett, Associated First National Pictures, Inc., 11/20/1920. Codirectors: Richard Jones, Erle Kenton; Scenario: Mack Sennett.
Cast: Ford Sterling, Charles Murray, Phyllis Haver, Marie Provost, George O'Hara, Charlotte Mineau, Billy Bevan, Kalla Pasha, Eddie Gribbon, Fanny Kelly, Billy Armstrong, Baldy Belmont, Eva Thatcher.

Judge Fawcett's court is disrupted by an arguing pair of newlyweds. They are in dispute because the girl found a photo of another woman and believes her husband to be unfaithful. The judge relates a story that happened to him that demonstrates the error of believing such circumstantial evidence. When he was a police judge, Fawcett was hired by a Mrs. Robin to follow her husband, haberdasher Milton Robin, and his mistress to the Gargle Inn. The judge is accompanied by Mrs. Robin and her brother but after some shenanigans there is a raid at the inn and the judge gets photographed in dubious but innocent circumstances planned by Robin's mistress and her friends, which opens the Judge up to blackmail. The judge is now forced to drop all charges against Robin.

1921

The Unhappy Finish, aka Bert the Penman

Paramount Sennett; 2/20/1921.
Cast: Ford Sterling.

A Pyjama Marriage

Cosmograph Comedies, Special Pictures Corporation, 10/17/1921.
Cast: Neely Edwards, Charlotte Merriam, Ford Sterling.
Note: This film is a *probable* inclusion in the Sterling filmography but it is not certain.

A Seminary Scandal

Cosmograph Comedies, Special Pictures Corporation, 1921.
Cast: Neely Edwards, Charlotte Merriam, Ford Sterling.
Note: This film is a *probable* inclusion in the Sterling filmography but it is not certain.

A Ballroom Romeo

Cosmograph Comedies, Special Pictures Corporation, 1921. Director: Reggie Morris.
Cast: Ford Sterling.
Note: Sterling signed with Special Pictures Corporation on November 3, 1920. These ComiClassic Productions were to be released under the banner of Cosmograph Comedies.

1922

Oh, Mabel Behave

Paramount Sennett, 6/20/1922. Director: Mack Sennett; Scenario and Titles; Joseph Farnham.
Cast: Mack Sennett, Ford Sterling, Owen Moore, Mabel Normand, Alice Davenport, Bobby Dunn.

The Strangers' Banquet

Marshall Neilan Production; 12/31/1922; seven/eight reels. Director: Marshall Neilan; Scenario: Brian Oswald Donn-Byrne (novel), Marshall Neilan.
Cast: Hobart Bosworth, Claire Windsor, Rockliffe Fellowes, Ford Sterling, Eleanor Boardman, Thomas Holding, Eugenie Besserer, Nigel Barrie, Stuart Holmes, Claude Gillingwater, Margaret Loomis, Tom Guise, Lillian Langdon, William Humphrey, Edward McWade.
Note: The original version of this film ran eight reels, but the shortened version was condensed to seven reels.

Quincy Adams Sawyer

Paramount Sennett, 1922.
Cast: Ford Sterling.

1923

The Brass Bottle
Maurice Tourneur Productions; Associated First National Pictures, 1/2/1923; six reels. Director: Maurice Tourneur; Scenario: F. Anstey (novel), Fred Kennedy Myton.

Cast: Harry Myers, Ernest Torrence, Tully Marshall, Clarissa Selwynne, Ford Sterling, Aggie Herring, Charlotte Merriam, Edward Jobson, Barbara La Marr, Otis Harlan, Hazel Keener, Julanne Johnston.

Roaring Twenties version of the Aladdin story, involving an English architect who finds the bottle. The genie from the bottle promises to grant every wish asked of him in return for his freedom but the wishes backfire, causing too much trouble. The architect tricks the genie back into the bottle and throws it out to sea.

The Spoilers
Maurice Tourneur Productions, Goldwyn Distributing Company, 5/8/1923; eight reels. Director: Lambert Hillyer; Scenario: Rex Beach (novel/play), Elliott J. Clawson (adapt.).

Cast: Milton Sills, Anna Q. Nilsson, Barbara Bedford, Robert Edeson, Ford Sterling, Noah Beery, Mitchell Lewis, John Elliott, Robert McKim, Tom McGuire, Kate Price, Rockliffe Fellowes, J. Gordon Russell, Louise Fazenda, Tilly Nelson.

"Slapjack" Simms is the foreman of the Midas mine and his bosses, Roy Glenister and his partner, are victimized by a crooked politician and his friend Stillman, who are trying to gain control of gold mines in Alaska by jumping the owners' claims. Roy befriends Helen Chester, Stillman's niece, believing she is an accomplice. He saves Stillman from hanging; however, Helen becomes suspicious of her uncle and makes some investigations of her own.

Hollywood, aka Joligud
Marshal Neilan Productions, Goldwyn Distributors, 7/26/1923.

Cast: Ford Sterling.

Destroying Angel
Arthur F. Beck, Associated Distributors, 8/19/1923; six reels. Director: W.S. Van Dyke; Scenario: Leah Baird, Louis Joseph Vance (novel).

Cast: Leah Baird, John Bowers, Noah Beery, Ford Sterling, Mitchell Lewis.

Hugo Whittaker meets a pregnant young girl who has been deserted by her lover. Whittaker decides to marry her to save her from disgrace; however, he only has a few months to live. He travels to Europe, where he recovers his health. On his return to New York, he falls in love with an actress but fears that this is complicated by his marriage. She, though, recognizes him as her husband but before she can tell him that she is kidnapped. Hugo goes in search of her and when he finds her she tells him who she really is.

The Day of Faith
Goldwyn Pictures, Goldwyn-Cosmopolitan Distribution Corp., 10/21/1923; seven reels. Director: Tod Browning; Scenario: Katharine Kavanaugh (adapt.), June Mathis (adapt.).

Cast: Eleanor Boardman, Tyrone Power, Sr., Raymond Griffith, Wallace MacDonald, Ford Sterling, Heinie Conklin, Ruby Lafayette, Jane Mercer, Edward Martindel, Winter Hall, Emmett King, Jack Curtis, Frederick Vroom, John Curry, Henry Hebert, Samuel Jackson.

John Anstell, the son of a selfish millionaire, falls in love with Jane Maynard, who has opened a mission in memory of the philanthropist, Bland Hendricks. Naturally, John's father disapproves and does everything in his power to ruin Jane's attempts to run the mission. He hires a reporter to write a slanderous article on the mission but the reporter, after seeing what Jane is doing, volunteers to help her. To gain public favor, John's father pretends to support the mission but a mob bent on revenge for the millionaire's scurrilous past has beaten his son to death. The millionaire sees the errors of his ways, reforms, and joins Jane in her work.

Guardian Angel
1923.

Cast: Ford Sterling.

1924

Wild Oranges
Goldwyn Pictures Corporation, Goldwyn-Cosmopolitan Distribution Corporation: 1/20/1924; seven reels. Director: King Vidor; Scenario: Joseph Hergesheimer (novel) King Vidor (adapt.).

Cast: Virginia Valli, Frank Mayo, Ford Sterling, Nigel De Brulier, Charles A. Post.

The Galloping Fish
Thomas H. Ince Corp., Associated First National Pictures, 3/10/1924; six reels. Director: Del Andrews; Scenario: Will Lambert.

Cast: Louise Fazenda, Syd Chaplin, Ford Sterling, Chester Conklin, Lucille Ricksen, John Steppling, Lloyd Ingraham, Eugene Pallette, Truly Shattuck, Freddy the Seal.

Undine is a fancy diver in a vaudeville show and her most valuable possession is her partner in the diving act, Freddie, a trained seal. Undine owes somebody some money and that somebody gets out a court attachment on the seal. A sheriff armed with the attachment starts out to take possession of the seal. Freddy, a young man of wealth who is estranged from his bride, volunteers to foil the sheriff by smuggling the seal out of the theater. He gets it away by calling an ambulance and telling the young intern that the seal, now wrapped in a sheet, is a man suffering from acute appendicitis. Freddy takes Freddie to his hotel and then to his rich uncle's house, but unfortunately the house is swept away and floats down the river when a dam breaks. Freddie the seal goes, too, but is eventually found again by Freddy, who also rescues all the guests and becomes reconciled with his wife.

Note: Selected, Inc., Capitol, released a sound version in the United States in 1930.

The Woman on the Jury
Associated First National Pictures; Paramount Pictures, 4/20/1924, seven reels. Director: Harry O. Hoyt; Scenario: Bernard K. Burns (play) Mary O'Hara (adapt.).

Cast: Sylvia Breamer, Frank Mayo, Lew Cody, Bessie Love, Mary Carr, Hobart Bosworth, Myrtle Stedman, Henry B. Walthall, Roy Stewart, Jean Hersholt, Ford Sterling, Arthur Lubin, Stanton Heck, Fred Warren, Edwards Davis, Arthur S. Hull, Kewpie King, Leo White.

Grace Pierce is to be tried for murdering George Montgomery, and Betty and her husband have been selected to be on the jury. Betty, the only woman, is shocked when she hears the evidence; the man Grace shot was the same man who betrayed Betty before she was married to Fred. The events that led up to the murder so parallel Betty's experience that she has only sympathy for the girl and manages to persuade the jury to see things her way, thus letting Grace off. When her husband realizes the way his wife has sacrificed her principles in public to free Grace, he forgives her.

Note: This picture was released on 6/8/1925 in Finland.

Love and Glory
Universal Pictures, 7/12/1924, seven reels. Director: Rupert Julian; Scenario: Elliott J. Clawson, Rupert Julian, Robert Hobart Davis and Perley Poore Sheehan (story, "We Are the French").

Cast: Charles de Rochefort, Wallace MacDonald, Madge Bellamy, Ford Sterling, Gibson Gowland, Priscilla Moran, Charles De Ravenne, Andre Lancy, Madam De Bodamere, Christian J. Frank, Rolfe Sedan.

During the uprising in Algeria in 1869, two Frenchmen, Anatole and Pierre, join the army and are reportedly killed. Gabrielle, Anatole's sister and Pierre's girlfriend, is kidnapped and whisked off to Paris. The two men were not killed and return to France as heroes. They are recognized for their deeds fifty years later, but on the way to the medal ceremony Anatole dies. Pierre sees Gabrielle and is reunited with his lost love.

Note: The original working title of this film was *We Are the French*.

He Who Gets Slapped
MGM, 11/9/1924; seven reels. Director: Victor Sjöström; Scenario: Leonid Andreyev (play), Victor Sjöström (adapt.).

Cast: Lon Chaney, Norma Shearer, John

Gilbert, Harvey Clark, Clyde Cook, George Davis, Paulette Duval, Brandon Hurst, Ruth King, Tully Marshall, Marc McDermott, Ford Sterling, Edward Arnold, Holly Bane, Bartine Burkett, Carrie Daumey, Bela Lugosi (uncredited).

Paul Beaumont is an inventor who is betrayed by his wife and his patron who, by seducing Beaumont's wife, claimed his work as his own and made a fool out of Beaumont when he tried to present his invention to an audience of scientists. Beaumont decides to make a career out of what his wife and the patron have made of him. He changes his name to HE and becomes a clown whose act consists of getting slapped by all the other clowns, led by Tricaud, the head clown. HE falls in love with another circus performer, Consuelo, but those who betrayed him enter his life yet again.

Note: Universum Film A. G. (UFA) released a version of this film in Germany in 1925.

So Big

First National Pictures, Inc., 12/28/1924; nine reels. Director: Charles Brabin; Scenario: Edna Ferber (novel), Adelaide Heilbron, Earl Hudson (adapt.).

Cast: Colleen Moore, Joseph De Grasse, John Bowers, Ben Lyon, Wallace Beery, Gladys Brockwell, Jean Hersholt, Charlotte Merriam, Dot Farley, Ford Sterling, Frankie Darro, Henry Hebert, Dorothy Brock, Rosemary Theby, Phyllis Haver.

1925

The Great Divide

MGM, 3/15/1925; eight reels. Director: Reginald Barker; Scenario: Benjamin Glazer (adapt.), William Vaughn Moody (play).

Cast: Alice Terry, Conway Tearle, Wallace Beery, Huntley Gordon, Allan Forrest, George Cooper, ZaSu Pitts, William Orlamond, Ford Sterling.

Note: Universum Film A. G. (UFA) released this film in Germany in 1926.

My Lady's Lips

PB Schulberg Production, Preferred Pictures, July 1925; seven reels. Director: James P. Hogan; Scenario: John F. Goodrich (also story).

Cast: Alyce Mills, William Powell, Clara Bow, Frank Keenan, Matthew Betz, Gertrude Short, Ford Sterling, John Sainpolis.

Forbes Lombard, the newspaper editor, finds out his daughter Lola has been misbehaving with a gang of gamblers. His star reporter, Seddon, sees Lola's activities as a good way to get an exclusive story on the gang, so he poses as an ex-con and joins the gang too. The leader, Dora, is a beautiful woman and Seddon falls in love with her. When the police raid the gang's hideout he tries to help her escape. They get caught by the police and are brutally interrogated; Seddon signs a false confession, believing the promise Dora makes to go straight. On their release she reneges on the deal and returns to gambling, but when Seddon tells her he loves her and wants them to get married she turns her back on the gang and they go off to begin anew.

Daddy's Gone A-Hunting

Metro-Goldwyn Picture Corp., 8/3/1925; six reels. Director: Frank Borzage; Assistant Director: Bunny Dull; Scenario: Zoe Akins (play), Kenneth B. Clarke (adapt.).

Cast: Holmes Herbert, James O. Barrows, Edythe Chapman, Charles Crockett, Helena D'Algy, Alice Joyce, Percy Marmont, Virginia Marshall, Ford Sterling.

Julian discovers that being married and the father of a little girl don't mix with being an artist, and he has lost his gift for creativity. In the hope of regaining his inspiration he persuades his wife, Edith, to take a menial job to support him through art school in Paris. After a year there he returns a changed man; he is no longer in love with his wife and feels he needs to be among his fellow artists, so he moves the family to an artists' colony. His wife has a male friend who offers to marry her and Julian gives them his blessing. Now alone, he realizes what he has given up and expresses his loss in a painting he names *Realization*. The public acclaim the painting to be a masterpiece. Not all is well with Edith, her new husband, and Julian's daughter Janet. Janet is involved in an accident that subsequently ends her short life; Julian is only just in time to be with her when she dies. The tragedy brings Edith and Julian back together.

The Trouble with Wives

Famous Players–Lasky Corp. Paramount Pictures, 8/28/1925; seven reels. Director: Malcolm St. Clair; Scenario: Sada Cowan, Howard Higgin.

Cast: Florence Vidor, Tom Moore, Esther Ralston, Ford Sterling, Lucy Beaumont, Edward Kennedy, Etta Lee, William Courtright.

Grace and William Hyatt own an exclusive bootery. The Hyatts are content in their marriage until Al Hennessey inadvertently tells Grace that Will has been seen dining with pretty Parisian designer Dagmar. Will sorts the problem out with Grace just fine until Hennessey tells Grace that he and Will have been visiting Dagmar in her apartment. This was a business trip, but Grace believes Will has been unfaithful so, in return, goes about making his life hell. Will eventually beats a retreat to a summer hotel and Grace follows him. Surprise! Dagmar is there too, but this time it is fine with Grace because Dagmar is there to marry Hennessey. Equilibrium returns once again to the Moore household.

Steppin' Out

Columbia Picture Corporation, 10/15/1925; six reels. Director: Frank R. Strayer; Scenario: Bernard Vorhaus.

Cast: Dorothy Revier, Ford Sterling, Robert Agnew, Cissy Fitzgerald, Ethel Wales, Tom Ricketts, Harry Lorraine.

Stage Struck

Famous Players–Lasky Corp., Paramount Pictures, 11/16/1925; seven reels. Director: Allan Dwan; Scenario: Frank R. Adams (story), Forrest Halsey.

Cast: Gloria Swanson, Lawrence Gray, Gertrude Astor, Oliver Sandys, Ford Sterling, Carrie Scott, Emil Hoch, Margery Whittington.

Jennie Hagen is a stage-struck waitress in a diner who is in love with the cook, Orme. He naturally has a weakness for something else: actresses. When a showboat arrives, the *Water Queen*, run by Waldo Buck, Orme pays the show a visit and falls in love with the leading lady, Lillian Lyons. Jennie, not wanting to be outdone, takes a correspondence course in acting to try to win him back. Buck, who has taken a liking to the girl, gives her a chance by letting her have a spot in the show, billing her as "The Masked Marvel" in a boxing fight with Lillian. It does not have the results Jennie had anticipated. Orme is horrified by the exhibition and in despair Jennie jumps overboard. Orme heroically dives in to save her and all works out well. They reconcile and later open a diner of their own.

Note: This picture was filmed in two-strip Technicolor.

1926

The American Venus

Famous Players–Lasky, Paramount, 1/31/1926; eight reels. Director: Frank Tuttle; Scenario: Townsend Martin, Frederick Stowers.

Cast: Frederick Stowers, Esther Ralston, Lawrence Gray, Ford Sterling, Fay Lanphier, Louise Brooks, Edna May Oliver, Kenneth MacKenna, William B. Mack, George De Carlton, W.T. Benda, Ernest Torrence, Douglas Fairbanks, Jr.

There are two rival beauty cream factories out West, and the son of one proprietor is engaged to marry the daughter of the other. A publicity man enters the daughter in "The American Venus" beauty competition. The plan was to have her endorse a cold cream if she wins and sell millions of jars, putting the other man out of business. The girl is told that her father is ill (which he is not) and she is called back home. She finds out the truth and returns to Atlantic City a second time but arrives too late for the final. Her friend, "Miss Alabama," wins. The winner endorses her father's cold cream anyway.

The Road to Glory

Fox Film Corp., 2/7/1926; six reels. Director: Howard Hawks; Scenario: Howard Hawks (story), Gordon Rigby.

Cast: May McAvoy, Leslie Fenton, Ford Sterling, Rockliffe Fellowes, Milla Davenport, John MacSweeney, Carole Lombard, Hank the Dog.

Judith Allen is gradually going blind after the car accident that killed her father. Bitter about what has happened to her, she renounces God, turns away from her boyfriend, and goes to live alone in a cabin in the mountains. David Hale, her ex-fiancé, is still in love with her and follows her to the mountains. While he is on the way to the cabin he is caught in a storm and badly injured by a falling tree. When Judith finds out, she rushes to his bedside and, returning to God, prays for his survival. Her newly regained faith not only gets her prayers answered, she also regains her sight.

Miss Brewster's Millions

Famous Players–Lasky Corp., Paramount, 3/22/1926; seven reels. Director: Clarence G. Badger; Scenario: Monte Brice (adapt.), Lloyd Corrigan, Harold Schumate.

Cast: Bebe Daniels, Warner Baxter, Ford Sterling, Andre de Beranger, Miss Beresford.

Polly Brewster has about as much money as the other Hollywood extras she works with, if not less, that is until she inherits a million dollars. There is a catch though: her lawyer tells her that a stipulation in the will states she has to invest the money and cannot spend it. Uncle Ned Brewster, on hearing the news, goes to visit Polly with a proposition. He never liked his brother, Polly's father, because of the indignities he made him suffer so, to get his own back, he offers to give Polly five million dollars if she can spend the inherited million in thirty days. She falls for it and invests some, has a ball with a fashion show, and runs over a man so that he can sue her; this soon disposes of the million dollars. Now she finds out Uncle Ned is in fact penniless and isn't about to give her five million anything. Fortunately a movie company she had invested in proves to have been a sound investment and compensates for Uncle Ned's tricks.

Mike

MGM, April 1926; seven reels. Director: Marshall Neilan; Scenario: Marion Jackson, Marshall Neilan (story).

Cast: Sally O'Neil, William Haines, Charles Murray, Ned Sparks, Ford Sterling, Frankie Darro, Frank Coghlan, Jr., Muriel Frances, Sam De Grasse.

Note: Universum Film A. G. (UFA) released this film in Germany in September 1926.

The Show Off

Famous Players–Lasky Corp., Paramount, 8/16/1926; seven reels. Director: Malcolm St. Clair; Scenario: Pierre Collings, George Kelly (play).

Cast: Ford Sterling, Lois Wilson, Louise Brooks, Gregory Kelly, Claire McDowell, Charles (C. W.) Goodrich, Joseph W. Smiley.

Aubrey Piper is a big show-off who boasts of his importance in business. He has purchased a ticket for a raffle, for which the grand prize is a new car. Aubrey proposes to his girlfriend, Amy Fisher, who is completely taken by his business acumen and his demeanor; her family, however, sees right through him. Amy's brother, Joe, is involved with Clara, the girl next door, and she tells the Fisher family that Aubrey is really only a clerk. Joe is an inventor, trying to peddle his new rust-proof paint to a corporation, but he has no money to finance this venture. Joe finally does get the money from his father, money needed to pay the house mortgage. Meanwhile, Amy and Aubrey have wed and are living in rather destitute means; they eventually have to move back with her family, who is grieving from the death of Amy's father. Aubrey has won the car in the raffle but he tells his wife that he inherited money from his uncle and used it to purchase the auto. However, he has no end of trouble with the new car and promptly wrecks it on the

Note: This picture features two-strip Technicolor scenes, and was released by Universum Film A. G. (UFA) in Germany in 1926.

way home. He tells his wife that, swerving to avoid hitting a child, he crashed and totaled the new car. Amy believes him but the police know better. His case comes to court and he is about to go to jail, when Amy's brother Joe pays his $1,000 fine (with the money for his invention). Now the family is in a pretty financial pickle. Aubrey sees the light and uses his powers of gab to sell Joe's invention, making back the money and becoming a hero in the process.

Note: Instead of the studio employing a double, Sterling did his own driving for the automotive scenes. In addition, Sterling used his given name, George Stitch, for the name of his uncle.

Everybody's Acting

Famous Players–Lasky Corp., Paramount, 11/8/1926; seven reels. Director: Marshall Neilan; Scenario: Benjamin Glazer, George Marion, Jr. (titles).

Cast: Betty Bronson, Ford Sterling, Louise Dresser, Lawrence Gray, Henry B. Walthall, Raymond Hitchcock, Stuart Holmes, Edward Martindel, Philo McCullough, Jed Prouty, Jocelyn Lee.

Young Doris Poole is left orphaned when her father is charged with the murder of her mother and is subsequently executed. They were members of a traveling show, and the little girl is adopted by four members of the company and a newspaper reporter, who decide to settle in the San Francisco Bay area. The girl, now the ingénue of a local stock company, meets and falls in love with a taxi-cab driver; the complication is that he is not who he pretends to be. In reality he is the son of a wealthy domineering businesswoman and is driving a cab as research for a novel he is writing. His mother naturally disapproves of such a match for her son but the five surrogate fathers get around this by persuading the boy to take a job his mother has offered him in China and secretly booking passage for the girl, too. The boy's mother, knowing love has won out, gives them her blessings.

Stranded in Paris

Famous Players–Lasky Corp., Paramount, 12/13/1926; seven reels. Director: Arthur Rosson; Scenario: Hans Backwitz (play), Ethel Doherty.

Cast: Bebe Daniels, James Hall, Ford Sterling, Iris Stuart, Mabel Julienne, Tom Ricketts, Helen Dunbar, Ida Darling, George Grandee, André Lanoy.

Good and Naughty

Famous Players–Lasky Corp., Paramount, 1926; seven reels. Director: Malcolm St. Clair; Scenario: Pierre Collings, Henry Falk (play).

Cast: Pola Negri, Tom Moore, Ford Sterling, Miss DuPont, Stuart Holmes, Marie Mosquini, Warner P. Richmond.

Mike, a girl, lives in a converted railroad boxcar with her father, the railroad section boss, and three younger siblings. One of the siblings gets into trouble and Harlan, a section hand, saves the child's life. Mike is grateful and spends some time with Harlan, who confides in her that he was once a telegrapher but when he allowed the Transcontinental Limited to go through an open switch he was fired by the railroad. He invites her to the village dance, where Mike overhears Slinky and his gang discussing their plans to rob the mail train. They catch her and lock her in a boxcar, which they send off down the tracks. Harlan, seeing what has happened, goes after the boxcar and rescues her; he then telegraphs the nearest government agency, which more or less sends out the cavalry. It is actually a flight of marine aviators who, with the aid of their bombs, foil Slinky and his gang's plans and capture them. In thanks, the railroad reinstates Harlan and he marries Mike.

1927

Casey at the Bat

Famous Players–Lasky Corp., Paramount, 3/8/1927; six reels. Director: Monte Brice; Scenario: Monte Brice, Reggie Morris (adapt.), Grant Clarke, Sam Kellerman (titles), Ernest Lawrence Thayer (poem), Hector Turnball (story).

Cast: Wallace Beery, Ford Sterling, ZaSu Pitts, Sterling Holloway, Spec O'Donnell, Iris Stuart, Sydney Jarvis, Lotus Thompson, Anne Sheridan, Doris Hill, Sally Blane, Robert Livingstone.

In turn-of-the-century Centerville, Casey, the local junk dealer, is the hardest hitting batsman in the village baseball club. But he has competition on another front. Putnam, the town barber, is a very persistent suitor of Camille, whom Casey is also in love with. O'Dowd is supposedly a big-league scout who arrives in town and sees a way to get Casey out of the picture, allowing himself to be Camille's only suitor. Putnam encourages O'Dowd to sign Casey with the New York Giants, which he does and then subsequently leaves town. Once the party arrives in New York they do just that, party, but this is all part of Putnam's plans. He foots the bill for Casey's enthusiasm to buy people drinks, which makes Casey very popular; he also sets Casey up with Trixie, who is with the Florida Sextette. The disreputable bunch make their way to Coney Island, where they meet up with Camille and Spec. Camille forgives Casey, and Spec convinces Casey he has been hoaxed. At the game, Casey comes to bat, but to spoil his game O'Dowd throws the pitcher a trick ball to pitch at Casey, which causes him to strike out. After some investigation, the truth comes to light and Casey is exonerated.

Drums of the Desert

Paramount Famous–Lasky Corp., Paramount, 6/4/1927; six reels. Director: John Waters; Scenario: Zane Grey (novel), John Stone.

Cast: Warner Baxter, Marietta Millner, Ford Sterling, Wallace MacDonald, Heinie Conklin, George Irving, Bernard Siegel, Guy Oliver.

When oil is discovered on a Navajo reservation, a group of white men under a leader named Will Newton tries to force them off the land so they can steal their oil rights. Meanwhile, a traveling charlatan named Perkins is hired as a guide for a party of explorers in the desert. Various escapades bring the explorer party, Newton's gang, and the Indians all into conflict with one another, but the U.S. cavalry arrives in time to save the day.

The Trunk Mystery

Pathé Exchange; 6/12/1927. Director: Frank Hall Crane; Scenario: Frederick Chapin, Forrest Sheldon (story).

Cast: Charles Hutchison, Alice Calhoun, Richard Neill, Ben Walker, Ford Sterling, Otto Lederer, Charles W. Mack.

Mysteriously, shortly after buying a trunk of unclaimed stolen and lost property, a retired secret service agent, Jim Manning, has his house broken into twice. There were three perpetrators, two men, Fawcett and Turner, and a woman, Margaret Hampton. Margaret explains to Manning why she tried to rob him. Her father had been employed by a jewel merchant who had accused her father of steeling a valuable necklace; he was arrested and put in prison. She suspects it was Fawcett and Turner who were the real thieves. Manning, convinced she is right, offers to help her. He catches them and their boss, who is none other than Olaff Stevanov, the jeweler who had employed Margaret's father. Manning produces the necklace, which he had taken out of the trunk before the robberies.

For the Love of Mike

Robert Kane Productions, First National Pictures, Inc., 7/31/1927; seven reels. Director: Frank Capra; Scenario: J. Clarkson Miller, John A. Moroso (story).

Cast: Claudette Colbert, Ben Lyon, George Sidney, Ford Sterling, Hugh Cameron, Richard "Skeets" Gallagher, Rudolph Cameron, Mabel Swor.

Three unlikely candidates, German delicatessen owner Herman Schultz, Irish street cleaner Patrick O'Malley, and Jewish tailor Abraham Katz, find an abandoned baby on the landing of a tenement building in New York's Hell's Kitchen. The three men have all sorts of plans for the baby they name Mike. Unlike them, he will go to high school and college. But Mike doesn't want the men to have to support him through college and, even though he has been accepted at Yale, he wants to stay home and help support the three men. Their Italian neighbor, Mary, who works for Herman as his cashier, joins with the men to persuade Mike to go to college. Mike ends up going to Yale as planned, and for his twenty-first birthday the men plan a lavish banquet for him. He has been doing very well at college, and they invite many notables who could be useful to Mike when he tries to get a job. Unfortunately, on the way to the party Mike meets up with Evelyn Joyce and she lures him to a cocktail party where he gets drunk. He arrives at his banquet much the worse for wear and promptly insults the guests, who leave in disgust. Mike turns against the three men and during a row Patrick knocks him out. Back at college, Mike gets into more trouble, this time gambling. He is not good at it and becomes indebted to a crooked gambler, Henry Sharp. Sharp uses his hold over Mike to try to blackmail him for writing bad checks and insists that Mike lose the upcoming Yale–Harvard crew race. Mike is the captain of the varsity crew and knows if the truth comes out about his debts he will be expelled from Yale. The three men and Mary come to watch the race and when Mike sees them, he goes all out to win and he and his crew do win. Sharp then threatens the three men, telling them he is going to send Mike to jail for his misdemeanors. They just push Sharp overboard and Mike, reconciled, rows the family home.

Figures Don't Lie

Paramount Famous–Lasky Corp., Paramount, 10/8/1927; six reels. Director: Edward Sutherland; Scenario: Ethel Doherty, Grover Jones (adapt.), Louise Long, B. F. Zeidman, Herman Mankiewicz (titles).

Cast: Esther Ralston, Richard Arlen, Ford Sterling, Doris Hill, Blanche Payson, Natalie Kingston.

"Howdy" Jones's secretary is beautiful and an efficient worker who spends her day at the beck and call of Mr. Jones. Unfortunately, Janet's work is disrupted at the office by the behavior of Jones's violently jealous wife. Soon Janet's mind is taken off the problem by the attentions of the new sales manager, Bob Blewe, although she considers him to be a bit too fresh. When she refuses his invitation to the office picnic by the sea, he takes Dolores, the office's stenographer, instead. Janet demonstrates she can be jealous, too, and to get back at Bob she plays up to Mr. Jones at the picnic. Janet goes for a swim and when she gets tangled up in seaweed she is rescued by Bob. Later, the enraged Mrs. Jones finds Janet and her husband in a somewhat compromising situation and decides the only solution is to shoot Janet. Bob fortunately thwarts her plan.

Hearts and Flowers

Cast: Ford Sterling.

Note: This film is probably different from the 1919 short of the same title, which Sterling also appeared in, but it could be a rerelease.

1928

Wife Savers

Famous Players–Lasky Corp., Paramount, 1/7/1928; six reels. Codirectors: Malcolm St. Clair, Ralph Ceder; Scenario: Thomas J. Geraghty, Grover Jones.

Cast: Wallace Beery, Raymond Hatton, ZaSu Pitts, Sally Blane, Tom Kennedy, Ford Sterling, George Y. Harvey, August Tollaire.

After World War I, two American soldiers, Louis Hozenozzel and Rodney Ramsbottom, have been left stationed in Switzerland. Ramsbottom has fallen in love with a local girl and when he is ordered back the America he puts Hozenozzel in charge of looking after her. A Swiss general is also in love with the girl but she is not interested. In revenge, he issues an order that all single girls must get married, believing the girl will now marry him. She doesn't: she marries Hozenozzel instead. The general, angered, writes to Ramsbottom to tell him he has been double-crossed by his friend. Ramsbottom returns to Switzerland to confront his friend in a duel of honor. The girl tells Ramsbottom why she was forced to marry Hozenozzel and the friends are back on good terms. The local mayor grants her a divorce when he knows the situation. She doesn't marry Ramsbottom, but a good-looking young major instead.

Note: This film was released in Finland on 4/29/1928.

Gentlemen Prefer Blondes

Famous Players–Lasky Corp., Paramount, 1/22/1928. Director: Malcolm St. Clair; Scenario: John Emerson Anita Loos (novel and titles).

Cast: Ruth Taylor, Alice White, Ford Sterling, Holmes Herbert, Mack Swain, Emily Fitzroy, Trixie Friganza, Blanche Frederici, Edward Faust, Eugene Borden, Margaret Seddon, Luke Cosgrave, Chester Conklin, Yorke Sherwood, Mildred Boyd.

A wealthy button king and his fellow transatlantic traveler, Gus Eisman, find themselves onboard ship with two girls, gold digger Lorelei Lee and her friend Dorothy Shaw. They are on the trip to try to capture one of America's richest bachelors, Henry Spoffard, who is traveling to Paris to investigate reports of immoral activities of American tourists in Paris. The girls don't have any money for tickets, especially not for ones in first class, where they'll need to be in order to snare their catch. This is solved by Lorelei, who purloins money from Gus Eisman to finance their trip.

That's My Daddy

Universal Picture Corp., 2/5/1928, six reels, Director: Fred C. Newmeyer; Scenario: Pierre Couderc (adapt.), Albert DeMond.

Cast: Reginald Denny, Barbara Kent, Lillian Rich, Tom O'Brien, Jane La Verne, Mathilde Brundage, Wilson Benge, Ford Sterling.

Sporting Goods

Paramount Famous–Lasky Corp., Paramount, 2/11/1928; seven reels. Director: Malcolm St. Clair; Scenario: Thomas J. Crizer (also story), Ray Harris (also story).

Cast: Richard Dix, Ford Sterling, Gertrude Olmstead, Philip Strange, Myrtle Stedman, Wade Boteler, Claude King, Maude Turner Gordon.

A young socialite, Alice Elliott, thinks that a traveling sporting goods salesman (and the inventor of a new type of golf suit), Richard Shelby, is millionaire Timothy Stanfield. Shelby falls in love with Alice and so as not to disillusion her allows himself to be installed in an expensive California hotel. Realizing he is going to need to be able to produce at least some cash, Shelby comes up with a get-rich-quick brain wave. He persuades Jordan, who is the head of a department store and a keen golfer, to wear his golf suit made of "elasto-tweed" on the golf course. Shelby hopes that Jordan will think the suit so wonderful that he will buy a great quantity of them. At first Jordan is suitably impressed so to speak, but then it begins to rain. The rain soaks the elasto-tweed suit and it gradually stretches to the ground. Jordan, no longer impressed, cancels his order, leaving Shelby with no cash and an exorbitant hotel bill. Later, as Jordan returns to the hotel, Shelby is caught trying to sneak out. Jordan has a reason for returning and seeking out Shelby; he has heard that these golf suits are all the rage in the East and doubles his order. Stanfield, who owns the company that manufactures the suits, promotes Shelby to sales manager. This gives Shelby enough income to marry Alice Elliott.

Chicken a La King

Fox Film Corp., 6/9/1928; seven reels. Director: Henry Lehrman; Assistant Director: Virgil Hart; Scenario: Izola Forrester, Harry Wagstaff Gribble (play).

Cast: Nancy Carroll, George Meeker, Arthur Stone, Ford Sterling, Frances Lee, Carol Holloway.

A prosperous businessman tires of his drab wife and becomes involved with two gold-digging chorus girls. The wife decides to smarten up to win back her husband. After spending a large amount of her husband's money on clothes and beauty treatments, she gets her wish and gets back her husband.

Note: Stage play and working title *Mr. Romeo*.

Oh Kay!

First National Pictures, Inc., 8/26/1928; six reels. Director: Mervyn LeRoy; Scenario:

Guy Bolton (play), Elsie Janis (adapt.), P. G. Wodehouse (titles).

Cast: Colleen Moore, Lawrence Gray, Alan Hale, Ford Sterling, Claude Gillingwater, Julanne Johnston, Claude King, Edgar Norton, Percy Williams, Fred O'Beck.

Lady Kay Rutfield is not particularly enthusiastic about marrying wimpy Lord Braggot, so on the day before her nuptials she goes for a sail in her small boat. She is swept out to sea when a storm blows up but is rescued by rumrunners. When the gang drop anchor in New York Sound, Kay escapes and hides in a deserted mansion. Unbeknownst to her, the mansion belongs to wealthy Jimmy Winter who is on his way there. He is about to get married. A detective has followed Kay to the mansion, believing she is a member of a gang; when Jimmy arrives, she manages to persuade him to pretend she is his wife so as to throw the detective off her tracks. One of the bootleggers has hidden a barrel of rum in the cellar. Vowing to guard it until he can make his escape, he pretends to be the butler. Neither Jimmy nor Kay marry their intended ones, they decide to marry each other instead.

1929

The Fall of Eve

Columbia Pictures Corp., 6/17/1929; eight reels. Director: Frank R. Strayer; Scenario: John Emerson (story), Fanny Hatton (dialogue).

Cast: Patsy Ruth Miller (Eve Grant), Ford Sterling (Mr. Mack), Gertrude Astor (Mrs. Ford), Arthur Rankin (Tom Ford, Jr.), Jed Prouty (Tom Ford, Sr.), Betty Farrington (Mrs. Mack), Fred Kelsey (cop), Hank Mann, Bob White (bit parts).

Tom Ford, Jr., has a secret: he and his father's secretary, Eve Grant, are in love. When an out-of-town buyer, Mr. Mack, arrives with his wife, Ford, Sr., enlists Eve's help. It just so happens that Mrs. Ford is away on vacation at the moment so he has to entertain them. When Mack's wife insists on joining the nightclub party, Eve is introduced as Mrs. Ford. A radio broadcast from the nightclub alerts the vacationing Mrs. Ford that something is amiss when she hears that a certain dance tune has been requested by Mr. and Mrs. Tom Ford. Ford calls his son to help extricate him from his difficulties with the boorish couple. Ford, Jr., agrees to come if Ford, Sr., will consent to his marriage. The party returns to the Ford home. The intoxicated Mr. Mack and his corpulent wife, having decided to stay the night, are about to go to bed when Mrs. Ford returns and calls the police, having seen an unfamiliar figure raiding her icebox. Ford, Jr., explains the situation to everyone's satisfaction and introduces Eve as his bride.

Note: Two versions of this film were produced, one silent (running 1,903 meters, or 6,243 feet), and one Movietone sound (2,072 meters, or 6,798 feet).

The Girl in the Show

MGM, 8/31/1929, nine reels. MovieTone sound. Director: Edgar Selwyn; Scenario: Joseph Farnham (titles), John Golden (play).

Cast: Bessie Love, Raymond Hackett, Edward J. Nugent, Mary Doran, Jed Prouty, Ford Sterling, Nanci Price, Lucy Beaumont, Richard Carlyle, Alice Moe, Frank Nelson, Jack McDonald, Ethel Wales, John F. Morrissey.

A tale about a touring company doing *Uncle Tom's Cabin* finding itself in trouble after its manager walks out. Love decides to settle with Prouty, who offers marriage and to take care of her little sister. Hackett organizes an impromptu show and stops the marriage. Love and Hackett fall for each other. After some confusion Love becomes star of the show.

Note: This was director Edgar Selwyn's first feature. His name served as the "wyn" in Goldwyn when the company was founded in 1916.

Fatal Forceps

Christie Film Corp., Paramount, 11/2/1929; two reels. Director: William Watson; Scenario: C.L.V. Duffy.

Cast: Ford Sterling, Bert Roach, Will King, Natalie Joyce.

Sally

First National; 12/23/1929; Twelve reels; Vitaphone.

Director: John Francis Dillon. Scenario: Guy Bolton (play), P.G. Wodehouse (play), Waldemar Young (adapt. Dialogue).

Cast: Marilyn Miller, Alexander Gray, Joe E. Brown, T. Roy Barnes, Pert Kelton, Ford Sterling, Maude Turner, Gordon E.J. Ratcliffe, Jack Duffy, Ethel Stone, Nora Lane, Adrienne Ames, Anita Garvin.

Sally is an orphan whose name was derived from the telephone exchange where she was abandoned as a baby. Despite her troubles, she finds refuge in dancing. The only work she was qualified to do was as a waitress and she is delighted when she finds a job which allows her to combine her waitressing with dancing. She meets Blair Farrell and they fall for each other, but she does not know that Farrell is engaged to Marcia. Sally is hired to impersonate a famous Russian dancer named Noskerova. However, at that engagement her true identity is revealed and she also finds out that Farrell is engaged to marry another. She pushes ahead, headlining with the Ziegfeld Follies, and eventually does win the heart of Blair Farrell.

Note: *Sally* featured some of the largest sets built at that time, as external scenes needed to be shot inside to control sound and lighting for colors. Two-strip Technicolor scenes were featured in the dance sequences and it was decided to use dancers who were redheads, as they apparently photographed better. The picture was also released in Germany in 1930.

1930

Spring Is Here

First National Pictures, Inc., 4/13/1930, seven reels. Codirectors: Edgar Selwyn, John Francis Dillon; Scenario: Owen Davis (play), James A. Starr (adapt.).

Cast: Lawrence Gray, Alexander Gray, Bernice Claire, Ford Sterling, Louise Fazenda, Inez Courtney, Natalie Moorhead, Frank Albertson, Gretchen Thomas, Bobbe Brox, Lorraine Brox, Kathlyn Brox.

Showgirl in Hollywood

First National Pictures, Inc., 4/20/1930; nine reels; Vitaphone with Color sequences. Director: Mervyn LeRoy; Scenario: J.P. McEvoy (novel), Harvey F. Thew (adapt.).

Cast: Alice White, Jack Mulhall, Blanche Sweet, Ford Sterling, John Miljan, Syd Saylor, Spec O'Donnell, Virginia Sale, Lee Shumway, Herman Bing, Walter Pidgeon, Noah Beery, Noah Beery, Jr., Maurice Black, Billy Bletcher, Lew Harvey, Al Jolson, Ruby Keeler, Loretta Young (guests).

White plays a New York nightclub star whisked to Hollywood by a producer (Sterling) in this parody of filmmaking. It is an interesting and accurate behind-the-scenes account of how silent films were made. Silent star Blanche Sweet plays a fading actress who sings "There's a Tear for Every Smile in Hollywood."

Bride of the Regiment, aka Lady of the Rose

First National Pictures, Inc., 5/21/1930; twelve reels. Director: John Francis Dillon; Scenario: Ray Harris Humphrey Pearson.

Cast: Vivienne Segal, Allan Prior, Walter Pidgeon, Louise Fazenda, Myrna Loy, Lupino Lane, Ford Sterling, Harry Cording, Claude Fleming, Herbert Clark.

Note: Reviewed as an "unremarkable musical comedy featuring Segal as the wife of a proud Italian count fighting off Austrian invading army."

Kismet

First National Pictures Inc., Warner Bros., 10/30/1930; ten reels. Director: John Francis Dillon; Scenario: Howard Estabrook Edward Knoblock (play).

Cast: Otis Skinner, Loretta Young, David Manners, Sidney Blackmer, Mary Duncan, Montagu Love, Ford Sterling, Theodore von Eltz, John St. Polis, Edmund Breese, Blanche Frederici, Richard Carlyle, John Sheehan, Otto Hoffman.

Note: The film was shot in Warner Brothers' Vitascope on 65mm stock to give a widescreen image; it had to be reduced to the standard 35mm for showing in general theaters that were not equipped with the larger format projectors.

Our Nagging Wives

Christie Film Corp., Gayety Comedies; Educational Film Exchange, 11/9/1930. Director: Arvid E. Gillstrom; Scenario: Harry McCoy, Jimmy Starr.

Cast: Ford Sterling, Eleanor Hunt.

1931

Come to Papa

Gayety Comedy, Al Christie Production, Educational Film Exchange, 2/2/1931; two reels. Director: William Watson; Scenario: George Bentley, Leon Barry (dialogue).

Cast: Ford Sterling.

Stars of Yesterday

Warner Brothers, Vitaphone, 3/19/1931; one reel.

Cast: Ford Sterling, Betty Blythe.

Note: This documentary short may have been made up from stock footage that Warner Bros had acquired in one of their buyouts.

Twenty Horses

Al Christie Comedy, Paramount, 4/28/1931; two reels. Director: Albert Ray; Scenario: Nunnally Johnson.

Cast: Ford Sterling, Jed Prouty, Aileen Cook.

Foolish Forties

Al Christie Production, Gayety Comedies, Educational Film Exchange, 6/6/1931; two reels. Director: William Watson.

Cast: Ford Sterling, June MacCloy, Stella Adams, Eddie Baker, Billy Engle, Lyle Tayo.

Mr. Adolph Krause, ladies' tailor, is much perturbed. One of his salesmen has gotten himself involved with a blonde and the scandal has brought a lot of unwanted publicity to Krause's business house. He expresses himself strongly on the subject of blondes, on husbands who chase them around, and the fact that when Googlemeyer bought expensive gowns for his fair flame he didn't buy them from Krause. Mrs. Krause knows that her husband would never do a thing like that. Still, she sees him speaking to a pretty blonde in the store and decides it might pay to be careful. She tries to call her husband away before any harm can come. But she is a little too late. The blonde has already asked the tailor to come to her apartment that evening to bring her a selection of gowns for her inspection. Adolph shows up at the apartment dressed in his very best attire. The blonde seems in no hurry to examine the gowns and suggests they have a little refreshment before settling down to the business of the evening. When Adolph says he doesn't drink, the blonde assures him it is nothing but apple cider. It may be only apple cider but it has an awful effect on the tailor. He is soon chasing butterflies all over the apartment and finally passes out in a blaze of glory. The plot thickens when the blonde's husband appears on the scene. The two of them hoist the unconscious Adolph into bed, but not before photographing him in a very compromising pose. They strip dates from the calendar and when Adolph awakes he is told he has been in the apartment for a week. As if that were not enough, Adolph is informed that he is going to marry the girl. As Mrs. Krause is still very much alive, Adolph knows he is in a bad hole. When he tells the couple he can't marry the girl, the supposed brother-to-be pulls a gun and threatens Krause. The blonde finally says she will have to go away to hide her shame but that she hasn't any money. Adolph, anxious to get her out of the way, gives her a check for $10,000, enough to get her far, far away. In the meantime, Mrs. Krause, alarmed at her husband's overnight absence, calls the police. At the station house she recognizes a picture of the blonde and is told she is Mrs. Montaine who, with her husband, comprised a formidable blackmail team. The detectives go to the bank and trail the pair of blackmailers to their apartment, arresting them just as they are leaving for parts unknown. Mrs. Krause finds Adolph in the apartment but he manages to think up a convincing explanation for his dereliction and everything is forgiven.

Trouble from Abroad

RKO, 8/22/1931; two reels. Director: Mark Sandrich; Scenario: Johnnie Grey, Lloyd French, Mark Sandrich.

Cast: Ford Sterling, Lucien Littlefield, James Finlayson, Cecil Cunningham, Ruth Renick, Renee Damonde.

Sgt. Joe Widgett and Captain Bill Wimble are two friends and army buddies who had fought together in France during World War I in Company A of the White Mule Division. They are staying at the Embassy Club Hotel with their wives for their company's first reunion. Their wives attend a bridge party also being held in the hotel. Bill and Joe reveal secretive tattoos to each other. Both got them in France and both tattoos are similar, reading "Fifi." Bill had told his wife it was a war wound; Joe told his wife that the tattoo represented the "Fi Fi" fraternity that Company A had started in France. Both men, however, are aghast to realize that their tattoos each honor the same woman! Meanwhile, the wives listen in on their husbands' banquet, which is being broadcast on the radio. Bill is introduced as the heartiest love in the Company. His wife is horrified! Later, when Bill recognizes Joe as the *real* company Casanova, *his* wife's angst can be imagined. Both men are in for a surprise, as their Fifi is the special guest who will serenade the troops. The two men spend the better part of the rest of the evening trying to hide Fifi from their wives, with very humorous results.

It Ought to Be a Crime

Al Christie Comedy, Paramount, 9/17/1931; two reels. Director: Albert Ray; Scenario: Nunnally Johnson.

Cast: Ford Sterling.

Her Majesty Love

First National Picture Corp., Warner Brothers, 12/15/1931; eight reels. Director: William Dieterle; Scenario: R. Berbrauer (story), Arthur Caesar.

Cast: Marilyn Miller, Ben Lyon, W.C. Fields, Leon Errol, Ford Sterling, Chester Conklin.

Auto Intoxication

Al Christie Comedy, Paramount, 1931. Director: Albert Ray.

Cast: Ford Sterling, Lucia Bacus Seger, Frank Allworth, Bert Gardner, Herschel Mayal, Ed Gargan, Walter Eilson, Anitra Frazen, Aileen Cook, Edward Keen.

Otto Krausmeyer tells his tale, in flashback, of his numerous adventures with a certain Celebrity 8 automobile, thanks to the wily efforts of "Smiling Sam, The Sales Man."

Walking the Dog

Al Christie Comedy, Paramount, 1931.
Cast: Ford Sterling, Francetta Malloy.

Screen Snapshots

Series 9, Number 10; 1931.

Cast: Ford Sterling, Louise Fazenda, Buster West, Glenn Tryon, John Dillon, Eddie Cline, Frank Fay.

Note: In this variety short, the stars are seen without a sound track.

1932

Pretty Puppies

Educational Film Exchange, 1932.
Cast: Ford Sterling.

Stout Hearts and Willing Hands

RKO Radio Pictures, Inc., Masquers Club of Hollywood, 1932; two reels; Director: Bryan Foy.

Cast: Ford Sterling, Mary Carr, Lew Cody, Chester Conklin, Clyde Cook, Frank Fay, James Finlayson, Alec B. Francis, Laura La Plante, Hank Mann, Matt Moore, Owen Moore, Tom Moore, Eddie Quillan, Mack Swain, Bobby Vernon, D. Bryan Foy.

Note: This film won the Academy Award for Best Short Subject Comedy in 1933.

1933

The Fisherman

Flamingo Film Company, July 1933. Director: Marshall Neilan.

Cast: Buster Keaton, Ford Sterling.

Note: Only a small amount of footage was shot for this film before it was abandoned. It was to be filmed at the Kennedy Studios, Weedon's Island, St. Petersburg, Florida, and in New York.

The Tomcat

July 1933. Director: Ford Sterling.

Note: Sterling was flown out to make this short for Aubrey M. Kennedy at the Kennedy Studios, Weedon's Island, St. Petersburg, Florida, but after funds ran out the project was dropped.

Playthings of Desire

Kennedy Studios, Eagle Picture Company, 9/2/1933. Director: George Melford.

Cast: Ford Sterling, Linda Watkins, James Kirkwood, Josephine Dunn, Reed Howes, Molly O'Day.

Note: Filmed at the Kennedy Studios, Weedon's Island, St. Petersburg, Florida.

Alice in Wonderland

Paramount Pictures Inc., 12/22/1933; eight reels. Director: Norman McLeod; Scenario: Lewis Carroll (novels), Joseph Mankiewicz.

Cast: Ford Sterling, Charlotte Henry, Leon Errol, Louise Fazenda, Richard "Skeets" Galagher, Raymond Hatton, Polly Moran, Ned Sparks, Sterling Holloway, Roscoe Ates, Alison Skipworth, Lillian Harmer, Richard Arlen, Edward Everett Horton, Jackie Searl.

Note: This picture was released on 1/5/1939 in Finland.

1934

Sterling is not known to have made any films during 1934.

1935

Behind the Green Lights

Mascot Pictures, 3/11/1935; seven reels. Director: Christy Cabanne; Scenario: Colbert Clark, James Gruen.

Cast: Norman Foster, Judith Allen, Sidney Blackmer, Purnell Pratt, Theodore von Eltz, Ford Sterling, Kenneth Thomson, Lloyd Whitlock, Edward Hearn, Jane Meredith, Edward Gargan, J. Carrol Naish, John Davidson, Hooper Atchley, Marc Loebell.

Ruthless criminal attorney Raymond Cortell is not above bending and twisting the law to suit his purposes, making him a well-paid pariah among his peers. Practically the only person who believes that Cortell's tactics are ethical is his faithful assistant, Mary, the daughter of police lieutenant Jim Kennedy. There is a diamond robbery that is in fact a setup, but there is a witness, the janitor. Cortell frightens and bribes the janitor into hiding out and refusing to give evidence, but Mary's police detective fiancé is out to get the attorney and the gang and he persuades the janitor to come forward at the trial. Mary finally gets a wake-up call when a criminal she's helped to acquit shoots down her father during a robbery. She then switches her allegiance to a young detective, Dave Britten, who's been waiting a long time to get the goods on the unscrupulous Cortell.

The Headline Woman

Mascot Pictures Corporation, Republic Pictures Corporation, 5/13/1935; seven reels. Director: William Nigh; Scenario: Claire Church, Jack Natteford.

Cast: Heather Angel, Roger Pryor, Jack LaRue, Ford Sterling, Conway Tearle, Franklin Pangborn, Jack Mulhall, Morgan Wallace, Russell Hopton, Theodore von Eltz, George J. Lewis, Ward Bond, Harry Bowen, Wade Boteler, Wheeler Oakman.

In a popular but crooked gambling venue frequented by society folk as well as gangsters, a murder is committed. It is the third murder where the police suspect the victim is part of a gambling war. Hugo Meyer is a bumbling and inept police officer who is pounding his beat just around the corner from the venue. He sees the murderer running toward him, yet the ever helpful Meyer inadvertently lets the man go by, even hailing a cab for him. Bob Grayson, star reporter, sees this as an opportunity to embarrass the police chief, who is having a war of his own with the newspaper's editor. The police chief refuses to give out any bulletins to the editor, so Grayson has the idea to use Meyer. They get him to feed the reporters information on current crimes, which they solve; they get an exclusive story and Meyer in return gets the credit. The reporters then start a publicity campaign to promote Meyer and help him rise in the ranks.

Black Sheep

Fox Film Corp., 6/14/1935; eight reels. Director: Allan Dwan; Scenario: Allan Dwan (story), Allen Rivkin.

Cast: Edmund Lowe, Claire Trevor, Tom Brown, Eugene Pallette, Adrienne Ames, Herbert Mundin, Ford Sterling, Jed Prouty, Billy Bevan, David Torrence.

On an oceangoing liner, the SS *Southampton*, a professional gambler meets up with a gold-digging young lady. There is a young society man on board who is in trouble; he has gotten into debt through gambling and a rich (but none too honest) woman has given him money on his notes. She intends to blackmail the young man into taking a valuable pearl necklace she has stolen off the ship in return for the notes. He feels he can't do it and eventually confides in the gold digger and gambler, who help foil her plan. It turns out that the young man is the gambler's long-lost son. The gambler doesn't want his son or his son's new family to know this. It wouldn't be a good thing for a young society man to be known as the son of a professional gambler.

Keystone Hotel

Warner Brothers; 1935; two reels. Director: Ralph Staub; Scenario: Joe Traub.

Cast: Ford Sterling, Ben Turpin, Chester Conklin, Hank Mann, Marie Prevost, Vivien Oakland, Dewey Robinson, Bert Roach, Leo White, Jack Duffy, Keystone Kops.

The Keystone Hotel is hosting a prestigious beauty contest, which all the noted members of town want their wives and girlfriends to win. They all try to bribe or threaten the cross-eyed judge, Count Drewablanc, but in the confusion he presents the prize to an elderly cleaning lady. Angry members of the audience respond by hurling custard pies at the victor. It is not until the end that the Keystone Kops arrive, but they are still in time to get plastered with pastries.

Note: The version that was theatrically released measured two reels, while a show-at-home variety was one reel in length.

All Business
1935.
Cast: Ford Sterling.

Vitaphone Shorts
Fox. 1935–1937.

1936

Human Cargo

Twentieth Century Fox Corp., 5/29/1936; seven reels.

Director: Alan Dwan; Scenario: Doris Malloy, Jefferson Parker.

Cast: Claire Trevor, Brian Donlevy, Ralph Morgan, Rita Hayworth.

Note: Sterling is listed in the film's production charts, but not credited.

Framing Father

RKO Radio Pictures, Inc., 9/2/1936; two reels. Director and Scenario: Leslie Goodwins.

Cast: Ford Sterling.

Return Engagement

RKO Radio Pictures, 1936. Director: Leigh Jason.

Cast: Ford Sterling, Marjory Gateson, Tom Kennedy, Dorothy Kent, Kitty McHugh, George Stuart.

During breakfast at the Randall household, their son calls to say he is going to marry a manicurist, much to his parents' horror. They go to see him and stay at the hotel where the girl works. All the staff seem to know Mr. Randall very well, except they all call him Mr. Smith. He denies being Smith to his suspicious wife, who decides to go shopping while her husband has their trunks taken to their room. He asks the bellhop to send up Betty, the manicurist his son wants to marry, but Betty is busy and another girl is sent. Randall and the girl recognize each other as they had a fling together on Randall's previous visit as Smith. He notices the engagement ring on her finger and assumes it is his son she is engaged to. It isn't. It's the house detective who appears outside the room and knocks on the door. She has to hide and, while pushing her into a room, Randall tears off her dress, which he now has to hide, as well. The detective searches the room, making a big mess, but he can't find the girl, who is now in the bathroom. Randall throws her dress out the window and it lands on Mrs. Randall, who looks up to see her husband and the half-dressed girl in the window. On her return to the room, Randall tries to convince her it was the house detective she saw him with and then, running out of excuses, he pretends to be having a heart attack. Mrs. Randall goes to get him a drink and while she is away he tries to get rid of the girl; he returns her dress and she goes to put it on. Meanwhile, their son arrives with Betty to introduce her. He goes to speak with his mother and Randall sees Betty in the other room. He thinks she is the other girl and throws a blanket over her and stuffs her into a trunk. He explains to his son that a woman is trying to frame him and she is in the trunk, which they must hide from his mother. They push it into the closet, but they push the other girl out just as Mrs. Randall comes in. They pretend this is their son's fiancée and Randall pays her off with a check for $5,000. The trunk gets taken into the hall, where the son hears Betty inside and frees her. Meanwhile, the detective has also heard her and called the manager to come and see what he's found. The manager comes up and they open the now empty trunk. The detective is fired. When he tells his fiancée, the other girl, what has happened, she says it's OK, as she has enough money for them to have their honeymoon in Paris. She shows him the check then realizes it is signed. She is just in time to see the family leave in the elevator; Randall waves and says, "Good-bye everybody."

Bridle Grease

RKO Radio Pictures, Inc., 1936.
Cast: Ford Sterling.

1937

Many Unhappy Returns

RKO, 1937. Director: Charles Roberts.
Cast: Ford Sterling, Velma Wayne, Barbara Pepper, Richard Lane, Bud Jamison, Ed Dunn, Max Wagner.

It is Mrs. Morgan's birthday and her husband has bought her a doll, something she has a passion for. She comes down to breakfast early and Morgan hides the doll under his coat. She goes back out and he places the doll on the mantelpiece for her to find. Unfortunately, it falls into the fire and is burnt. He tells the butler not to let her know a doll burnt under any circumstances, as it would break her heart. When she returns, he tells her he was too late to pick up her gift last night, but he would have it at the office for her later. Then she notices a blonde hair on his waistcoat. He tells her about the doll and that is where the hair came from. Suspicious, Mrs. Morgan asks the butler, who denies any knowledge of a doll being burnt. This gets Morgan into trouble. He leaves for the office, where on his way in he picks up his papers. Among them is a photo, erroneously delivered to his office, of the cigar store girl. She had it to give to her boyfriend and had inscribed it. Mrs. Morgan comes to the office and sees the photo on her husband's desk. He has no knowledge of it but now she is convinced. On her way out to her attorney, she confronts the cigar girl, who thinks she's crazy. The newspapers are delivered and there is the photo on the front page. Back at home, the butler calls Morgan and tells him of a plan to get out of this; he must burn another doll so he has evidence. Mrs. Morgan overhears the call and realizes her mistake. Morgan orders another doll to burn and sends his secretary to buy one. Convinced Morgan is crazy, the secretary gets a doctor, too. When they see him set fire to the doll, they put him in a straightjacket. At that moment, Mrs. Morgan arrives and explains the situation. All is well until another newspaper arrives with an incriminating photo of Morgan and the cigar girl on the front. This had been taken when he picked up the fainting girl, but it doesn't look good for Morgan at the end!

Note: Information on this film was obtained from a viewing copy in the collection of the author.

Notes

Chapter 1

1. In early twentieth-century America, German stereotype comedians were referred to as Dutch comedians. Dutch was a corruption of the German word for "German," *Deutsch*. With thanks to Glenn Mitchell.

2. Index to early Notre Dame students, annual catalog, 55. 180. Stich, George F. is listed as age fifteen in 1898. As his birthday was in November, after registration, he would have been sixteen that year; hence, his birth year was 1882.

3. Fourteenth census, 1920, Los Angeles Township, California.

4. Roberta Courtland, Chats with Players, *Motion Picture*, December 1914, 115.

5. Jenny built what is considered the first skyscraper, which rose to ten stories.

6. Chicago Public Library; Chicago Historical Society.

7. The Eighteenth Annual Report of the U.S. Commissioner of Labor.

8. Mary Stich corresponded with the fathers at Notre Dame regularly and these letters are preserved in their archives. By October 15, 1899, she had sent the college $100 via Adams Express Company. On May 15, 1900, she sent a check for $119 to pay for fees and books and on June 15, 1900, she sent another letter to confirm the check had been sent.

9. Mary Stich to the Fathers of Notre Dame, 9 October 1898, Archives of the University of Notre Dame.

10. *Ibid.*, 16 September 1898.

11. *Ibid.*

12. *Ibid.*, 10 October 1899.

13. *Notre Dame Scholastic* (1899) 32: 168.

14. Mary Stich to the fathers of Notre Dame, October 1898, Archives of the University of Notre Dame.

15. *Ibid.*, May 1899.

16. *Ibid.*, 21 May 1899.

17. "Political Meetings Today; Republican," *Chicago Daily Tribune*, October 21, 1900. p. 5.

18. "Thousands Hear the Attorney Discuss Bryanism in the Auditorium," *Chicago Daily Tribune* November 3, 1900. p. 3.

19. Mary Stich to the Fathers of Notre Dame, 10 September 1899, Archives of the University of Notre Dame.

20. *Ibid.*, 28 August 1900.

21. Chats with Players, Roberta Courtland, *Motion Picture* December 1914. p. 115.

22. This can be found in Notre Dame's financial records as well as the letters dated October 15, 1899, where Mary Stich states she had sent the college $100 via Adams Express Company, and again on May 15, 1900, she sent a check for $119 to pay for fees and books, and on June 15, 1900, she sent another letter to confirm the check had been sent (after some queries).

23. Mary Stich to the Fathers of Notre Dame, 15 May 1900, Archives of the University of Notre Dame.

24. All letters after this date had this as their address.

25. After he left Notre Dame, James's life was marked by a downward spiral of drinking, prostitutes, and lengthy periods of living off his parents. He tried acting, mainly in the first decade of the twentieth century. Even if already jaded, he could still affect a stylish presence, with a voice to rival even his father's.

26. Index to early Notre Dame students; annual catalogs record O'Neill as attending the school during these years.

27. Mary Stich to the Fathers of Notre Dame, 28 August 1900, Archives of the University of Notre Dame.

28. Chats with Players, Roberta Courtland, *Motion Picture,* December 1914, 115.

29. Records with the dates of Sterling's early career are hazy at best. It would be safe to say that he worked in the circus for at least four years between 1901 and 1905. Concurrently, Sterling began playing farm-team baseball in 1904 and had begun getting theater reviews by 1905.

30. Educational Pictures, "Sterling Was Once Big

Top Clown," press release for *The Foolish Forties*, 6/28/1931.

31. Flying Lees act as described by circus performer and historian Natasha Gerson.

32. Educational Comedies press release for *The Foolish Forties*, 7/20/1931. p. 2.

33. "Notes of the Stage," *Washington Post*, 3/22/1904.

34. "A Woman's Pity," *New York Times*, 3/26/1905. p. 5.

35. At the Bijou, *Atlanta Constitution*, 2/4/1907. p. 6.

36. This is not the current Majestic Theater on Forty-fourth St. in New York City that was built later.

37. Brooklyn Amusements, *New York Times*, 11/10/1907.

38. At the Bijou, *Atlanta Constitution*, 1/27/1908. p. 7.

39. Chats with Players, Roberta Courtland; *Motion Picture*, December 1914 p. 115. Hollywood in Sport, "Surprise Athlete," *Los Angeles Times*, 7/11/1937.

40. "Keystone Kop Dreamed of O.B. Career," Al Kermisch, *Baseball Research Journal* 14 (1985) p. 17.

41. "Fired into Fortune, *Lima Daily News*, 5/2/1914. p. 6.

42. *Los Angeles Times*, 3/31/1914. p. iii3.

43. Harry A. Williams, "Chance Day Turns Out to Be Howling Success," *Los Angeles Times*, 11/16/1916. p. 19.

44. "Screen Stars vs. Wrestlers" and Nagurski Joins Grapplers for S. B. Game Sunday," *Los Angeles Times*, 8/24/1937. p. A10.

45. Sterling was still playing as late as 1937, although not up to his old standards.

46. *Chicago's American* was an afternoon newspaper in Chicago, Illinois. Its first edition came out on July 4, 1900, as Hearst's Chicago American. In 1939 Hearst sold the *American* and his *Herald Examiner*. As an afternoon paper it relied on street sales rather than subscription. Aggressive reporting of the sensational was the order of the day as this is what sold papers. Sales were also increased by breaking news and its updates. It was not unknown for reporters to help stories along to get the scoop, often posing as officials such as police officers.

47. *Atlanta Constitution*, May 16, 1915. p. A13.

48. Otis Skinner (1858–1942) had a career that lasted over sixty years. The American actor played hundreds of roles in theaters throughout the world. His first stage appearance was at the Philadelphia Museum in 1877 in Woodleigh. He was born in Cambridge, Massachusetts.

49. William Gillette (b.1853), the American actor, stage manager, and playwright, was most famous as an actor in his own dramatization of Sherlock Holmes, which he adapted for the stage from Sir Arthur Conan Doyle's stories. He left college in 1875 and joined a stock company in New Orleans, Louisiana; He was born in Hartford, Connecticut.

Chapter 2

1. The Mutoscope & Biograph dates back to 1895, founded by a syndicate that included W. K. L. Dickson, who worked at the Thomas Edison laboratory. He discovered how to put moving images onto film but Edison considered the new novelty of no importance. Dickson, though, could see its potential. He left Edison in 1895, to form the first ever company that focused solely on the production of moving pictures. He named the new company the American Mutoscope & Biograph Company. Biograph was soon Edison's main competitor, and in 1896 the Biograph Projector showed the first projected images to an audience in America by an American company. By 1908 Biograph was producing films in New York and California. The New York studio boasted the services of D. W. Griffith. Many early stars spent their formative years at Biograph under the direction of Griffith, including Mary Pickford, Lionel Barrymore, and Lillian Gish. Technically, Biograph were ahead of most studios using elements such as close-ups, crosscutting, dissolves, innovative editing, moving shots, fade-outs, and the iris shot.

2. William Desmond Taylor (1877–1922) is remembered primarily for his unsolved murder in Hollywood. He was also an actor and a director, notably of Mary Pickford films for Famous Players-Lasky. He had a reputation as a ladies' man and was reputedly involved with Mabel Normand, Mary Miles Minter, and several other female stars and starlets.

3. "Film Stars Will Aid in Rite for Miss Normand," *Chicago Daily Tribune*, 2/28/1930. p. 14.

4. Howard Walls was employed by the U.S. Copyright Office when he discovered the paper print collection. His interest and the potential historic value of the material led him first to catalogue the reels and, by the mid 1940s attempt to have the collection reproduced onto a film base.

Carl Louis Gregory, from the National Archives Motion Picture Division, modified the printer he had designed for running old and shrunken film to utilize reflected instead of transmitted light. In the mid to late 1940s various groups, including the National Archives, Richard Fleischer of RKO/Pathé, and the George Eastman House made attempts to copy this material. In the early 1950s, under the direction of Kemp Niver, the collection was prepared for copying using a printer and printing process he had designed to transfer the collection onto 16mm film stock. In the mid 1980s the Library of Congress contracted with UCLA Film and Television Archive to remaster the material onto 35mm film stock with more efficient equipment. To date, the LOC has been continuing the reconstructions with state-of-the-art equipment with excellent success.

5. Sterling has been credited with being in *The Inventor's Secret* (October 1911), *Lucky Horseshoe* (1911), *Too Many Burglars* (October 1911), *Abe Gets Even with Father* (December 1911), and *Mix Up in Raincoats* (December, 1911). There is no evidence to support this to date.

6. Paramount press release, date unknown.

7. *Moving Picture World*, 4/26/1913. p. 361.

Chapter 3

1. Adam Kessel and Charles Bauman. Until 1908, when Governor Charles Evans Hughs signed into law a bill banning racetrack gambling in New York, Kessel and Bauman were successful bookmakers. Kessel had saved much of their earnings and among some debts he collected was a small film exchange. He expanded this, with Bauman eventually rejoining him in the new venture. They were so successful competitors tried to cut off their product supplies. In retaliation, Kessel and Bauman went into production, hiring Fred Balshofer as cameraman; this new venture became the Bison Company. Soon they were selling to others and formed the New York Motion Picture Company.

2. Ince was a former actor and now director and producer of spectacles and of the westerns of William S. Hart.

3. Echo Park can still be visited today. Although smaller, a section having been used to run a road through, the lake, boathouse, and lake surround are recognizable as the place in these shorts.

4. Waddy Film Facts and Reel Chatter, *Los Angeles Times*, 2/28/1913.

5. In these days film did not register color as we see it. Some colors were emphasized while others were toned down. Reds (a component color of skin) photographed black, eventually theatrical makeup companies produced greasepaint sticks called "motion picture yellow," for women and "motion picture orange" for men.

6. Gene Fowler, *Father Goose: The Story of Mack Sennett* (New York: Covici-Fried, 1934), p. 163.

Chapter 4

1. Kalton Lahue and Terry Brewer, *Kops and Custard* (Norman: University of Oklahoma Press, 1968).

2. Kalton Lahue and Sam Gill, *Clown Princes and Court Jesters* (New York: A.S. Barnes, 1970).

3. Series of Western Union telegrams, night letters, and day letters sent from the NYP Company in 1913 and 1914.

4. Kalton Lahue and Terry Brewer, *Kops and Custard*, p. 73. Mack Sennett and Cameron Shipp, *King of Comedy* (New York: Doubleday, 1954), p. 150. In *Father Goose: The Story of Mack Sennett*, p. 223. Sennett claims he was paying Sterling $200 per week.

5. Mack Sennett and Fred Balshofer in his biography, *One Reel a Week*, and his interviews as interpreted by Kalton Lahue in his books *Kops and Custard*, and *Clown Princes and Court Jesters* and Mack Sennett's *Keystone*.

6. Kalton Lahue and Terry Brewer, *Kops and Custard*, p. 74.

7. Cameron Shipp and Mack Sennett, *King of Comedy*, p. 150.

8. Ibid.

9. Gene Fowler, *Father Goose*, p.224.

10. Mack Sennett and Cameron Shipp, *King of Comedy*, p. 229.

11. Gene Fowler, *Father Goose*, p. 228.

12. Charles Chaplin, *My Autobiography* (New York: Simon and Schuster, 1964), p. 142.

13. Fred J. Balshofer and Arthur C. Miller, with Bebe Bergsten, *One Reel a Week* (Berkeley: University of California Press, 1967).

Chapter 5

1. Sterling's homes have not had a good survival rate; this address also is now part of a freeway.

2. "Lehrman to Make New 'Big U' Brand Comedy," *Atlanta Constitution*, August 9, 1914.

3. *Moving Picture World*, 12/19/1914.

4. In Movie Land, *Chicago Daily Tribune*, 1/3/1915.

5. This address no longer exists as the freeway now runs over it.

6. Author's interviews with June MacCloy 2002–2005

7. David Robinson, *Chaplin* (New York: McGraw-Hill, 1985), p. 103.

Chapter 6

1. *Variety* 1/16/1915. p. 26.

2. Kitty Kelly, Flickerings from Film Land, *Chicago Daily* Tribune, 2/11/1915. p. 10.

3. *Variety*, 4/9/1915. p. 17.

4. "Comedian's Career in Films Told," *Los Angeles Times*, 7/5/1925. p. D10.

5. *Chicago Daily Tribune*, 4/11/1916. p. 18. Flickerings from Film Land Kitty Kelly.

6. "Is Your Favorite Film Star Married?" *Washington Post*, 1/28/1917. p. SM3

Chapter 7

1. "Oh, Mabel Behave," C. B. Sewell, *Moving Picture World*, 12/17/1921. p. 855.
2. Billie Ritchie (1874–1921) was born in Glasgow, Scotland. He was a member of Fred Karno's company, with which he appeared on the Orpheum Circuit. There were similarities between Chaplin and Ritchie in costume, act, and mannerisms going back to the Karno days and both did a similar drunk act. Lehrman signed Ritchie to imitate Chaplin in 1914 for L-KO, taking him with him to Fox after Lehrman had a disagreement with Universal and moved on. Lehrman had been given the name "Suicide" Lehrman by his performers because of the dangerous stunts he required them to do. Ritchie fell victim to Lehrman's requirements and often sustained injuries while filming. Lehrman, with his insistence on a rapid turnout of his product, didn't give Ritchie time to heal before Ritchie was injured again. The final straw was an attack by ostriches that were being used in one of his comedies; Ritchie was forced to retire and later died from the effects of his injury. Lehrman promised to support Ritchie's widow and daughter but failed to keep his promise; Chaplin instead took the family under his wing and hired Ritchie's widow as his wardrobe mistress.
3. Eddie Cline would go on to direct Buster Keaton, W. C. Fields, Wheeler & Woolsey, and Olsen & Johnson.
4. "Stars to Lend Talent for National Defense," *Los Angeles Times*, 11/4/1917. p. V12.
5. Flashes, "Mack Sennett's New One," Grace Kingsley, *Los Angeles Times*, 7/3/1920. p. II7.
6. *Atlanta Constitution*, 10/9/1921. p. 2.
7. "Ford Sterling is Latest Comedy Star to Be Signed by Special Pictures," *Moving Picture World*, 9/4/1920 p. 64.
8. The New York offices were at 126 West Forty-sixth St., New York City, and the California offices were at 7100 Santa Monica Blvd., Hollywood, California.
9. "Radio Special Moves In, Takes Possession of J. D. Hampton Studio," Edwin Schalbert, *Los Angeles Times*, 9/15/1920. p. II4.
10. "Radio's New Studio," Edwin Schalbert, *Los Angeles Times*, 11/17/1920. p. II4.
11. "Contract Covers Orient," *Los Angeles Times*, 11/3/1920. p. III2.
12. Sam Gill interview with Eddie Baker, used with permission.
13. *Atlanta Constitution*, 10/9/1920. p. 2.
14. Flashes, "Sterling to Tour" Grace Kingsley, *Los Angeles Times*, 10/14/1920. p. B1. "Ford Sterling Booster," *Atlanta Constitution*, October 24, 1920. p. 2F.
15. *Atlanta Constitution*, May 1, 1921. p. E5.

Chapter 8

1. "Comedian Wins Honor as Artist in Photography," *Los Angeles Times*, 6/29/1924. p. B37.
2. *Atlanta Constitution*, 7/7/1918. p. 4. Movie Notes.
3. Artistic Photographer, "Ford Sterling — In Private," *Wisconsin Rapids Daily Tribune*, p. 9.
4. C. B. Neblette, *Photography: Its Principles and Practice* (New York: Van Norstrand, New York City copyright 1927).
5. After developing his bromide print in the normal way, Sterling would have bleached and tanned the print by soaking it in water. The softer highlights absorbed more water then the harder dark areas, causing them to swell more. Working on the premise that oil repels water and vice versa, the lighter the highlight the less oil-based inks used to color the print are absorbed; in contrast the darker drier areas soak up much more color.
6. *Photography: Its Principles and Practice*, C. B. Neblette.
7. *Wisconsin Rapids Daily Tribune*, p. 9. Artistic Photographer.
8. "Ford Sterling Highly Skilled in Photography," Educational Pictures press release for *Foolish Forties*, 7/20/1931. p. 1.
9. "The Photographic Salon," by Anthony Anderson, *Los Angeles Times*, 1/12/1919. p. III3.
10. "World's Best Pictorial Artists Exhibit Here," Henrietta Boeckman, *Los Angeles Times*, 12/11/1921. p. ii10.
11. "Comedian Wins Honor as Artist in Photography," *Los Angeles Times*, 6/29/1924. p. B37.
12. "Takes Medals," *Washington Post*, 12/10/1933. p. A1.
13. "Movie Sidelights," Associated Press, *Washington Post*, 6/26/1927. p. 12.

Chapter 9

1. *Wisconsin Rapids Daily Tribune*, p. 9. Artistic Photographer.
2. *Los Angeles Times*, 6/8/1942. p. B13.
3. Playdom, Pick Wanderer, *Los Angeles Times*, 2/8/1923.
4. "First Beauty Quest Winners Next Sunday," *Los Angeles Times*, 3/5/1922. p. 111.
5. *Los Angeles Times*, 5/14/1923. p. ii16.
6. New York State Archives, http://www.iarchives.nysed.gov/
7. Identified as such by Edward Hulse.
8. Identified by the author.
9. Titles researched by Joseph Moore.
10. "Nome's Heyday Is Revived," *Los Angeles Times*, 7/18/1923.
11. *Variety*, October 1923.
12. "Work Night and Day," *Atlanta Constitution*, 8/19/1923. p. B5.

13. Flashes, "Will's at It Again," Grace Kingsley, *Los Angeles Times*, 11/28/1923. p/ii11.
14. "Off for Georgia," *Los Angeles Times*, 8/2/1923. p. i18.
15. Flashes, Grace Kensley, *Los Angeles Times*, 9/26/1923. p. B11.
16. *"He Who Gets Slapped*, Howard's Big Feature," *Atlanta Constitution*, 2/15/1925. p. C2.
17. *New York Clipper*, June 28, 1913.
18. Flashes, "All Star Cast," Grace Kinsley, *Los Angeles Times*, p. A11.
19. "Ford Sterling in Julian's Picture," *Los Angeles Times*, 4/1/1924. p. A9.

Chapter 10

1. *Atlanta Constitution*, May 1, 1921. p. E5.
2. "On the Set and Off," *Movie World*, 9/13/1924.
3. Like all major studios, Paramount sent information out to newspapers and magazines about its stars and upcoming movies in the form of press releases. Often what was included in these releases was printed verbatim as articles under the byline of a staff reporter, with no credit given to Paramount.
4. "What I Want My Wife to Be Like," Paramount press release, date unknown.
5. Charles Chaplin, *My Autobiography* (1964).
6. Educational Comedies press release for *Foolish Forties*, 7/20/1931.
7. "Painted Desert Forms Setting in Barker's Picture," *Los Angeles Times*, 2/15/1925. p. 35.
8. American Film Institute.
9. "Ford Sterling Tries Prison in Steppin' Out," *Los Angeles Times*, 8/9/1925. p. D13.
10. Two-strip Technicolor. The 1915 invention of J. G. Capstaff, an employee of the Kodak Research Laboratory. A beam-splitting camera was used to obtain two negatives that recorded the red and blue-green content of the image. After the negatives were processed they were printed onto opposite sides of a film base that had previously been coated on both sides with emulsion. The final stage of processing converted the black and white images to red-orange and blue-green. The resulting combined image gave a satisfactory, but not natural, reproduction of the original. The technique required far more lighting than black and white.
11. Gloria Swanson, *Swanson on Swanson* (New York: Pantheon Books, 1984).
12. "Ford Sterling Awarded Long Lasky Contract," *Los Angeles Times*, 10/18/1925. p. 3.
13. *Ibid*.
14. Flashes, "Comedian in It," *Los Angeles Times*, 12/9/1925.
15. Paramount press release, date unknown.
16. "Visit to a Screen Wizard's Workshop," *New York Times*, 2/13/1927. p. X7.

17. Paramount press review, date unknown.
18. *Variety*, January 1924.
19. "Attractions at the Local Playhouses," *Washington Post*, 6/28/1926. p. 5.
20. *Washington Post*, 6/28/1926. p5.
21. "Strong Cast in Picture Now at Uptown Theater," *Los Angeles Times*, 2/7/1926. p. 31.
22. "Nency gives big performance for Shriners," *Los Angeles Times*, 10/21/1936. p. G13.
23. "Seen on the Screen, Writer, 'The Film Girl,'" *Syracuse Herald*, 10/29/1915. p. 12.
24. "Under the Lights," *Los Angeles Times*, 8/29/1926, p. 12.
25. "Ford Sterling, Almost a Perfect, Bumptious, Bombastic Show Off," *Chicago Daily Tribune*, 7/27/1926. p. 29.
26. "Service Tells Story of Automobile," *Los Angeles Times*, 4/17/1927. p. G7.
27. Robert Lusk, "Strike Stalks at Paramount," *Los Angeles Times*, 1/30/1927. p. C22.
28. Grace Kinsey, "Open Season for Directors," *Los Angeles Times*, 4/25/1927.
29. Joseph McBride, *Frank Capra: The Catastrophe of Success* (New York: Simon & Schuster, 1992), p. 181.
30. "Celluloid golfers at Rancho," *Los Angeles Times*, 7/24/1927. p. A4.
31. Paramount press release, writer, Snell.
32. Paramount press release, writer, Holloway. *Los Angeles Times*, 9/1/1927. "Players Suffer in Desert Heat."
33. Paramount press release, Holloway.
34. *Ibid*.
35. *Ibid*.
36. *Ibid*.
37. *Ibid*.
38. *Ibid*.
39. *Ibid*.
40. *Ibid*.
41. *Ibid*.
42. Paramount press release, Wright.
43. *Ibid*.
44. Paramount press release, "Burns Prevent Actor from Playing Role," *Los Angeles Times*, 11/12/1927. p. A9. "Sterling Burned," *Moving Picture World*, 11/12/1927. p. 16.
45. *Variety*.
46. "Elks Temple to Broadcast on KNRC Set," *Los Angeles Times*, 2/19/1928. p. B6.
47. "Wife of Player Seeks Divorce," *Los Angeles Times*, 2/27/1928.
48. "Teddy Sampson to Travel," *Los Angeles Times*, 2/23/1928. p. 14.
49. "Crash Maims Film Beauty," *Los Angeles Times*, 10/28/1927.

Chapter 11

1. "Actors Given Equity Edict," *Los Angeles Times*, 6/21/1929. p. A20.
2. Screen Actor's Guild, http://www.sag.org/history/
3. The Masquer's Club, http://www.masquersclub.org/scrapbook.htm/
4. *Los Angeles Times*, 2/24/1929. p. C23.
5. Vitaphone, synchronized disc. The first commercial release (August 1926), *Don Juan* with John Barrymore, was with a music track only; *The Jazz Singer*, released in October 1927, was the first film to include synchronized dialogue using sixteen-inch discs; one disc was supposed to run the length of one reel.
6. The American pioneer and wireless engineer, Lee De Forest, who after many setbacks perfected sound on film in 1923, which he called the Phonofilm system. It was demonstrated throughout the U.S. but the public showed little interest in it. However, Fox bought up the patent and incorporated the technique with two other systems it had bought and named it Movietone. This "sound on film" worked by using a clear and solid pattern recorded along the edge of the film, which was scanned during projection by a light-sensitive photoelectric cell. This process converted the pattern into an alternating current that was then amplified and sent through wires to loudspeakers. The loudspeakers consisted of a circular permanent magnet surrounding a freely moving coil that had a cone-shaped diaphragm attached to it. The alternating current sent from the amplifier alternated at the same frequency as the sound waves that had generated the sound track on the film and this in turn induced an alternating magnetic field in the coil of the speaker. As the polarity of the magnetic field of the coil alternated, it was attracted to and repelled by the permanent magnet. This made the coil and the attached diaphragm vibrate at the same frequency as the sounds originally picked up by the microphone in the studio and this is what was heard coming out of the speakers.
7. "Ford Sterling and Patsy Ruth Miller Take Leads in *Fall of Eve*," *Los Angeles Times*, 7/5/1929. p. A13.
8. "Red Hair Given Preference in Color Picture," *Los Angeles Times*, 1/16/1930. p. A13.
9. "Income Lien Served Against Sterling," *Los Angeles Times*, 6/26/1929.
10. "Collector Files Back Tax Liens," *Los Angeles Times*, 10/22/1930. p. A17.
11. "Eye Attracted in Music Film," *Los Angeles Times*, 6/3/1930. p. A11.
12. Ibid.
13. "Christy Signs Ford Sterling for Comedies," *Los Angeles Times*, 8/19/1930. p. B11.
14. "Ford Sterling Ill in Arizona," *Los Angeles Times*, 12/23/1930. p. 1.
15. Author's interviews with June MacCloy 2002–2005.
16. "Library Tastes of Stars Run Varied Fare," *Los Angeles Times*, 8/25/1931. p. B9.
17. "Sterling Makes Comedies," *Los Angeles Times*, 8/25/1931. p. 17.
18. "Elks to Show Keystone Cops," *Los Angeles Times*, 12/10/1932. p. A5. Elks to show Keystone Cops.
19. Eddie Quillan interview with Brent Walker, with permission
20. "Ford Sterling in Black Sheep film," *Los Angeles Times*, 3/23/1935. p. 5.
21. "Famous Film Comedian Directs Pictures for Kennedy Company, *St. Petersburg Times*, 6/16/1933.
22. "Just Another Day's Work for Comedian of Screen," *Florida Times*, June 1933.
23. *St. Petersburg Times*, 7/18/1933.
24. "Famous Film Comedian Directs Pictures for Kennedy Company," *St. Petersburg Times*, 6/16/1933. "Sterling Cast in Keaton Film," *Evening Independent*, 7/27/1933. p. 9.
25. "Cheer Rules City Today," *Los Angeles Times*, 12/25/1934. p. 1.
26. "Comedian Is Fancier of Blooded Dogs and Persian Cats," *Syracuse Herald*, 8/8/1926. p. 3.
27. Seen by author to be a vacant lot in 2004.

Chapter 12

1. "Ford Sterling in Black Sheep Film," *Los Angeles Times*, 3/23/1935. p. 11.
2. "Two Signed for Headlines," *Los Angeles Times*, 4/4/1935. p. 19.
3. *Harrison's Report*, 5/25/1935. p. 83.
4. "Keystone Cops and Ex-Mayor," Sidney Skolsky, *Washington Post*, 5/29/1935. p. 20.
5. *Harrison's Report*, 3/30/1935.
6. Although Sterling didn't sign with R. K. O. until 1937, he made several short subjects as a freelance actor.
7. "Sterling Signs for Comedies," *Los Angeles Times*, 5/26/1937, p. 16.
8. Around and About in Hollywood, Read Kendal, *Los Angeles Times*, 5/17/1938. p. A14.
9. "Ford Sterling Critically Ill," *Nevada State Journal*, 2/18/1939. p. 8.
10. "Ford Sterling Seriously Ill," *Los Angeles Times*, 2/19/1939. p. 5.
11. Associated Press, 8/10/1939. *Chicago Daily Tribune*, 8/11/1939. p. 17. *New York Times*, 8/11/1939. p. 17. "Ford Sterling's Leg Amputated," *Los Angeles Times*, 8/11/1939. p. A1.
12. "Ford Sterling, Movie Actor, Has Chance of Hope," *Oshkosh Daily Northwestern*, 8/11/1939.

"Ford Sterling, Fight for Life," *Ironwood Daily Globe*, 8/11/1939. p. 1.

13. Jed Prouty (1879–1956), born in Boston, Massachusetts. He began his career on the stage, mostly as a song and dance man then as a character actor. He made numerous sound and silent films. He was a member of the Shriners and Masquer's. The first time he appeared with Sterling was in *Everybody's Acting*.

14. In Hollywood With Hedda Hopper, *Washington Post*, 8/24/1939. p. 10.

15. *Ironwood Daily Globe* 9/14/1939. p. 13. "Veteran Silent Film Comic Growing Weaker."

16. "Hollywood Cavalcade Is a Smash — So We Hear!" Nelson B. Bell, *Washington Post*, 10/3/1939. p. 10.

17. "Ford Sterling Paid Tribute," *Associated Press*, 10/17/1939.

18. Brian Anthony interview with Joe Kavigon.

19. "Critical Moment," Hedda Hopper Hollywood, *Los Angeles Times*, 10/21/1939. p. A7.

Bibliography

American Film Institute Catalogue 1911–1937.

Balshofer, Fred J., Arthur C. Miller, with the assistance of Bebe Bergsten. *One Reel a Week.* Foreword by Kemp R. Niver. Berkeley: University of California Press, 1967.

Blum, Daniel. *A Pictorial History of American Theater, 1900–1951.* New York: Greenburg, 1951.

_____. *A Pictorial History of the Silent Screen.* New York: G. P. Putnam's Sons, 1953.

Bowser, Eileen. Introduction. *Biograph Bulletins, 1908–1912.* New York: Octagon Books, 1973.

Capra, Frank. *The Name Above the Title.* Cambridge, MA: Da Capo Press, 1997.

Chaplin, Charles. *My Autobiography.* New York: Penguin Putnam, 1973.

D'Agostino, Annette M. *Filmmakers of the Moving Picture World: An Index to Articles 1907–1927.* Jefferson, NC: McFarland, 1997.

Film Daily Yearbook of Motion Pictures, 1920–21. N.p.: Ayer, 1971.

Fowler, Gene. *Father Goose: The Story of Mack Sennett.* New York: Covici-Fried; Rahway, N.J.: Quinn and Boden, 1934.

Gregory, Carl Louis. *Motion Picture Photography.* New York: Falk, 1927.

International Celebrity Register. Celebrity Register, 1959.

Kaplan, Mike. *Variety Film Reviews. Vol 1: 1907–1920, Vol. 2: 1921–1925, Vol. 3, 1926–1929, Vol. 4, 1930–1933. Vol. 5, 1934–1937.* N.p.: R.R. Bowker, 1983.

Kennedy, Joseph P. *The Story of the Films.* Englewood, NJ: Jerome S. Ozer, 1971.

Lahue, Kalton C. *Dreams for Sale: The Rise and Fall of the Triangle Film Corporation.* South Brunswick, NJ: A. S. Barnes, 1971.

_____. *Mack Sennett's Keystone: The Man, the Myth, and the Comedies.* South Brunswick, NJ: A.S. Barnes, 1971.

_____. *World of Laughter: The Motion Picture Comedy Short, 1910–1930.* Norman: University of Oklahoma Press, 1966.

Lahue, Kalton C., and Terry Brewer. *Kops and Custard.* Norman: University of Oklahoma Press, 1968.

Lahue, Kalton C., and Samuel Gill. *Clown Princes and Court Jesters.* South Brunswick, NJ: A.S. Barnes, 1970.

Lauritzen, Einer, and Gunner Lundquist. *American Film Index.* Vol. 1, 1908–1915. Vol. 2, 1916–1920. 1984. Distributed by Tonnheims.

Los Angeles City Directories, 1911–1939.

McBride, Joseph. *Frank Capra: The Catastrophe of Success.* New York: St. Martin's Press, 2000.

Ragan, David. *Who's Who in Hollywood, 1900–1976.* New York: Arlington House, n.d.

Robinson, David. *Chaplin, His Life and Art.* New York: McGraw-Hill, 1987.

Shipp, Cameron. *Mack Sennett: King of Comedy.* New York: Doubleday, 1954. Reprinted. N.P.: Mercury House, 1990.

Swanson, Gloria. *Swanson on Swanson.* N.p.: Random House, 1980.

Taylor, Deems. *A Pictorial History of the Movies.* London: George Allen and Unwin, 1943.

Vazzana, Eugene. *Silent Film Necrology.* Jefferson, NC: McFarland, 1995.

Wing, Ruth, ed. *The Blue Book of the Screen.* CA, 1923.

Periodicals, News Agencies, and Newspapers

This section is a listing of paper resources used in researching this book. The material came in various formats, including original, photocopies, cuttings, and microfilm. They were found in public libraries, either in the library's own collections or through interlibrary loans, university libraries, personal collections, and searchable online newspaper collections. The dates included are for the periods used in compiling the book and do not represent the extent of the run of that particular publication or source.

Associated Press, 1927–1939
Atlanta Constitution, 1907–1925
Baltimore Evening Sun, 1930
Baseball Research Journal #14, 1985 (Cooperstown, NY)
Chicago Daily Tribune, 1900–1939
Clearfield Progress, 1914
Daily News, Frederick, Maryland, 1914
Daily Tribune, 1939
Davenport Daily Leader, 1892
Davenport Democrat and Leader, 1927
Educational Comedies Press Sheet, 1931
Eighteenth Annual Report of the U.S. Commissioner of Labor
Evening Independent (Florida), 1933
Film Flashes, 1924
Film Fun, 1926
Florida Times, 1933
Fort Wayne Daily News, 1914–1915
Fort Wayne Journal-Gazette, 1907
Frederick Post, Frederick, Maryland, 1924
Gazette and Bulletin, Williamsport, PA, 1914
Harrison's Reports, NY, 1919–1937
Independent, St. Petersburg, 1933
Ironwood Daily Globe, 1939
Kinema Comic, Vol. 9, no. 474, May 25, 1929
Lima Daily News, 1914
London Times, 1912–1939
Los Angeles Examiner, 1924
Los Angeles Record, 1930
Los Angeles Times, 1913–1939
Mack Sennett Weekly, 1920
Mansfield News, 1915
Motion Picture, 1914–1919
Motion Picture Classic, 1927
Motion Picture News (NY) 1913–1928
Motography, 1912–1916
Movie Weekly
Moving Picture News, 1914
Moving Picture World (NY) 1920 — 1927
Nevada State Journal, 1939
New Movie, 1930
New York Clipper, 1912–1923
New York Herald, 1922
New York Morning Telegraph, 1907–1939
New York Times, 1905–1939
Nineteenth Annual Report of the U.S. Commissioner of Labor
Oakland Tribune, 1921–1924
Oshkosh Daily Northwestern, 1939
Paramount press releases, 1926–1927
Photoplay, 1911–1939
Photoplayers Weekly, 1915
Picture Play (NY) 1915–1939
Picture Show, 1921–1925
Pictures and Picture Goers, 1915
Reel Life, 1914–1915
Reno Evening Gazette, 1930
St. Petersburg Evening Independent, 1933
St. Petersburg Times, 1933
Screen Book, 1931
Society for American Baseball Research, Inc.
Syracuse Herald, 1915 — 1926
Twelfth Biennial Report of the Illinois Bureau of Labor Statistics
Universal Weekly, 1914 — 1915
Variety, 1915 — 1939
Washington Post, 1904 — 1939
Wisconsin Rapids Daily Tribune, 1926–1939

Index

Acker, Edward 145
Ackroyd, Jack 70, 71, 160
Across the Hall 44, 56
Aitken, Harry 64–66
Aitken, Jane 160
Aitken, Judith 176
Aitken, Roy 64
Alexandria Bar 41
Algy on the Force 150
Alice in Wonderland 123, 124, 132, 136, 176
All Business 177
Allen, Phyllis 150
Almost Married 156
Ambitious Butler 147
American Academy of Dramatic Arts (AADA) 13
American Journal of Photography 87
The American Venus 102–106, 117, 166
Among Those Present 160
Anderson, Claire 159
Anderson, Dave 156
Andrews, Dell 164
Angel, Heather 136
Angels (Los Angeles baseball team) 17
Arbuckle, Roscoe (Fatty) 29, 32, 33, 35, 36, 42, 54–57, 59, 76, 119, 120, 151–158
Arlen, Richard 114, 170
Arling, Charles 158
Armstrong, Billy 70, 71, 73, 74
Arnold, Edward 165
Asher, Max 36, 49, 50
Associated Actors and Artists of America (4As) 118
Associated Exhibitors 92
Astor, Gertrude 103, 166, 172
Astor, Mary 122
At Coney Island (a.k.a. *Cohen at Coney Island*) 147
At It Again 147
At Three O'clock 46, 156
Auto Intoxication 121, 126, 175

Avery, Charles 33, 57, 59, 65, 145, 152, 153, 157, 159

Baby Day 152
A Bad Game 153
Badger, Clarence 66, 159, 167
Baffles, Gentleman Burglar 38, 154
Baird, Leah 163
Baker, Eddie 78, 79
A Ballroom Romeo 79, 162
Balshofer, Fred 35, 38–41, 43–48
Barker, Reginald 97
Barney Oldfield — A Race for a Life 28, 29, 31, 151
Barrie, Nigel 92, 162
Barrymore, Lionel 59
Barty, Billy 122, 124
Baseball 5, 8, 16, 17, 71, 77, 110
The Battle of Who Run 148
Bauman, Charles 26, 39, 40, 43, 44, 64, 65
Baxter, Warner 111, 167, 169
A Bear Escape 147, 157
The Beating He Needed 146
Beaudine, William 145, 146
Because He Loved Her 158
Beck, Arthur C. 92, 163
Bedford, Barbara 163
Beery, Noah, Jr. 173
Beery, Noah, Sr. 92, 94, 163, 172
Beery, Wallace 101, 106, 109, 110, 165, 169, 170
Behind the Green Light 139, 176
Bellamy, Madge 98, 164
Belmont, Joseph 160
Bennett, Charles 159
Bernard, Harry 60, 157, 158
Bernard, Sam 66, 158
Besser, Eugenie 162
Between Showers 41, 154
Bevan, Billy 73, 74, 160–162, 177
Beware of Boarders 68, 159

B. H. Dyers (department store) 17
Big Moments from Little Pictures 36, 37, 94
Biograph Company 19–28, 40, 88, 125, 145
Black Hands 157
Black Sheep 132, 133, 136, 137, 177
Blane, Sally 169, 170
Boardman, Eleanor 94, 162, 163
A Bogus Baron 156
Bond, Ward 136, 176
Booth, Elmer 145
Boswell, Hobart 92
Bosworth, Hobart 89, 162, 164
Bow, Clara 165
Bowers, John 165
The Bowling Match 153
Boyd, Lois 160
The Brass Bottle 163
Braybin, Charles 165
Breaking into Society (play) 19
Breamer, Sylvia 89, 164
Brennan, John E. 9
Brennan, Walter 118
Brice, Monty 168
Bridal Grease 140, 178
Bride of the Regiment 124, 173
Bromo and Juliet 56
Bromoil process 80–82
Bronson, Betty 107, 168
Brooks, Louise 25, 105, 108, 114, 166, 167
Brown, Bothwell 75
Brown, Joe E. 173
Browning, Tod 91, 92, 94, 134, 163
Bruce, Kate 145
Bull's Eye (studio) 57
Bunny, John 39
Bunting, Walter S. 145
Burkett, Bartine 165
Burham, Daniel H. 6
Busch, Mae 158

191

Butler, Kathleen 145
Butler, William J. 145
By Golly 161

Cabanne, Christy 145, 176
Calhoun, Alice 169
Camera Pictorialists of Los Angeles 82–84, 86, 87
Capra, Frank 110, 169
Carmen, Jewel 153
Carmen's Washday 157
Carr, Mary 164
Carroll, Nancy 117, 171
Casey at the Bat 109, 168
Cavander, Glen 158
Chaney, Lon, Sr. 13, 89, 98, 164
Chaplin, Charles 5, 6, 29, 32, 39–43, 45, 53, 57, 59, 68, 78, 101, 113, 142, 154, 155
Chaplin, Syd 164
Chase, Charley (Parrott, Charles) 31, 56, 57, 68, 93, 142, 157, 158
Chicago 6–12, 17, 79
Chicago Cubs (baseball team) 17
Chicken a La King 117, 171
Chief Seginitso 111, 112
The Chief's Predicament 149
Chisholm, Scotty 79
Christie Comedies 49, 56, 125, 126, 128, 174, 175
Circus 12, 13, 26, 28, 98
Clark, Harvey 165
Clark, Marguerite 39
Clifton, Emma 45, 154, 155
Cline, Eddie 60, 61, 69, 160, 175
The Close Call 156
Cody, Lew 20, 60, 164
Cogley, Nick 35, 57, 59, 148, 151, 153
Cohen Collects a Debt 27, 146
Cohen Saves the Flag 29, 30, 153
Cohen's Outing 152
Colbert, Claudette 169
Coleman, Dan 15, 16
A Colored Villainy 57
Come to Papa 126, 174
ComiClassic Productions 79
Conklin, Charles 161
Conklin, Chester 5, 41, 59, 77, 92, 94, 106, 116, 132, 154, 155, 160, 164, 171, 175, 177
Conklin, Heinie 111, 160, 163, 169
Cook, Aileen 127, 129, 174, 175
Cook, Clyde 165
Cooper, Earl 153
Cosmograph Comedies 77, 79, 161, 162

Courthouse Crooks 56–58, 158
The Crash 47, 155
Creative Art (magazine) 126
Crocker, Zeph 37
Cullingham, Margaret 78
Culver City Studio 94
The Cure That Failed 148

Daddy's Gone A-Hunting 165
Daniels, Bebe 103, 110, 111, 119, 167, 168
Daro, Jack 17
Darro, Frankie 165, 167
Davenport, Alice 26, 27, 30, 32, 33, 54, 147, 148, 150, 152–154, 157, 159, 162
Davenport, Dorothy 27
Davenport, Harry Bryant 27
Davenport, Milla 167
Davis, Edward 89, 164
The Day of Faith 91, 92, 94, 95, 163
The Deacon Outwitted 148
The Deacon's Troubles 147
A Deaf Burglar 149
De Brulier, Nigel 96, 164
De Grasse 94, 165, 167
Del Ruth, Hampton 159
Denny, Reginald 171
Depp, Harry 159
De Rochefort, Charles 98, 164
Destroying Angel 92, 163
Diegel, Leo 79
Dillon, Edward (Eddie) 20, 145, 146, 156
Dillon, John Francis 52, 121, 124, 173, 175
Diltz, Elva 161
Dirty Work in a Laundry (a.k.a. *A Desperate Scoundrel*) 30–32, 39, 56, 60, 158
Dix, Richard 115, 171
The Dog Raffles 157
Done in Oil 159
Donnelly, James 159
Don't Weaken 161
Double Crossed 38, 154
A Double Wedding 147
Down the Pike (play) 15
A Dramatic Mistake 156
Dresser, Louise 167
Drums of the Desert 111, 113, 169
Duffy, Jack 78, 118, 121, 173, 177
Duluth baseball team 16, 17
Dunn, Bobby 17, 159, 160, 162
Dunn, Ed 178
Dunn, Josephine 176
Durfee, Minta 31, 32, 35, 56, 58, 60, 61, 153, 154, 157, 158, 160

A Dutch Gold Mine 21, 145
Dwan, Allan 102, 105, 136, 166, 177

East Lynne with Variations 160
Echo Park, Los Angeles California 27
Edendale, California 26, 27, 41, 66
Educational Comedies 52, 125, 126
Edwards, Gus 49
Edwards, Neely 78, 79, 162
Edwards, Vivian 159
The Elite Ball 148
Elks Club 117, 126
Emory, May 158
Empire Exchange 65
Equity 118, 119
Errol, Leon 140, 175, 176
Essenay 18
Evans, Frank 145
Everybody's Acting 107, 168

Fairbanks, Douglas, Jr. 166
Fairbanks, Douglas, Sr. 78, 94, 125, 142, 143
The Faithful Taxi Cab (a.k.a. *Fatal Taxi Cab*) 152
The Fall of Eve 120, 121, 172
A False Beauty (a.k.a. *A Faded Vampire*) 27, 30, 154
Famous Players–Lasky 23, 25, 52, 102, 108, 166–168, 170, 171
Farley, Dot 118, 149, 150, 165
Farnham, Joseph 162
Fatal Forceps 125, 172
The Fatal Wedding 155
Father's Choice 150
Fatty and the Broadway Stars 158
Fazenda, Louise 24, 44, 70, 71, 77, 91, 94, 118, 121–125, 159–161, 163, 164, 173, 175, 176
Federal Film Exchange of America 79
Fellowes, Rockliffe 92–94, 162, 163, 167
Fenton, Leslie 167
Fickle Fancy 161
Fields, W. C. 113, 123, 175
Figures Don't Lie 113–115, 170
A Film Johnnie 154
Film Supply Company of America 65
Finlayson, James 60, 130, 160, 161, 175
The Firebugs 152
"The Firefly" 81
First National Pictures 21, 51,

52, 69, 110, 124, 162–165, 169, 171, 175
The Fisherman 132, 133, 175
A Fishy Affair 150
Fitzgerald, Cissero 102
Flamingo Film Company 133
Fleckenstein, Louis 82, 83, 86
The Flirt 46
The Flirting Husband 147
Flying Lees 12, 13
Foiling Fickle Father 149
Fontaine, Frances 14
Foolish Forties 52, 125, 126, 174
Fools and Duels 68, 160
For the Love of Mabel 151
For the Love of Mike 110, 169
Forde, Victoria 146
The Foreman of the Jury 151
Forepaughs Amalgamated Circus 13
Four Mortons 18
Fox, Virginia 72, 74, 161
Fox Films 51, 52, 57, 68, 110, 117, 120, 140, 167, 171, 177
Fox Sunshine Comedies 50, 66, 68, 69, 159, 160
Foy, Eddie 160
Framing Father 140, 177
Franklin car 110
Franklyn, Chester 44
Freddy the Seal 164
Fredericks, Pauline 106
Fresh from the City 72–74, 161
Freuler, John R. 65
Friganza, Trixie 171

Gallagher, Richard "Skeets" 169
The Galloping Fish 21, 164
A Game of Poker 150
A Game of Pool 152
The Gangsters 151
Garvin, Anita 173
Gay, Alden 119
Gentlemen Prefer Blondes 116, 171
George Whittier's Repertory Company 12
Gilbert, Billy 17
Gilbert, John 165
Gillette, William 18, 23
Gillingwater, Claude 162
Gillstrom, Arvid 159
Gilroy, Bert 140
The Girl in the Show 120, 172
Goldman, Sam 15
Golf 8, 75, 79, 91, 110, 116
Good, Frank B. 45
Good and Naughty 106, 140, 168
Good Samaritan Hospital 141–143
Goodwins, Leslie 140, 177

Gordon, Lewis 73, 74
Goreman, Charles 145
Gowland, Gibson 164
Graham, Ernest 6
Grand Prix Auto Races 45
Grant, Eve 120
Gray, Alexander 172, 173
Gray, Lawrence 102, 103, 166, 167, 172, 173
The Great Divide 101, 165
Great Scott! 72, 78, 161
Greenwood, Charlotte 113
Gregory, Carl Louis 20
Grey, Ray 160
Grey, Zane 169
Gribbon, Eddie 72, 74, 160–162
Gribbon, Harry 17, 159–161
Griffith, Beverly 44
Griffith, D. W. 20, 49, 57, 58, 65, 78
Griffith, Raymond 94, 110, 163
The Grocery Clerk's Romance 147
Guardian Angel 163
Guise, Thomas 162
Gulfport Crabs (baseball team) 16
The Gusher 31, 73, 153

Hackett, Raymond 120, 172
Hagart, Dot 55, 158
Haggerty, Charles 15, 154
Haines, William 167
Hale, Alan 172
Hall, Charlie 7
Hall, James 168
Hamilton, Laurel Lee 160
Hamilton, Lloyd 57, 59
Hammond, Harriett 72, 78, 160, 161
Hampton Studios 78
The Hansom Driver 151
Hardy, Oliver (Babe) 57, 113, 130
Hatton, Raymond 106, 170
Hauber, William 151, 153
Haver, Phyllis 16, 70, 77, 160–162, 165
Hawks, Howard 167
Hayes, Frank 160
He Must Have a Wife 22, 145
He Who Gets Slapped 13, 89, 96, 98, 164
He Wouldn't Stay Down 31, 56, 60, 157
Headline Woman 136, 138, 176
A Healthy Neighborhood 153
Heart to Heart 122
Hearts and Flowers 16, 23, 24, 48, 69, 160, 170
Hearts and Swords 51, 155
Heck, Stanton 89, 164

Heinie's Outing 156
Heinze's Resurrection 148
Help! Help! Hydrophobia! 150
Henderson, Dell 145, 146, 158
Henderson, Grace 145
Her Birthday Present 148
Her Majesty Love 175
Her Screen Idol 68, 161
Her Torpedoed Love 159
Herbert, Henry 165
Herbert, Holmes 116, 165
Hersholt, Jean 89, 164
Hide and Seek 33, 34, 149
His Chum the Baron 150
His Crooked Career 151
His Father's Footsteps 158
His Last False Step 77, 160
His Lying Heart 65, 159
His New Job 156
His Pride and Shame 65, 159
His Ups and Downs 150
His Smashing Career 52, 156
His Wife's Flirtation 156
His Wild Oats 65, 159
His Youthful Fancy 161
Hitchcock, Raymond 106, 167
Hoffmeyer's Legacy 147
Hogan, James P. 165
Hogan's Romance Upset 54, 157
Holding, Thomas 162
Holloway, Sterling 169
Hollywood (a.k.a. *Joligud*) 163
Hollywood Cavalcade 136, 142, 143
Hollywood Forever Cemetery 142
Holmes, Helen 149
Holmes, Stuart 162, 168
Home Sweet Home 49
Hopper, Hedda 118, 142, 143
Horsley, David 45
How Hiram Won Out 148
Hoyt, Harry O. 164
Hughs, Lloyd 122
Hull, Aurther S. 89, 164
Human Cargo 140, 177
Humphrey, William 162
The Hunt 55, 159
The Husband 153
Hyde, Harry 145
Hypnotic Power 156

If I Were a King (play) 10
An Ill Wind 156
L'Illustration (magazine) 126
IMP 27, 64
In and Out 156
In the Clutches of the Gang 154
Ince, Thomas H. 27, 31, 98
Ince Corporation 164
Inceville Studio 27

Ingraham, Lloyd 164
International Exhibitors of Photographers 84
The Interrupted Elopement 22, 23, 25, 145
Inventor's Secret 145
Irving, George 111
It Ought to Be a Crime 175
It's a Cinch 159

Jackson, Samuel 163
Jacobs, Paul "Little Billy" 33, 44, 45, 152, 155
Jason, Leigh 140
The Jazz Band (a.k.a. *That Ragtime Band*) 41, 150
The Jazz Singer 120
The Jealous Husband 155
The Jealous Waiter 148
Jenny, William LeBarron 6
Jenson, Jens 7
Jeske, George 44, 50, 52
John Robinson's Circus 12
Johnson, Nunnally 174, 175
Johnson, Olive 44
Joker Comedies 50
Joyce, Alice 165
Julian, Rupert 164
June, Mildred 161
The Jury 157
Just Brown's Luck 148
Just Kids 153

Kales, Arthur F. 82, 83, 86
Karno, Fred 41
Karno Company 40, 41, 68
Kavigon, Joe 142, 143
Keaton, Buster 35, 36, 76, 113, 13–134, 176
Keeler, Ruby 173
Keenan, Frank 165
Keith, Isabelle 161
Kelly, Fanny 72
Kelly, Gregory 108
Kelly, Pat 72–74
Kelsey, Fred 120, 172
Kennedy, Aubrey M. 133, 176
Kennedy, Edgar 17, 71, 149–151, 153, 160, 166, 170
Kennedy, Tom 106, 159, 160, 177
Kennedy City Studios 132, 133, 176
Keno the Boy Clown 12, 98
Kenton, Earl 160
Kessel, Adam 26, 38–40, 43, 44, 64, 65
Kessel, Charles 38
Keystone Hotel 5, 138, 139, 177
Keystone Kops 5, 28, 31, 33–35, 44–46, 64, 75, 126, 132, 138, 142, 177
Keystone Studio 5, 6, 12, 14, 18, 20–29, 31, 35, 37–45, 48, 49, 54, 56, 57, 59, 60, 62, 65–69, 71, 80, 88, 94, 98, 102, 113, 123, 142, 146–158
King, Emmett 163
King, Kewpie 89, 164
King Bee Studio 57
King Casey 15
Kingston, Natalie 169
Kirkland, David 156
Kismet 18, 125, 173
Kitchen, Karl K. 39
Kitley, Virginia 154
The Knockout 56
KNRC (radio station) 117
Kokusai Film Corporation 78

La Crosse, Wisconsin 6, 11, 12
A Lady's Tailor 154, 160
Laemmle, Carl 42–44, 51, 64, 65, 68, 98
Lake, Alice 84, 85
The Land Salesman 149
A Landlord's Troubles 148
Lane, Lupino 124, 173
Langdon, Harry 17, 110
Langdon, Lillian 162
Langham, Margaret 14
La Plante, Laura 175
La Rue, Carmen 44
La Rue, Jack 136, 176
Lasky Corporation 98, 103, 166–170
Laurel, Stan 57, 79, 113, 130
Lehrman, Henry "Pathé" 6, 19, 26, 29, 31, 35, 37, 41–45, 48–52, 66, 68, 69, 117, 146–148, 150–155, 160, 171
Le Roy, Mervyn 171
Levine, Nat 52
Library of Congress Motion Picture Preservation Laboratory 21
Lind, Myrtle 160, 161
Life in the Balance 150
Littlefield, Lucien 129, 175
L-KO (Lehrman-Knock Out) 68, 69, 159, 160
Lloyd, Frank 157
Lloyd, Harold 57–59, 107, 132, 142, 157, 158
Long, Baron 49, 51, 142, 143
Loomis, Margaret 162
Loos, Anita 171
Los Angeles International Photographers Salon 83
Love, Bessie 90, 120, 164, 172
Love and Dynamite 154
Love and Glory 98, 164
Love and Pain 149
Love and Rubbish 33, 152
Love and Vengeance 6, 29, 45, 46, 155
Love, Honor and Obey 162
Love Sickness at Sea 153
Low, Edmund 177
Loy, Myrna 124, 173
Lubin, Arthur 89, 164
Lucas, Wilfred 152, 153
Lucky Horseshoe 145
Lugosi, Bela 165
Lynn, Charles 160
Lyon, Ben 165, 169, 175

Mabel at the Wheel 6, 14, 45
Mabel's Adventure 147
Mabel's Awful Mistake 151
Mabel's Dramatic Career 152
Mabel's Lovers 147
MacCloy, June 52, 125, 126, 174
MacDonald, Wallace 94, 111, 164
Mace, Fred 15, 20, 26–28, 30, 37, 40, 45, 146–152
Mack, Hughie 76
Madison, Ethel 157
A Maiden's Trust 159
Majestic Film Company 64
Malloy, Francetta 128
The Man Next Door 149
The Manicurist 157
Mann, Hank 5, 15, 120, 150, 151, 153, 154, 172, 175, 177
Mansfield, Squire William D. 17
Many Unhappy Returns 141, 178
Marked Men 92
Marmont, Percy 119, 165
Married Life 161
Marshal, Frank H. 78
Marshall, Tully 163, 165
Masquers Club 59, 60, 118, 119, 121, 132, 140, 142, 143
Mayo, Frank 89, 96, 97, 164
McAvoy, May 167
McCoy, Harry 148, 152, 158, 174
McEvoy, Tom 19
McEvoy and Sterling (act) 19
McGee, E. W. 30
McGuire, Kathryn 160, 161
McKim, Robert 94, 163
McWade, Edward 162
Meeker, George 117, 171
Meighan, Thomas 113
Menjou, Adolph 110
Mercer, Jane 95, 163
The Merchant of Venice (play) 10
Merriam, Charlotte 78, 79, 162, 163, 165
A Midnight Elopement 147
Mike 167
Miller, J. Clarkson 169

Index

Miller, Marilyn 121, 123, 173, 175
Miller, Patsy Ruth 120, 172
Miller, Rube 154
Millner, Marietta 111
Mineau, Charlotte 69, 161
Miss Brewster's Millions 103, 105, 167
A Missed Engagement 121, 140
Mississippi river boat 18, 19
The Mistaken Masher 148
Mr. Fix-It (a.k.a. *Mr. Fixer*) 147
Mitchell, Grant 119
Mobile Seagulls (baseball team) 16
Molly O' 68
Monte Carlo or Bust 29
Moonshine 159
Moore, Owen 64, 67, 162
Moore, Tom 99, 140, 166, 168
Moran, Polly 37, 55, 158, 159, 176
Moran, Priscilla 164
Morgan, Ralph 119
Morris Reggie 77–79
Mosquini, Marie 168
Movietone 120
A Muddy Romance (a.k.a. *Muddled in Mud*) 32, 153
Mulhall, Jack 136, 173, 176
Murray, Charlie 54, 72, 76, 78, 91, 117, 160–162
Murray, Mae 83
Murphy's IOU 150
Mutual Film Corporation 26, 38, 62, 64, 65
My Lady's Lips 166
Myers, Harry 163
Myton, Fred Kennedy 163

Navajo (tribe) 111–113
Negri, Pola 106, 168
Neilan, Marshall 52, 92, 94, 133, 143, 162, 167, 168, 175
Nestor Studio 26, 45
The New Conductor 150
The New Neighbor 146
New York Motion Picture Company (NYMP Co.) 26, 38, 39, 42, 43, 62, 64, 65
Nichols, George 41, 48, 92, 147–150, 153, 154
Nigh, William 176
Nilsson, Anna Q. 94, 163
Normand, Mabel 6, 20, 26–29, 31–34, 37, 39, 41, 43–45, 49, 54, 56, 66–68, 119, 120, 145–153, 157, 162
North, Robert 52
Notre Dame College 9–12

Oakland, Vivian, 5, 177
Oakman, Wheeler 118, 136, 176
O'Brian, Tony 171
O'Donnell, Spec 109, 169, 173
Oh Kay! 171
Oh, Mabel Behave 67, 162
O'Hara, George 72, 161
Old Arizona 120
Old Blondeau's Tavern 45
Oldfield, Barney 29, 30, 142, 143, 151
Oliver, Edna May 105, 106, 166
Oliver, Guy 111
Olive's Love Affair 157
Olmstead, Gertrude 171
On His Wedding Day 149
O'Neil, Sally 167
O'Neill, Eugene 11
O'Neill, James 11
Only a Messenger Boy 32, 56, 62, 158
Orpheum Circuit 54
Our Dare Devil Chief 35, 56, 60, 157
Our Nagging Wives 174
Out and In 151

Pallette, Eugene 137, 164, 177
Pangborn, Franklin 136, 176
Papa's Boy 155
Paper print positives 21, 22
Paramount Studio 22, 52, 65, 66, 69, 72, 77, 100, 103, 105, 110–112, 117, 125, 126
Parkyakarkus 17
Parrott, Charles 157–159; see also Chase, Charley
Pasha, Kala 71, 74, 160–162
Pat's Day Off 147
Payson, Blanch 170
Peanuts and Bullets 57
Pearce, Peggy 44–46, 155, 156
The Peddler 152
Pedro's Dilemma 146
Peeping Pete 151
Perkins, Dwight 6
Photoplayers Club 60
Pickford, Mary 39, 64, 68, 78
Pidgeon, Walter 124, 173
Pinched in the Finish 159
Piper, C. Welborn 80
Pitts, ZaSu 101, 109, 110, 165, 169, 170
Pixley, Gus 145–146
Playthings of Desire 132, 133, 176
Post, Charles A. 96, 164
Powell, William 165
Power, Tyrone, Sr. 91, 163
Prescott, Vivian 20
Pretty Puppies 132, 175

Prevost, Marie 5, 72, 74, 77, 177
Price, Kate 94, 163
Producing Manager's Association 118
Professor Bean's Removal 152
The Professor's Daughter 149
Prouty, Jed 9, 12, 120, 136, 142, 143, 168, 172, 174, 177
Pryor, Roger 136, 137, 176
Purviance, Edna 20
A Pyjama Marriage 79, 162

Quick, Evelyn 148
A Quiet Fourth 140
Quillan, Eddie 132
Quincy Adams Sawyer 162

Ralston, Esther 99, 105, 114, 115, 166, 170
Rand, John 161
Rappe, Virginia 35
Rastus and the Game Cock 152
Ray, Johnny 17, 18
Ray, Johnny and Emma 15, 16
A Red Hot Romance 149
Reel Club 60
Reeves, Alf 40
Reggie Morris Productions 78
Reliance Pictures 65
Rent Jumpers 57
Return Engagement 177
Revier, Dorothy 102
Richardson, Jack 161
Ricketts, Tom 102
Rickson, Lucille 164
Riley and Schultz 146
The Riot 152
Ritchie, Billy 68
Ritz Brothers 17
The Rivals 147
RKO 16, 59, 121, 129, 132, 140, 141
Roach, Bert 72–74, 77, 160, 161, 172, 177
Roach, Hal 56, 57
Roach Studio 56, 57, 93
The Road to Glory 167
Roberts, Charles 141
Roberts, H. J. 77
A Robust Romeo 38, 154
Rogers, Will 7, 36, 37, 93–95
Ross, Bud 161
Rough on Husbands 68, 159
Royal Photographic Society, London, England 82, 83
The Rube and the Baron 149
Rubin, Benny 17

Safe in Jail 152
Saginaw Wa-Was (baseball team) 16

Index

St. Clair, Mal 23, 25, 52, 108, 160, 166–168, 170, 171
St. John, Al 17, 61, 150, 151, 154, 157, 158
Sally 121–123, 173
Salome vs. Shenandoah 160
Sampson, Teddy (Nora) (Mrs. Ford Sterling) 49–51, 66, 79, 99, 101, 117
San Gabriel Golf Club 79
Santa Fe Rail Road 30
Saving Mabel's Dad 147
Saylor, Syd 173
Schade, Betty 148–150
Schade, Fritz 158, 159
Schulberg, B. P. 52, 111
Screen Actor's Guild (SAG) 118
Screen Club of San Francisco 51
Screen Snapshots 123, 124, 175
Secret Service Snitz 49, 51, 52, 157
Selwyn, Edgar 172
A Seminary Scandal 79, 162
Semon, Larry 17
Sennett, Mack 5, 6, 10, 15, 19, 20, 22, 23, 25–31, 35, 38–46, 48, 49, 51, 52, 54, 56, 57, 60, 65–69, 71, 76, 77, 80, 88, 91, 113, 132, 142, 145–155, 160–162
Sergeant Hofmeyer 45, 46, 155
Shakespeare, William 9, 10, 12
Shattuck, Truly 164
Shearer, Norma 164
Sheridan, Anne 169
A Shooting Match 156
The Show Off 23, 105, 107, 167
Showgirl in Hollywood 125, 173
Sidewalk Chatter (play) 19, 22
Siegel, Bernard 111
Sills, Milton 94, 163
Sjöström, Victor 89, 164
Skinner, Otis 18, 23, 125
The Sleuths at the Floral Street Parade 149
The Sleuth's Last Stand 149
A Small Time Act 153
Snitz Joins the Force 155
Snitz the Tailor 153
Snookee's Day Off 39, 157
Snookee's Disguise 156
Snookee's Flirtation 46, 155
The Snow Cure 159
So Big 100, 165
Some Nerve 154
Sparks, Ned 167
Special Pictures Corporation 77–79, 119, 161, 162
The Speed Kings 29, 153

The Speed Queen 151
The Spoilers 94, 163
Sporting Goods 115, 116, 171
Spring Is Here 121, 123, 173
Stage Struck 102–105, 166
Stars and Bars 159
Stars of Yesterday 174
Staub, Ralph 5, 177
Stedman, Myrtle 171
Steppin' Out 101, 102, 166
Steppling, John 164
Sterling, Ford: art 80; baseball 5, 8, 16, 17, 71, 77, 110; birth 5; burns hands, arms and face 115; Chief Teheezal 5, 24, 28, 29, 31, 33–36, 46, 60–62, 71, 94, 137, 138, 143; Cohen 24, 30, 31; death 143; divorce 49, 99, 117; Dutch character 5, 6, 23, 24, 28, 30, 43, 45, 72; father 6, 8, 10; golf 8, 75, 79, 91, 110, 116; homes: (4142 Grand Blvd., Chicago IL) 8, 9, 11, (305 36th Place, Chicago IL) 11, (3139 Michigan Ave, Chicago IL) 11, (427 Lake, Venice CA) 52, (5636 Carlton Way, Los Angeles CA) 49, 85, 123, 135, (5272 Hollywood Blvd, Los Angeles CA) 135; illness 11, 12, 51, 52, 125, 136, 141–143; mother 10, 11, 99; musical comedy 12, 15, 16, 19, 121, 125; name change 12; Navajo (Indian) name 112; Sergeant Hofmeyer 31, 45, 46; Snookee 36, 45, 52; stage career 11–13, 18–20, 22, 23, 25, 54, 80, 121, 125; "Sterling Kids" (cartoons) 18, 80; tax lien 123; tennis 91; wife (Teddy Sampson) 49, 51, 66, 79, 99, 101, 117; wedding 51, 52
Sterling Motion Picture Corporation 42–47, 49–51, 54, 68, 71, 98, 119, 151–157
Stern, Abe 68
Stern, Julius 68
Stern Papa 22, 146
Stewart, Roy 80, 164
Stich (Stitch), George F., Jr. *see* Sterling, Ford
Stich (Stitch), George F., Sr. (father) 6, 8, 10
Stich (Stitch), Mary Kirby (mother) 10, 11, 99
Stolen Glory 29, 146
The Stolen Purse 148
Stout Hearts and Willing Hands 59, 60, 132, 175

Stowers, Frederick 166
Stranded in Paris 110, 168
The Stranger's Banquet 92, 162
Strayer, Frank 120, 166, 172
A Strong Revenge 149
Summer Girls 68, 161
Sutherland, Edward 106, 110, 113, 114, 170
Swain, Mack 54, 60, 116, 152, 153, 157, 159, 171, 175
Swanson, Gloria 102, 103, 105, 166
Sweet, Blanche 125, 173
Swickard, Joseph 159

Tango Tangles 29, 32, 155
Tavares, Arthur 46
Taylor, Ruth 116, 171
Tearle, Conway 101, 136, 138, 165, 175
Teddy (Sennett Studio Great Dane) 73, 161
A Temperamental Husband 147
Ten Dollars or Ten Days 161
Terry, Alice 101, 165
Terry-Thomas 29
Tezlaff, Teddy 153
That Little Band of Gold 54, 157
That Minstrel Man 156
Thatcher, Eve 72, 78, 160–162
That's My Daddy 171
Their First Execution 151
A Thief Catcher 38, 154
Thomson, Kenneth 119
Thornby, Bob 44
Those Good Old Days 150
Those Magnificent Men in Their Flying Machines 29
Three Keatons (act) 18, 76
Three Stooges 17, 56, 57
Tijuana 37
The Time Lock Safe 33
Todd, Thelma 122
Toledo Mud Hens (baseball team) 16
The Tomcat 133, 134, 176
Too Many Brides (a.k.a. *The Love Chase*) 154
Too Many Burglars 145
Toplitsky and Co. 27, 28, 31, 32, 151
Torrence, David 177
Torrence, Ernest 163, 166
Tourneur, Maurice 163
Townley, jack 140
Tragedy in a Dress Suit 22–24, 145
Trask, Wayland 159, 160
Traub, Joe 5
Treating Them Rough 161
Trevilla, Sibyl 161

Trevor, Claire 177
Triangle Film Corporation 65
Triangle-Keystone 65, 66, 71
Trouble from Abroad 16, 121, 129, 175
The Trouble with Wives 99, 103, 166
Troublesome Pets 47, 156
The Trunk Mystery 169
Trying to Get Along 160
Turpin, Ben 5, 77, 160, 161, 177
Tuttle, Frank 166
Twenty Horses 126, 127, 129, 174
The Two Widows 149

The Unhappy Finish (a.k.a. *Bert the Penman*) 162
United Artists 78, 110
Universal Studios 17, 39, 42–46, 49, 51, 52, 54, 68, 98, 102, 120, 155–157, 159, 160, 164, 175

Valentine's Day Ball 60
Valli, Virginia 96, 97, 164
Vanderbilt Cup 45, 109

Vaudeville 9, 18, 19, 22, 23, 49, 54, 56, 113, 121, 123
Vernon, Bobby 158, 159, 175
Vernon Country Club 49
Vidor, Florence 99, 166
Vidor, King 92, 96, 97, 164
Vitagraph 20, 39
Vitaphone 120, 125
Vitascope 125
Vroom, Frederick 163

The Waiters' Picnic 151
Walking the Dog 126, 128, 175
Wall, E. J. 80
Waller, Fred 105
Walls, Howard Lamarre 20
Walsh, John A. 145
Walthall, Henry B. 168
Warren, Fred 89, 164
Watch Your Husbands 79, 161
The Water Nymph 27, 146
Waters, John 111, 169
We're in the Navy Now 106
West, Billy 57
Western Export Company 44
Weston, Edward 82, 86
Weston, Flora (Chandler) 82
Wheeler, Bert 17
When Dreams Come True 153

When Smaltz Loves 155
White, Alice 116, 171, 173
White, Jack 43
White, Leo 89, 164, 177
Wife Savers 170
A Wife Wanted 149
Wild Oranges 96, 97, 164
Williams, Harry S. 159
Wilson, Lois 25, 108, 167
Windsor, Claire 92, 162
Wine 153
The Woman on the Jury 89, 90, 164
A Woman's Pity (play) 14
Woodward, Guy 55, 158, 159
World War One 43, 69, 74, 98, 129
WRC (radio station) 125
Wrigley, William 17
Wrigley Field, California 17
Wrigley Field, Illinois 17

Yankee Doodle in Berlin 31, 72, 74, 76, 88, 160
Yarborough, Jean 140
Young, Loretta 125, 173

Zukor, Adolph 66
Zuzu, the Band Leader 15, 154

www.ingramcontent.com/pod-product-compliance
Lightning Source LLC
Chambersburg PA
CBHW081557300426
44116CB00015B/2921